Applied Ethics

A Non-Consequentialist Approach

David S. Oderberg

BLACKWELL
Publishers

BLACKWELL PUBLISHING
350 Main Street, Malden, MA 02148-5020, USA
9600 Garsington Road, Oxford OX4 2DQ, UK
550 Swanston Street, Carlton, Victoria 3053, Australia

First published 2000

2   2005

Library of Congress Cataloging-in-Publication Data

Oderberg, David S.
    Applied ethics : a non-consequentialist approach / David S. Oderberg.
        p.cm.
    Companion to: Moral theory.
    Includes bibliographical references and index.
    ISBN 0-631-21904-8 (hb : alk. paper) — ISBN 0-631-21905-6 (pbk. : alk. paper)
    1. Applied ethics. 2. Ethical problems. I. Title.
BJ1031.O34 2000
170 2 21—dc21   99-045660
                                                         CIP

ISBN-13: 978-0-631-21904-0 (hb : alk. paper) — ISBN-13: 978-0-631-21905-7 (pbk. :
alk. paper)

A catalogue record for this title is available from the British Library.

Set in 10 on 13 Sabon
by Ace Filmsetting Ltd, Frome, Somerset
Printed and bound in the United Kingdom
by Marston Book Services

The publisher's policy is to use permanent paper from mills that operate a
sustainable forestry policy, and which has been manufactured from pulp
processed using acid-free and elementary chlorine-free practices. Furthermore,
the publisher ensures that the text paper and cover board used have met
acceptable environmental accreditation standards.

For further information on
Blackwell Publishing, visit our website:
www.blackwellpublishing.com

Contents

Preface and Acknowledgements

In 1995, the philosopher Professor Peter Singer published a book entitled *Rethinking Life and Death*. The subtitle is *The Collapse of our Traditional Ethics*. Professor Singer announced the conquest of the view of morality coming down to us through the centuries, and rooted in what he calls the 'Judeo-Christian' ethical tradition. The 'old ethic', he says with undisguised relief, is dead; a 'new ethical approach' is on its way, though its 'shape' is still to be determined.

The purpose of this book, and of its companion *Moral Theory*, is to show that traditional morality is not dead. It may not be the official outlook of most moral philosophers, and one might even question how many people in Western societies believe it any more. I suspect, however, that the number is larger than the intelligentsia would have us think.

In seeking to show that traditional morality is not dead, I do not want to pretend that there has not been something of a revolution in moral philosophy, which has filtered down to the population at large. Indeed, Professor Singer is one of the thinkers most responsible for this startling change in our attitudes to a wide range of topics. Since his seminal work in the 1970s, he has been followed by hundreds of writers in the field he almost single-handedly invented, called 'practical' or 'applied' ethics, all of them in one way or another assisting in the overthrow of traditional morality. Professor Singer's moral theory, known as consequentialism, owes its modern form to the nineteenth-century British ethicists James Mill, Jeremy Bentham and John Stuart Mill (among others), and became the dominant ethical outlook in British moral philosophy in the twentieth century. Whatever the differences among its adherents, and whatever the challenges it now faces in the higher levels of moral theory (for example, from Kantianism), it is still the overwhelmingly pre-eminent theory used in applied ethics in Britain, the USA, Australia, and elsewhere in the West.

Traditional ethics has had its defenders, to be sure, but they are small in number and influence. This book and its companion, it is hoped, will help to redress the imbalance in the kind of material available to students. If I do not succeed in convincing the reader of the truth of the positions I defend, at the very least I hope to show that traditional ethics is a coherent system of thought, that it can be done in the modern age, and that it provides a method for dealing with even the most difficult problems in practical ethics. In other words, the pronouncement of its demise is, I believe, premature.

I will not describe here what the traditional ethic amounts to: that is the work of the following chapters. What I will say, however, is that even if the bulk of moral philosophers find the conclusions I reach unpalatable, disagreeable, ridiculous, absurd, anachronistic, barbaric, bizarre, or just plain wrong, I console myself with the following thought: that every single one of the major positions I defend was believed by the *vast majority* of human beings in Western society for thousands of years, right up until some time in the 1960s, when the Western Cultural Revolution took place. (I do not speak of the non-Western societies, which even today subscribe to most or all of the views defended here.) Naturally, this does not make the views for which I argue right; but it is a fact that offers some solace in an age in which traditional ethics is held up to such ridicule. Furthermore, I also believe that there is such a thing as the common sense of humanity, which extends to morals as well as to everything else. In this I follow Aristotle, for whom the investigation of morality began with common sense and was in large part its systematisation. Hence the much-derided Principle of Double Effect, which is central to traditional moral theory (and which I defend in chapter 3 of *Moral Theory*), is nothing but the codification and elaboration of what we all know intuitively to be correct, however much the principle is considered by some to be obscure and repugnant to rationality. Indeed, it has its difficulties, like many other philosophical principles, traditional or not, but it begins with common sense on its side, and therefore starts at an advantage.

Moral Theory and *Applied Ethics* are companion volumes, designed to be read in sequence. Either book makes sense on its own and could be read without the other, but there is a dependence between them that makes this undesirable. *Moral Theory* presents ethical ideas and principles in the abstract, and looks to their application to concrete cases; *Applied Ethics* discusses concrete cases, and presupposes the prior defence of the ideas and principles applied to them (although the main lines of defence are recapitulated). They were written together, and are best read together.

The structure of the two books is simple. In *Moral Theory* I set out in elementary fashion the system of traditional morality as I understand it. I start with a critique of moral scepticism, not because I have anything especially new to say or because it has not already been refuted by others. The reason is that scepticism about the very possibility of arriving at moral truth pervades universities throughout the Western world. It has seeped into culture at all levels, in fact, so that students come to university sceptical about moral objectivity and leave with their scepticism intact and even reinforced by their teachers. This is one topic on which traditional moralists, and consequentialists such as Peter Singer, are in substantial agreement. (Although not even consequentialism, on analysis, escapes from ethical relativism born of pluralism about values, resort to subjective preferences, and a lack of belief in human nature. See further Janet E. Smith, 'The Pre-eminence of Autonomy in Bioethics', in D. S. Oderberg and J. A. Laing (eds), *Human Lives: Critical Essays on Consequentialist Bioethics* (London/New York: Macmillan/St Martin's Press, 1997), pp. 182–95.) No student can be receptive to what traditional morality has to say without first shaking off his sceptical prejudices, and this is what chapter 1 is designed to help him to do.

Chapters 2 and 3 of *Moral Theory* set out the basic concepts and principles of traditional morality. The exposition is on the whole elementary and non-technical. It is not designed as a comprehensive or definitive statement of the traditional ethic. I do not engage with all the alternative ideas explored in recent literature on virtue theory, or Kantianism, or natural law ethics. I am concerned only to present the leading ideas of traditional morality in a straightforward way, showing their main interconnections, in order to prepare the ground for a discussion of specific problems in the second volume. The vast majority of applied ethics books share the vice of not giving sufficient space to the theoretical justification of the positions adopted on particular issues. Far too often, an author gives a twenty-page exposition of his ethical viewpoint and then launches into discussion of difficult concrete cases. I believe this is wholly inadequate, hence my desire, at the risk of 'over-egging the pudding', to state and defend at length the traditional ethicist's theoretical presuppositions and general approach and to explain the concepts used in later discussion. Applied ethics is not like riding a bicycle: you don't just 'do it', as some applied ethicists seem to think, and convince your reader by doing it well rather than badly. You start with a theory, explicit or implicit, and you *apply* it. I have, then, stated the theory of traditional morality as explicitly as possible for my purpose of applying it to concrete cases. There is also some discussion that has no direct bearing on later applications, but seemed to me worthwhile for the purpose of elaborating and defending traditional moral theory for its own sake. These passages, some of which are abstruse and somewhat technical, can safely be skipped by the reader who wants to focus on the main points, in particular on the application of the theory to specific problems.

Chapter 4 is the link between the two books, setting out the fundamental moral principle of the sanctity of human life. Here I draw the reader away from general theory and towards my main focus, which is issues of life and death. The doctrine of the sanctity of human life has come under merciless attack in recent years, and is the first principle that most applied ethicists seek to undermine. Without it, there is no traditional morality. With it, much of what passes for contemporary ethical opinion can be shown to be false, even morally repugnant and dangerous to society.

The main negative focus of *Moral Theory* is the critique of consequentialism, which by far dominates current thinking and writing in applied ethics. (For those who doubt that this is the case, a typical example to look at is A. Dyson and J. Harris (eds), *Ethics and Biotechnology* (London: Routledge, 1994), in addition, of course, to the well-known texts by Singer, Glover, Rachels, Harris, Beauchamp and Childress, among many others.) Hence the subtitle of both books: its aim is to make clear that they constitute an alternative to the staple fare of applied ethics books, in which the approach to theory and practice is overwhelmingly consequentialist. I do not set out every flaw in consequentialism, omitting even some major ones. Rather, I concentrate on its incompatibility with the basic demands of rights and of justice (due primarily to its 'maximising' and calculative nature), and hence its fundamentally inhuman character, and I explore some other of its more bizarre and morally objectionable features. Of course, consequentialism comes in various forms, and I have not explored the species and sub-species that have been formulated in the attempt to get around certain objections. Instead, I focus on the leading ideas central to any form of consequentialism worthy of the name. The trend in current ethical writing seems to be for consequentialists of a more enlightened outlook to alter their theories to such an extent – in order to make them conform to common sense and basic morality – that they are barely recognisable as consequentialist. This is a research programme with an uncertain future, one to which I am happy to leave its exponents.

In *Applied Ethics* I discuss particular controversies, all of them revolving around issues of life and death. In chapters 1 and 2 I argue for specific prohibitions on the taking of human life. In chapter 3 I draw the boundary separating those beings which possess the right to life from those which do not. Here, although the chapter is entitled 'Animals', the reader will soon see that I focus almost exclusively on the issue of whether animals have rights. There are all sorts of facets to the 'animals issue' which I do not explore. The main reason for this is that by concentrating on the question of rights, and drawing a logico-moral boundary between human and animal life, I aim to highlight, or to place in relief, what I say about rights for human beings. In this sense the question of animal rights is an integral conceptual part of the overall project of expounding traditional morality. Second, however, it seems that the animal rights movement is growing strongly and distorting the common-sense approach that most people still have towards the animal kingdom. Only by seeing the flaws in the idea that animals have rights will society recover a sane attitude both to them and to itself.

It might be thought that my position on the animals issue places me close to Peter Singer's, since he too does not believe in animal rights. While Professor Singer is to be commended for much of what he has written and done about the suffering of animals, it remains the case that his attitude is fundamentally unsound, since it stems from his consequentialist belief that *no* being has rights – 'I am not convinced that the notion of a moral right is a helpful or meaningful one' – and that '[t]he language of rights is a convenient political shorthand. It is even more valuable in the era of thirty-second TV news clips'. (See *Practical Ethics*, Cambridge: Cambridge University Press, 1993; 2nd edn, p. 96; and *Animal Liberation*, London: Jonathan Cape, 1990; 2nd edn), p. 8.) Whereas, then, Professor Singer seeks to demote human beings to the same level as animals inasmuch as *none* of them have rights, traditional morality maintains a fundamental conceptual and moral distinction between human beings and every other living creature. Professor Singer's viewpoint may have meant an improvement in the lot of many animals, which is praiseworthy; but it also means, for the traditional ethicist, a change for the worse in the fate of mankind.

In chapters 4 and 5 I argue for cases where it is permissible to take human life. It is at this point that some people who see themselves as partisans of traditional morality will part company with me. They have, according to my diagnosis, overreacted to the contemporary attack on the sanctity of life by falling into the opposite error of regarding all killing as wrong simply by virtue of the victim's being human. Like all overreactions, this one may be understandable in the present death-oriented climate but, like all overreactions, it too is mistaken. It simply is not in conformity with traditional morality to oppose, *on principle*, war or capital punishment. Nor, when the issues are thought through, is it in accord with traditional moral thinking to oppose either activity in certain very real cases that have obtained in our recent history or that obtain today. In other words, it is untraditional to say *either* 'War/capital punishment is wrong' or 'War/capital punishment is permissible in principle, but the circumstances in which it is legitimate today are so rare that it is, for all practical purposes, always wrong.' Chapters 4 and 5 are designed to show why this is so.

The choice of topics for the second volume has given the book a certain natural structure, though it was in the first instance motivated more by personal interest and a concern to present the traditional view of certain hotly debated issues. In each case, I pursue the topic in as much depth as space allows, because it seemed to me early on that an in-depth examination of a limited number of topics would ultimately be more useful to students than a more superficial overview of a wider range of issues. My objective is to show how traditional moral philosophy works, how its fundamental concepts and categories apply to an issue. Also, I have been concerned to tackle at length many of the most common objections to traditional positions, objections that recur time and again in the literature and in popular discussion, and also most significantly in the way students talk about the traditional viewpoint. Hence I have, at the risk of obsessiveness on my part and potential annoyance on the reader's, discussed some apparently minor issues at substantial length. Moreover, it seems to me that the right approach to many disputed topics not covered here – such as genetic engineering, embryo experimentation, and cloning – depends in a straightforwardly logical way upon the position to be taken on what should be called the *fundamental* issues, such as abortion and euthanasia. I hope this approach will be excused because of its ultimate usefulness, not least for other traditional ethicists. Once it is seen how to tackle a small number of foundational issues in detail in the traditional way, the student may then be in a better position to apply the same method to topics I have not covered here. Perhaps, if the opportunity becomes available, I will expand the list myself.

In writing this book and its companion I have benefited greatly from discussions with a number of people, some of whom have also commented on portions of them. In particular I would like to thank (in no special order) John Andrews, Elaine Beadle, Tim Chappell, John Cottingham, Brad Hooker, Andrew Mason, and Dale Miller. I am especially indebted to Helen Watt, with whom I have discussed at length the contents of both volumes; and to Jacqueline Laing, for many stimulating and profitable discussions not just on ethics, but on all aspects of philosophy, as well as for her encouragement in the preparation of both books. Finally, I would like to express my immense debt of gratitude to Steve Smith of Blackwell Publishers for his unfailing support and encouragement, even at times that would have taxed an editor with the patience of Job.

Needless to say, the fact that someone has assisted me with these books does not imply that they hold any or all of the views I defend. Some will disagree with almost everything I say. I hope that they find the project encapsulated in *Moral Theory* and *Applied Ethics* of some worth, nevertheless.

David S. Oderberg
Reading, May 1999

Note: References throughout the book to the male gender are used in the generic sense unless the context suggests otherwise, and are in no way intended to cause offence.

1

Abortion

1.1 The Problem of Abortion Today

In terms of contemporary applied ethics, abortion is perhaps the 'oldest' topic of dispute, the one most likely to figure in textbooks or to be covered in an applied ethics course. Historically, this is mainly because modern applied ethics began to come into its own at around the time abortion was *the* issue on the public moral agenda. Since the late 1960s, however, abortion, once a criminal offence in nearly every single country outside the then communist bloc (and an offence in those countries before communism), has been legalised the world over, the handful of exceptions remaining (such as Ireland) wholly likely to go the way of every other country in the near future.

One might have thought that made abortion a non-issue: just as slavery does not figure as a topic in applied ethics books, why should abortion, now the issue has been 'settled' throughout the world? No doubt some ethicists (and many pro-abortionists, whether philosophers or not) would wish it were that way. Two reasons show, nevertheless, why abortion is and must remain the number one issue of public policy. First, although a kind of legal settlement has descended upon the abortion issue, it is far from true that there has been a social settlement. No issue stirs up the intensity of feeling, often verging on blind hatred, and the commitment to public action, which is seen in the case of abortion. It is rare that a meeting between pro- and anti-abortionists does not involve some violence, or at the least the most fearsome verbal abuse. The media excel themselves in hysteria whenever it merely looks as though abortion is back on the agenda, such as in one of the hundreds of cases, since the legalisation of abortion, when elected politicians have introduced legislation to restrict its availability, only to be met with a stream of media and popular abuse of the kind usually reserved for the corrupt or the lecherous. Anti-abortion electoral broadcasts have often been the subject of censorship. In the USA in particular, abortion is still the occasion of regular demonstrations; abortionists and their assistants have been killed in recent years; clinics bombed and vandalised; pro-life organisations have been subjected to vicious hate campaigns; politicians find themselves pressured into treating abortion as a crucially important election issue when they would on the whole prefer it to go away. In short, a legal consensus does not mean a social consensus, and the intensity of feeling still generated by abortion in all quarters means that moral philosophers must continue to have it at or near the top of their list of most important issues.

Second, and much more significant philosophically, is the simple fact that the legalisation of something does not make it right. Slavery, racism, the exploitation of child labour, the negligent sale of dangerous products – we do not need to think hard of the many kinds of immoral behaviour that have either been legal nearly everywhere at one time or other, or are still legal now. As has already been emphasised in *Moral Theory*, and cannot be underlined enough, the law must follow morality, not the other way around; and the blithe appeal to what is or is not legal here and now rarely amounts to more than an excuse for not thinking about ethics.

So, whatever the passions that are aroused, whatever the state of the law, we need to think carefully and rigorously about whether abortion is right or wrong, treating it just as we would treat any other moral issue, including the ones that do not generally arouse strong feelings. Having said that, however, we must immediately add an important point. For *if* abortion is wrong, then it is hard to see how it could be anything other than *seriously* wrong, and a serious wrong that is being committed on a scale that is hard to grasp. In the USA, around 1.4 million abortions are carried out every year. In Britain it is 180,000. In Australia the figure is 80,000. In Russia, some 3.5 million abortions occur annually, and in China, with its one-child and coercive abortion policy, the figure (though hard to verify) is well over 10 million. Throughout the world, according to the UN Population Fund, there are some 45 million abortions every year, or one for every three live births.[1]

Now, one *might* take the view that abortion is in general permissible, but that when it is wrong this will be for reasons to do with the lack of sufficient justification based on a calculation of costs and benefits; such would be the consequentialist approach. One might, then, conclude that

Emma's abortion was right because her life was in danger, but Fiona's was not because her only reason was that she wanted to go on a skiing holiday rather than be pregnant and stay at home. On this view of the morality of the issue, abortion would rarely, if ever, be a serious wrong. In particular, it would never be wrong in the way that murder is wrong, not least because it would not be seen *as* an instance of murder.

Since it has been argued in *Moral Theory* that we should take a non-consequentialist approach to ethics, one that recognises rights such as the right to life, it seems that on such an approach abortion, *if* wrong, would be wrong for serious reasons to do with *principle*. If it were wrong, it is hard to see how it could be wrong for any other reason than that it involved the deliberate taking of innocent human life. And if this were so, it would be a simple fact, however we dress it up, that homicides are and have for the last few decades been taking place on a scale unprecedented in human history, involving millions upon millions of innocent human beings. (We will see that there are non-consequentialists who also hold that abortion, *if* wrong, would be seriously wrong as a violation of the right to life, but who also hold that such a right can be overridden in many cases.) Whatever emotions such a thought arouses, ranging from horror to disgusted disbelief, must for present purposes be discarded. Whatever consequences of public policy follow from abortion's being permissible or impermissible are not our present concern. Nor are the human-interest stories that emanate from both sides of the debate, horrifying though many of those stories are. We are interested in one thing only – the correct philosophical position to take on abortion. Is it permissible or not? How is it to be characterised from the ethical point of view?

1.2 The Basic Argument and Some Responses

The position I will be defending in the rest of this chapter is that abortion – that is, the deliberate killing of the foetus in its mother's womb – is wrong, being an instance of the intentional taking of innocent human life. (The term 'foetus' will be used in conformity with standard practice – it is Latin for 'offspring' – though one must always be alert to the way terminology can be used to colour a debate. Strictly, 'unborn child' is perfectly accurate, as will be argued, but this might be regarded as too emotionally charged. Needless to say, terms such as 'product of pregnancy' or 'conceptus', often used by pro-abortionists, are also open to the accusation of being loaded by virtue of their very moral neutrality.) This position on abortion – what might be called absolutist, for want of a better name – follows from the general defence, in chapter 4 of *Moral Theory*, of the fundamental value of human life and of the right to life which is correlative with it. *If* the foetus is an innocent human being, and *if* it is always wrong deliberately to kill an innocent human being, then it must be wrong deliberately to kill a foetus. This, in fact, is the argument (which I will call the *basic argument*) with which debate about abortion most usually begins, with opponents seeking to defend both premises and supporters attacking either or both. Naturally there are all sorts of complications that lie behind such a bald statement of the way the debate tends to run, and we will explore some of them.

To begin, let us look briefly at, in order equally briefly to dispose of, three poor responses to the basic argument that are only too prevalent in popular debate. They are sometimes levelled at premise 1 of the basic argument (the foetus is an innocent human being) and sometimes at premise 2 (it is always wrong deliberately to kill an innocent human being). (1) Some people say that the foetus is only a human being, or that it only becomes wrong to kill it, once it is born, as though its becoming *visible* or *separate* from the mother makes a difference. The objection is absurd. How can being human, or morally protected from killing, depend on whether you can be seen? Or on your location? Did foetuses become human beings with a right to life with the invention of X-ray and ultrasound? If the objection has something to do with the thought that the foetus, once born, is at its highest level of development, are we to say that a premature baby deserves protection, being born, whereas a late-term foetus, although as fully developed as a baby born at full term, has no protection since it is not born yet? Advocates of the gruesome practice of partial-birth abortion (legal in the USA and many other countries) might think so, but it is hard to see how such a view is rational. And if the idea is that the born baby is *separate* from the mother, as though physical separation makes a difference, does that mean the born baby can be killed while still attached to the mother by the umbilical cord? Does it mean Siamese twins have no right to life? If not, why not? The arbitrariness and unreasonableness of such a position barely needs stating.

(2) Some people speak of *viability* as a crucial cut-off point, beyond which the foetus acquires either humanity or the right to life. Viability

means the capacity to survive outside the womb. In the landmark case in the USA effectively legalising abortion, *Roe v. Wade* (1973), the Supreme Court held that the state acquires a 'compelling interest' in protecting the life of the foetus at viability because at that stage it 'presumably has the capability of meaningful life outside the mother's womb'. Just what the Court meant by 'meaningful life' is anybody's guess, but most people see viability as important because it apparently implies a lack of total dependence upon the mother – the mother is no longer 'essential' to the foetus's survival. But the implication is indeed only apparent. A born baby is also totally dependent on its mother, only instead of being fed and sheltered by the mother's automatic internal processes, it is fed and sheltered by the mother's consciously controlled external behaviour. How can that make a difference to whether or not a foetus is a human being or has a right to life? Moreover, as we all know, the technology for keeping a baby alive outside the womb has advanced markedly, so that now it is not uncommon for babies to be born and kept alive at 20–22 weeks, and some have even survived at 18 weeks, something that was once unthinkable. Does your being human or having the right to life depend on whether the technology exists for keeping you alive in certain situations? Are we to say that 22-week-old foetuses have the right to life now, but did not in 1950 or 1370? Or that they were human beings at one time but not another? Does morality depend upon available hardware? And if the hardware exists in America but not Ethiopia, should we say that 22-week-old American foetuses have the right to life, but not 22-week-old Ethiopian foetuses?

(3) It is often said that, at least in the very early stages of pregnancy, the foetus does not *look* like a human being. 'After all,' it is objected, 'in the early stages the foetus – rather, the embryo – is only a clump of cells, with no discernible similarity to a human being. It might have human DNA, but then so does a clump of skin cells.' Now this latter point, about DNA, touches on questions of identity and individuality that we will look at later. For the moment, what is at issue is the relevance of what the foetus looks like. It must be accepted that what it looks like *does* matter, but only because what a thing *looks* like is powerful (though defeasible) evidence of what a thing *is*, and what matters is whether the foetus *is* a human being. The reply to the objection, however, is simple – it *begs the question*. The question is whether the foetus looks human; the objection is really that it does not look like an *adult* or *mature* human. And this is undeniable. But how does this prevent the response, 'Sure, the foetus doesn't

look like a mature human being, but it looks exactly like a *young* human being.' How do we know it looks like a young human? it might be countered. The answer is that we cannot merely assert it; we have to justify it on the basis of philosophical argument about foetal development, which will be done later in this discussion. Such argument necessarily appeals to empirical facts about what the foetus *looks* like – what characteristics it has – but not to the proposition that it looks like a mature human, which is both false and irrelevant. If by a combination of philosophical and empirical reasoning, then, it can be shown that the foetus really is a young human being, we will have shown that it is a human being pure and simple, which is the first premise of the basic argument. It will not look like a mature member of its kind, to be sure – because it *isn't* mature. But it will certainly look like an *immature* member of its kind, if that is what it in fact is.

1.3   Sentience: A Bad Argument Against Abortion

As well as weak arguments for abortion there are also weak arguments against, and one of the most common appeals to the capacity of the foetus to feel pain. It used to be standard opinion among abortionists and supporters of abortion that the foetus could not feel any pain, at least until relatively late in the pregnancy, perhaps not until the sixth month. Even now, some scientists – such as Harold Morowitz, a biologist, and James Trefil, a physicist – claim that sentience, which they plausibly link to brain development, which latter they implausibly link to 'the onset of humanness', is not clearly present earlier than 25 weeks (this, then, being for them the beginning of humanity for the foetus).[2]

Now although the measurement of pain sensation is a difficult matter, as a matter of empirical fact evidence is mounting that the foetus can feel pain as early as the *seventh week*, that is, before two months' gestation, if not earlier. The immunologist Peter McCullagh, citing research over 35 years, says:

> The first avoidance responses, in which cutaneous stimulation is followed by withdrawal from the stimulus, have been observed at 5 weeks gestational age in response to stimulation of the area around the mouth [citation of 1964 paper by T. Humphrey]. The sensitive area extends to include the remainder of the face in the sixth and

seventh weeks and the palms of the hands and soles of the feet in the eighth and ninth weeks respectively.[3]

Although there may be other explanations for the avoidance behaviour than conscious feeling, it seems an improbable coincidence that the behaviour applies to stimulation of parts of the body (face, hands and feet) that we *know* to be especially sensitive to the slightest touch. The 'father of foetology', Professor A. W. Liley, said: 'When doctors first began invading the sanctuary of the womb, they did not know that the unborn baby would react to pain in the same fashion as a child would. But they soon learned that he would.'[4] The evidence is overwhelming that the foetus displays at a very early age what would uncontroversially be called pain behaviour in you or me. It is not just a question of motor response to stimulus, which is found in insects and bacteria, but of much more finely-grained behaviour. It has been shown experimentally, for example, that the foetus swallows more amniotic fluid (in which it is bathed) if the fluid is sweetened with saccharine, and less if it is made to taste sour. (Since the fluid goes through both mouth and nose it cannot at present be said definitively that the foetus tastes the fluid rather than smells it; either case would involve sensation, of course.)

This sort of evidence can be multiplied,[5] but in the end its moral worth is dubious. For, in the words of a team led by Professor Fisk of the Centre for Foetal Care at Queen Charlotte and Chelsea Hospital, London, summarising their own experiments with intrauterine needling: 'the human foetus feels pain in utero and may benefit from anaesthesia or analgesia for invasive procedures'.[6] In other words, the pro-abortionist can say that all the capacity of the foetus to feel pain means is that it should be anaesthetised before the abortion, since it is wrong *deliberately* to cause pain to any living thing. (To say so, however, he would have to concede that the foetus was a human being, or else explain what other kind of living thing it was.) Perhaps the rule is not without exceptions: imagine a doctor trying to test the neural connections of a paralysed person – he might have to cause pain intentionally to see whether the patient had lost all feeling. On the whole, however, the deliberate infliction of pain should be avoided, even though suffering is not *the* criterion of morality, as Bentham and the classical utilitarians used to (and still) think. Pain should also be avoided when it is not the aim of the exercise: anti-abortionists do not disapprove of foetal surgery because it may involve pain; instead they, like everyone else, say the foetus should be anaesthetised. So sentience, as such, is not the nub of the debate. Opponents of abortion are against it even when the foetus, or rather embryo, seems obviously not to be able to feel pain, such as at one week of age. (A note about the term 'embryo', which etymologically means 'growing thing': again, the use of this term often can be ideologically loaded. Morowitz and Trefil unbelievably want to restrict the term 'foetus' to the unborn human after two months! Here I shall follow the common usage of applying 'embryo' to the unborn human in the first two weeks, when its ball-like shape has not yet developed into a more elongated, head-and-tail formation.)

1.4   A Return to the Basic Argument

In chapter 4 of *Moral Theory* it was argued that life is a fundamental good (if not *the* fundamental good, understood in a certain way) and that there is a right to life that protects this good. In elaboration it was further said, and will be explained in more detail later in this volume, that the right applies unconditionally to innocent human beings but can be forfeited in other cases. If, then, the foetus is an innocent human being, deliberately killing it must, as a matter of logic, be a homicidal act. This is all the basic argument says, and what the case against abortion rests on.

Defending the humanity of the foetus, however, requires further argument, and the argument most commonly used is the one based on *continuity of development*. The claim here is that there is no metaphysically significant dividing line in embryonic and foetal development separating something that is a human being from something that is not; hence the embryo/foetus is a human being from conception onwards. Contrary to the confused arguments of some anti-abortionists, the claim is *not* that the foetus is a *potential* human being, but that it is an *actual* human being.

A consideration of some of the facts – undisputed by all sides – shows the force of the argument from continuity of development. At fertilisation, the nucleus of the sperm, containing the DNA of the father, and that of the egg, containing the DNA of the mother, merge to form an entirely new nucleus. The *zygote* (from the Greek for 'yoke', referring presumably to the 'yoking together' or joining of the nuclei), or cell resulting from union of sperm and ovum, contains the *entire genetic blueprint* for the future development of the foetus, baby, child and adult. The actual physical constitution and appearance of the foetus, baby, and so on, is determined, if not wholly, then almost wholly, by the DNA of the zygote. About a day after conception, once the new genetic blueprint is formed, the zygote begins dividing, in other words, *growing*. It goes through the phase of *morula* (12–16 cells; from Latin for 'mulberry', referring to the rough shape of the entity; the cells are surrounded by a membrane, the *zona pellucida*, 'transparent girdle', and remain surrounded until the entity is able to implant itself in the womb). Then the growing entity is called a *blastocyst* ('germ bladder', referring to the fact that the entity has a hollow part), from day 4 to implantation at day 7. (All references to days are approximate.) Around days 7–9 the sex of the entity can already be determined, which is of course powerful evidence that it is a human being in its own right. A few days after implantation the embryo, which is now drawing nutrition from the lining of the mother's womb, begins sending out hormones and other chemicals that stop the mother menstruating. At about day 15 the embryo has a 'primitive streak', or the beginning of a body axis; the possibility of its dividing into identical twins ceases at this stage (we will return to the possibility of twinning later). At around day 17 the embryo's own blood cells are developing (hence it has its own blood type at this stage), as well as the placenta from which it will continue to feed until birth. By day 20 the brain is already beginning to form, and you can see the rudimentary hemispheres. The embryo is 2 mm (one-thirteenth of an inch) long. All of this, note, has occurred *before the mother knows she is pregnant* (detectable at present at about 3 weeks; at 2 weeks, when the mother misses her period, she may begin wondering if she is pregnant). Between days 21–24 the heart, now formed, begins regular beating, and by day 28 the three main parts of the brain, and the spinal cord, are formed. Ears and nose begin to form at day 30 (one month's gestation), and by 6 weeks (around day 42) the foetus has a face, fingers, toes and a complete skeleton, and shows reflex behaviour. Brain activity is detectable at around this time (and will probably be detectable earlier as technology improves), and increases in amount and complexity through the rest of gestation, birth *and beyond*. By 7 weeks the foetus has teeth and gums, by 8 weeks all major organs are functioning – stomach, liver, kidneys, and so on. No new structures are formed from this time. At 11–12 weeks the foetus is moving its arms and legs, sucking its thumb, breathing amniotic fluid, and its fingernails are growing. Most abortions (about 80 per cent) occur before 12 weeks. At 16 weeks (4 months) it has genital organs, it swims, kicks, somersaults, and grasps with its hands. The vocal cords are working by 18 weeks and the foetus also reacts to sounds. It has hair by 20 weeks, and is about 30 cm (12 inches) long. Rapid growth, with the continual addition of new kinds of behaviour, goes on until birth at 9 months.

It is interesting at this point to see what Peter Singer concludes from these undisputed facts of foetal development: 'there is no doubt that from the first moments of its existence an embryo conceived from human sperm and eggs [sic] is a human being'.[7] And again:

> the liberal search for a morally crucial dividing line between the newborn baby and the fetus has failed to yield any event or stage of development that can bear the weight of separating those with a right to life from those who lack such a right . . . . The conservative is on solid ground in insisting that the development from the embryo to the infant is a gradual process.[8]

Since for Singer it is *persons* who matter morally, not human beings, he is not perturbed by his conclusion; but since I have already argued at length against Singer's *personism* (in chapter 4 of *Moral Theory*), such a conclusion does have serious moral importance. It is the very continuity of development that makes it *metaphysically impossible* to say, 'Before stage S the foetus is not a human being, but after stage S it is.' Thus what the opponent of abortion claims is a *strict numerical identity* between zygote, embryo, foetus, baby, child and adult. Numerical identity follows from the fact of humanity: *if* the foetus *is* a human being, then *which* human being could it possibly be *other* than the one that is born from it? It is not as though foetal development involves a continual series of substitutions of one human being for another. (Twinning involves a substitution of sorts, but we will look at this later.) But now consider some objections.

1.4.1 Objection from brain activity

'The foetus displays no brain activity for the first 6 or so weeks. It does not even *have* a brain for the first 3 weeks. But to be human is to have a functioning brain. So how can the early foetus be human?'

By way of response, consider Singer's remark following the one cited above that 'an embryo conceived from human sperm and eggs is a human being'. He goes on to say: 'and the same is true of the most profoundly and irreparably intellectually disabled human being, even of an infant who is born anencephalic – literally, without a brain'. Here Singer is pointing out the fact that while a functioning brain is normally necessary for human life, a human being can live without one, whether it be for a number of weeks after conception or a number of weeks after birth. Clearly a baby without a brain is in a damaged state, just as if it had no legs, and an embryo without a brain, abnormalities aside, is genetically programmed to develop one. It is also clear that the brain plays a crucial if not essential role in normal psychological function. (This area is deeply ill-understood; there are documented cases of people with normal psychological function, and normal IQs, yet who lacked virtually all of their brain tissue.[9]) But none of this implies that being human *means* possessing a brain. The common rejoinder is to say, 'But we regard the cessation of brain activity – brain death – as the death of the human, so by parity of reasoning we should regard the onset of brain activity – brain life, as it were – as the coming into existence of the human being.' The response to this is simply that we are wrong to regard brain death as the ceasing to exist of the human being. In fact, according to current medical standards it is not brain death but brain*stem* death that is treated as the point of human death, since the brainstem is said to control basic reflexes such as blinking, eye movement, breathing, gagging and motor responses to stimulation. Brainstem death, as confirmed by tests for these reflexes, is supposed especially to be a criterion of the irreversible loss of consciousness. The question of brain death will be covered more fully in the next chapter when we look at euthanasia; for the moment what should be noted is that not all bodily functions cease when brain (including brainstem) activity apparently (and I stress apparently) ceases: heartbeat, circulation and blood pressure persist spontaneously, and hormones continue to circulate as well, among other things (exactly as in the case of the foetus of a few weeks' gestation, before brain function begins). Most doctors may well seem to regard a person in such a state as dead (and so 'harvest' his organs); but do they *really* regard such a person as dead? Would they, for instance, cremate him? The fact is that in the current state of medical and physiological knowledge, the only sure sign of death is something like generalised putrefaction of the body. This may be inconvenient for those who want to harvest organs, but inconvenient facts are facts nevertheless. There is, then, no sound reason for treating 'brain life' as human life any more than for treating 'brain death' as human death.[10]

1.4.2 Objection from sorites paradoxes

Michael Tooley objects that a continuous gradation between things does not mean all the things that are continuously graded have all the same properties. So, he says, consider a series of objects starting with a very heavy one and ending with a very light one, such that every object in the series is a hundredth of a gram lighter than the next. 'It is impossible to find two successive objects,' he says, 'one of which is heavy, and the other not. So [he pretends to infer] we must conclude that all of the objects are heavy.' The conclusion is absurd, and he adds: 'The point is simply that the absence of significant differences between successive members of some series, or between successive stages in some process, provides no reason at all for concluding that there are no significant differences between non-successive stages or members.'[11]

It should be noted that Tooley's concern is not whether the embryo/foetus is a human being, though in passing he uses the term 'human organism' to imply that this is true of the gestating entity at every moment of its development. Rather, he is concerned with *persons*, and denies that the foetus (or even infant!) is one; his argument cited above is that because of the phenomenon of *vagueness*, continuity of development does not entail that the clear existence of a *person* at some stage (for him, some point beyond infancy) means there will be a *person* at *every* stage of development. We will look at Tooley's *personism* in more detail later, but we can see now that his argument could have been applied to the claim that the foetus is always a human being, right back to conception. Unfortunately, however, it does not work. The argument from continuity of development is about the question of the *identity* of the foetus – is it the *very same thing* throughout its development? More precisely, is it *the same human being* as the baby/child/adult into which it develops? The argument is not based on the setting up of a series of entities that can be compared according to some characteristic admitting of degrees, such as *more or less heavy, more or less tall*, or *more or less bald*. The argument is not that the child is a human being because it has some large set of properties and you can (conceptually) go back in time to the foetus, observing those properties dropping away one by one and lessening by degrees, so that because there is no point at which humanity clearly ceases to apply to the gestating entity it must *therefore* be human all along. The argument is, rather, that there is a *single human organism* from zygote to adult, because at every stage of development the gestating entity is doing *precisely what any organism does* in its movement from immaturity to maturity, namely growing, differentiating, taking on a mature shape and form, and acting in a way that shows it to be numerically distinct from its environment (in the human case its mother and everything that belongs physically to her, such as her uterus) which it *uses for its own benefit.* These properties do not shows themselves to greater or lesser degree in the gestating entity at different stages of its existence: the gestating entity *always* has these properties, and they are essential properties of any organism (this is a simplification, since the definition of life and what is and is not an organism is a difficult and complex issue that cannot be explored here). The argument from continuity of development, then, says that the attributes of an organism, moreover one progressing from immaturity to maturity, are present at all stages of embryonic/foetal development. Hence there is one single organism at all stages; that organism can only be human; all human organisms are human beings; hence there is a single human being. (Human body cells – skin, bone, and so on – are most plausibly not organisms because they are parts of a whole and serve that whole rather than merely inhabiting an environment – the body – which they use for their benefit.)

By bringing vagueness into the question, defenders of abortion fall into equivocation over the terms they are using, thereby failing to make crucial distinctions. Judith Jarvis Thomson provides a notable example of this in her celebrated 1971 paper defending abortion. (We will look at her paper in some depth later on.) At first she says that she is 'inclined to think also that we shall probably have to agree that the foetus has already become a human person well before birth'[12] – but not as early as conception. By 'person' here she seems to mean simply 'human being'. Only a few lines later, however, she claims that '[a] newly fertilized ovum . . . is no more a person than an acorn is an oak tree',[13] arguing that our inability to say exactly when an acorn becomes an oak tree does not mean that we should call one the other, and by analogy does not mean we should call a fertilised ovum a person. But *here* by 'person' she seems to mean 'adult' or 'mature member of its kind'. By bringing vagueness into the equation, she confuses two propositions that need to be kept separate: (1) that the foetus is a human being, and sufficient attention to the continuity of development forces us to say the same even of a fertilised ovum; (2) neither the fertilised ovum nor the foetus is a mature member of its kind.

Hence the objection from fallacies about vagueness is both irrelevant and liable to lead to confusion. Furthermore, to use it, as supporters of abortion sometimes do, is what might be called a 'cheap shot'. Sorites paradoxes or paradoxes about vagueness – How many inches in height makes a tall person? How few hairs on the head make a bald person? A series of tiny changes can lead to a big change with absurd results, and so on – can be used *everywhere*. No one seems to have come up with a solution to them, though there have been some ingenious attempts. You can use sorites paradoxes to prove all sorts of things: you might insist that the zygote is human because the adult is, *or* you might insist that because the zygote is not human, neither is the adult! (One man's *modus ponens* is another man's *modus tollens*.) Depending on your presuppositions, you can wreak all sorts of havoc in philosophy with sorites arguments. They are not the special province of one sort of ethical or metaphysical view. As such they are best left to one side, well away from the abortion debate, while they await a general solution that makes everyone happy.

1.4.3   Objection from begging the question

'You say that there is continuity of development from conception to birth sufficient to prevent the drawing of a metaphysically significant dividing line during gestation that separates a human being from something that is not a human being. But 'conception' just *means* 'beginning (of human life)', so aren't you assuming what you are trying to prove, namely that human life begins at conception?'

The answer is that 'conception' is *not* being defined as 'the coming into existence of a human being'. If it were, it would of course be a tautology to say that the human being comes into existence at conception. Further, the term is not being defined as 'the union of sperm and egg', because of objections to such a definition that we will soon look at. 'Conception' can be *partially* defined as 'the event that typically consists in the union of sperm and egg', but that cannot be the full definition, which I will propose later. This leads us to the next objection, which for want of a better name can be called:

1.4.4   Objection from sperm and egg

'What is so special about the fertilised egg? If it is a human being, why aren't the sperm and egg collectively a human being before they unite?

Why can't any sperm and any egg, anywhere in the world, be taken collectively as a human being? But this is absurd. Does the use of a spermicide involve killing part of a human being? Do every pair of men and women collectively carry around millions of human beings, overlapping by sharing an egg or a sperm?'

Connected to these worries is the thought that because fertilisation is a *process* it is *gradual* and cannot really be marked off from what happens to sperm and egg before they unite. If continuity is so important, why not stretch it back *before* fertilisation, which is not some 'magic moment', and treat sperm and egg *as such* as a collective human being, with all the strange consequences that ensue? Again there is a related question sometimes posed (for example, by Tooley, though again in connection with *persons* rather than human beings), whether it is intrinsically wrong to refrain from procreation. After all, even if the sperm and egg are not a human being as such, they are, it might be thought, a *potential* human being, and since life is good, sperm and ova ought to be brought together wherever possible. But can this be right?

The answer is that all of these worries are specious. First, it is no part of the position being defended here that a sperm and an egg *per se* constitute a human being: it is a *fertilised* egg that is a human being. It is clear that fertilisation is a process and so occurs over time rather that at an instant. The same is true for, say, kicking a football: use a slow-motion camera and you will see the boot depressing the ball gradually, and the ball leaving the boot gradually, and no video camera, no matter how advanced, will record *the* mathematical instant at which the ball is *kicked*. But what are we supposed to infer from this – that it is metaphysically impossible to kick a football? The suggestion is absurd – it is as correct to say, 'Bill kicked the football at 2.13 p.m.', as it is to say that anyone ever does *anything*. The same goes for fertilisation: does it occur once the tail of the sperm is wholly inside the egg, or halfway, or will just the entry of the head suffice? There *is* no mathematically magic moment, but it is as true to say, 'Fertilisation occurred at 11.35 a.m.' as it is to say, 'Bill and Belinda had sex at 11.35 p.m.' That is as precise as we can be, and as precise as we need to be.[14]

Now, once we accept that there is such a thing as fertilisation and the fertilised egg, we can see how what goes on, from the moment the sperm enters the egg, is the complex sequence of events involving the union of the parts of each gamete. What is called *syngamy*, namely the merger of the genetic material of each gamete (complete after about 24 hours), is only the *end* of a process that *begins* when the sperm and egg start communicating information to each other via hormones and other chemicals, in a way still hardly understood. They are, as it were, 'made for each other', and once they are close enough to communicate (when sperm is inside egg if not before), absolutely *everything* they do is directed towards their own *extinction* and replacement by something else altogether. To regard sperm and egg separately as a collective human being is, then, spurious – they are clearly distinct organic entities with their own nuclei, that is, their own 'command and control' centres, their own nutritive and vegetative behaviour. True, they still seek each other out even when not united, but that does not make them a single entity any more than a hungry person and a cheesecake make a single entity before the former has digested the latter. (The analogy is imperfect but the point is similar; indeed, the facts as known thus far suggest that the ovum first digests all of the sperm except for the pronucleus containing the genetic material, which merges with the pronucleus of the egg, thus causing the zygote to have a full genetic complement.)

A sperm and an egg, then, are not a collective human being. Nor are they a *potential* human being in any sense different from that in which a pint of milk, a lump of cheese, some cream, flour and sugar are a potential cheesecake. The point of this analogy, again, is not to trivialise the status of sperm and egg as ingredients in that most precious of things, a human life – sperm and egg are not just any old cells like skin cells or bone cells – but to emphasise that a potential human being is not a *kind* of human being any more than a potential cheesecake is a kind of cake. Hence, whatever the moral issues surrounding procreation and contraception – and there *are* important issues that will not be discussed here – there can be no case for saying that there is a duty to procreate because the sperm and egg are a *kind of thing* – namely a potential human being – whose continued development would be thwarted if its parts did not come together.

1.4.5   Objection from fission and totipotency

There are two large and complex issues surrounding the metaphysical and moral status of the embryo that can only be touched on here and in the next section, but which should be mentioned because they are often raised especially by those more familiar with the facts of embryological development.[15]

The first concerns the fact that there is a kind of flexibility about the embryo in the early stages that seems to preclude its being counted as a single individual. Before the so-called 'primitive streak' appears at about 2 weeks' gestation (that group of cells which indicate the basic body plan of the embryo) it is possible for the embryo to divide into identical twins, each of which may also divide, and so on. So how can there have been an identifiable individual there at the beginning? Why not two? Or three? Or ten? Furthermore, up to the 8-cell stage (days 2–3), each cell of the embryo is 'totipotent': if removed from the embryo, it too begins dividing in such a way as to have the potential of developing into a foetus. So three cells could be taken from a 4-cell embryo and four identical foetuses would develop (and more, if any of them spontaneously twinned). Again, how can we speak of a single identifiable human being in the first place?

As interesting as these facts are, they do not refute the assertion that the early embryo is a single human being, albeit one with the potential to give rise to other, distinct human beings. In term of the metaphysics of embryo identity, twinning should be looked at in the same way as any case of the division of a cell (or group of cells). The 'parent' cell ceases to exist on division and the 'daughter' cells come into existence. The simple fact is that not all human beings come into existence at fertilisation – some do so a few days later if there is twinning. Twins (identical ones, that is) will *not* be able to trace their identities back to fertilisation. For them, conception occurs at division (hence one of the reasons why 'conception' and 'fertilisation' are not synonymous). What this means is that an embryo that subsequently twins *cannot* be identified with any post-division embryo – in *this* sense, it is not *identifiable*. But it *is* still identifiable as a living human being whose identity can be traced from fertilisation to division when it ceases to exist. Why should we regard it as really some indeterminate number of individuals simply because it can *give rise* to two or more individuals? Suppose I showed you a special kind of tree, the Twin Tree, which has the special property that on occasion it will begin to separate into distinct Twin Trees, its two halves gradually growing apart from the roots up. Would you then conclude I had not shown you a *single* tree in the first place? Were there really two all along? But if the two new trees can also divide, maybe ad infinitum, was there an *indeterminate* number of trees standing right where the original Twin Tree was? If so, this must mean there was *no tree at all*. (If it is *inherently* indeterminate how many *x*s of a certain kind there are at one place at one time, there can be *no x*s there at all. Think about why this must be true.) But isn't it absurd to say that I didn't show you a tree at all, even though what I showed you had roots, branches and leaves all connected up in a tree-like way, and behaved just like other trees do except for the peculiar twinning capacity?

The same goes for totipotency. Suppose I show you a Twin Bush which, like its cousin the Twin Tree, has a curious property. The Twin Bush is an interconnected bunch of shoots, any one of which can be separated from the rest and planted, whence it will develop into a genetically identical Twin Bush. I could break the original bush up into its shoots, all of which then grow into new Twin Bushes. Now, does this mean I do not have a single bush in the first place even though, without separation, the clump of shoots grows happily like any other bush, can be transplanted as a single object, can be destroyed by a poison applied to only one shoot, and so on? If there were an indeterminate number of Twin Bushes in the first place, how could there really be any? In the case of the embryo, say at the eight-cell stage, the removal and development of one totipotent cell looks like a case where the original embryo survives, having merely lost a cell. What happens if five cells are removed – has the original ceased to exist? Note that the same question arises if, say, ten shoots are taken from a fifteen-shoot Twin Bush. This is a difficult matter involving subtle questions about the beginning and end of existence of organisms – and we cannot enter into detailed discussion here. But note that the removal and development of totipotent parts of plants and trees happens all the time, namely when *cuttings* are taken! In such cases the original plant or tree survives though a small portion is removed and cultivated. We have no hesitation is saying, for instance, 'Here is a single rose bush', even though literally hundreds of cuttings could be taken from it! Moreover, it is fair to assume that there really *are* Twin Bushes (though not Twin Trees). So why should we have a problem in the case of, say, removing one shoot from a Twin Bush? And if not, why should we deny that there is a single embryo if one totipotent cell is removed? But if this is admitted, there is no problem in saying there is one embryo if *no* totipotent cells are removed. In other words, *there is no problem about how many embryos there are in the first place*, whether or not cells are removed, even if they are all totipotent. The only problem is how many cells need to be removed before that embryo ceases to exist, and this is a *different* problem that *presupposes* there was one embryo all along.

The moral of the story as far as fission and totipotency are concerned, then, is that the individuality of the embryo is not influenced by what it *might* do (for example, twin) or what *can* be done to it (separation into totipotent cells). But some lingering concern might remain. If the pre-twinning embryo really is an individual human being, is it the *parent* of the twins that result from it? Does it *die* when it divides? If it dies, should we *mourn* its death? There are complex issues raised by these questions, to do with our cultural practices, and only a few brief points can be made. First, parenthood involves far more than mere causation. The pre-twinning embryo *causes* the twins that result from it, but dividing cells or organisms are called 'parents' in a metaphorical sense only (their descendants always being called in biology 'daughters', not 'sons'). Parenthood involves one of three things: either a deliberate decision to bring another human being into existence; or a deliberate decision to do things that a couple knows may well lead to another human being's coming into existence; or well-founded social conventions about who should be *responsible* for someone else. The pre-twinning embryo makes no decisions and is incapable of responsibility. Therefore it cannot be a true parent. Second, the pre-twinning embryo does indeed cease to exist, though without leaving a corpse. This is a kind of death (as would be 'vaporisation' by a science-fiction vaporising gun). But we do not mourn the divided embryo, because of the bareness of its relationship to anyone. Suppose women had transparent stomachs with magnifying windows enabling anyone to see the embryos they carried at any stage of gestation. In such a world our practices would change, and justifiably so. Twinning would be mourned, though probably in a restrained and attenuated way, and there would be compensatory rejoicing for the new twins that had come into existence.

1.4.6   Objection from cloning and parthenogenesis

We have heard a great deal in recent years about developments in the technology of cloning. Sheep have been cloned, as have mice. Plants are routinely cloned. Probably human beings can be cloned. The main technique involves removing the nucleus of an ovum (containing the female's genetic material) and replacing it with some other nucleus, whether from a sperm or some body cell; the resulting organism will have the genotype of the sperm or body cell donor, it will be a 'twin' of the donor (which need not be male). Sometimes (as in famous experiments with carrot plants) a cell can be taken from an adult organism and induced to divide and develop into a 'twin' of that organism, without any nuclear injection. Another phenomenon, parthenogenesis, involves the development of an embryo from an unfertilised egg. This is the normal method of reproduction in some animals (the whip-tailed lizard, for example), while in others it can be induced (such as exposing frog eggs to salt water), although induced division usually stops at an early stage of development.[16]

It is sometimes argued that these phenomena must radically alter our understanding of the zygote (and embryo). After all, if an organism can be produced from, say, a skin cell or a bone cell, or even from an egg, rather than from the unification of egg and sperm, doesn't it follow that it is wrong to see fertilisation as the beginning of life? Suppose parthenogenesis could be induced in humans: shouldn't we then regard the *egg* as a human being? If a human could be cloned from a skin cell, shouldn't we say the skin cell was a human being? Suppose it were discovered that every human skin cell has the latent potential for being used to clone its owner: would it follow that we are all carrying around millions of tiny human beings? The suggestion is absurd, and if true, would mean we committed genocide every time we scratched an itch. Our concepts, it seems, need revising – in the direction of saying that the beginning of human life is not some magical event at which an organism, say a human being, comes into existence at a stroke: the beginnings of life are diverse, disparate, part of a flexible biological continuum.

This sort of response is, however, unwarranted. There is much we do not know about phenomena such as those mentioned above, and our metaphysical conclusions need to be firmly rooted in a correct understanding of what goes on in certain kinds of case. For instance, in the case of organisms for which parthenogenesis is the normal means of reproduction, we may be forced to conclude that the egg *really is the organism* at its earliest stage. More likely, however, is that what happens in such species involves the *triggering* of the egg in some biochemical way which brings the organism into existence and therefore *fundamentally changes the nature of the egg cell* from mere *precursor* of the organism to *the organism itself*. This, I would argue, is the key to understanding the metaphysics of embryogenesis. When cells are *induced* to divide embryonically, whether they be egg cells or other body cells, the induction is a *trigger* that *changes the nature of the cell*. Before that trigger is fired, the cell may indeed have the potential to be *turned into* a zygote, but that potential is *not* the same as the potential of an existing zygote to grow, take nutrition, expel waste, develop a mature form, and so on. The potential for these kinds of behaviour is *intrinsic*, part of the very *nature* of the thing itself. Given the right *extrinsic* factors – food and a hospitable environment being the primary ones – this intrinsic potential for development will be realised. But the potential of a skin cell to be used as a vector for cloning, or an egg cell to be used for (at least induced) parthenogenesis, is not intrinsic to it any more than a sperm cell has the intrinsic potential to develop into a mature member of the species of organism whose sperm it is. (Even if a human sperm cell could live forever in the most hospitable environment it could ever want, it would never develop into a human being.) In ordinary fertilisation both sperm and egg need triggers – namely each other – to turn their combination into a zygote. The same goes for an egg on its own, or body cell, or any other thing that could, through appropriate biochemical mechanisms, be transformed into an entity with the behaviour characteristic of immature members of the species from which the cell or other thing originates.

Our understanding of this area is very small compared to all that we could eventually find out. What has just been said is less a thorough argument for the claim that the phenomena under discussion do not undermine the proposition that human life begins at conception, than a proposal for how such phenomena could be *incorporated* into the overall position I have been defending. (I have given more detailed argument elsewhere, and refer the reader to the notes.) As things stand, the phenomena simply do not refute that position. But they do suggest the need for more precision in our *definition* of conception. Given the phenomena we have looked at, conception should be defined as follows: conception is that event, typically involving the union of sperm and egg, which consists in a change in the intrinsic nature of a cell or group of cells, where that change confers on the cell or group of cells (or their descendants in the case of division) the intrinsic potential to develop, given the right extrinsic factors, into a mature human being. Conception does not bring into existence a potential human being, but an *actual* human being with the potential to develop, given the right external factors, into a mature human being. I leave aside questions of intrinsic genetic defect, because that would require a more detailed discussion of potential which cannot be entered into here. Suffice it to say that an organism can have the intrinsic potential to develop into a mature member of its species even if intrinsic genetic defect means it will not be a *healthy* or *normal* member. (A more complicated case involves an intrinsic genetic defect that actually destroys – if possible – the very intrinsic potential to develop to maturity, say by ensuring radically stunted growth. While recognising the questions raised by such a case for my definition, I cannot pursue them here.)

1.5   A Feminist Argument for Abortion

Having spent some time on the first premise of the basic argument – that the foetus (and embryo and zygote) is a human being – it is time to return to the second premise concerning the permissibility of killing innocent human beings. Suppose we accept that the foetus is a human being with the right to life; might it still be permissible to kill it in certain cases? One strand of argument that has been prominent in the abortion debate from the very beginning, and which is probably what drove the debate into the headlines in the 1960s and 1970s, concerns the rights of the woman carrying the unborn child. The slogan was (and is) 'Woman have the right to choose what to do with their bodies' (hence the term 'pro-choice'), and the stigmatisation of abortion means no less than the denigration of this idea and the promotion of the opposite idea – namely, that women's bodies and fertility are subordinate to the rights of others, in particular the foetus, the father and society. In the Cultural Revolution of the 1960s, when feminism was at the very top of the social agenda, this view of abortion had great resonance – as it still does.

It is one thing, however, to assert women's total bodily independence, their 'right to control their fate', as feminists sometimes put it, and another to justify it. For one thing, if the observations made above about the nature of the foetus carry any weight, it is now beyond reasonable dispute – if it ever was not – that the foetus is not a female body part like breasts or the appendix. It is an independently subsisting organism which, from the first moment of its existence, *uses* its mother, takes *nourishment* from her, indeed, alters her whole being – body shape and size, chemical make-up, temperament – *for its own benefit*. The foetus does not *serve* its mother, but *is served* by her. So whatever 'the right to choose' may mean, it cannot entail that the choice to have an abortion is like the choice whether or not to have a nose job.

Second, the idea that women should have complete dominion over their own bodies is hardly one with a venerable history. Naturally the age and historical acceptance of an idea do not make it correct, but the point is that throughout history women have been seen as, among other things, potential mothers with a responsibility to care for and nurture their children for the benefit of society. The traditional notion has always been that, as a matter of socio-biological fact, women just do *not* have only themselves to answer to when fertility is in question. Other parties are involved. So if the 'right to control their bodies' is what women asked for in the 1960s, this was a radical idea that needed justification.

Judith Jarvis Thomson is thought by many feminists to have provided just such a justification, in her celebrated 1971 article defending abortion.[17] She is prepared to assume for the sake of debate that the foetus is an innocent human being with a right to life, but argues that this right is not absolute, because the foetus can be what is now sometimes called an 'innocent aggressor'. What she offers in defence of abortion is a simple thought experiment. Suppose that you are kidnapped by the Society of Music Lovers anxious to save the life of a famous violinist with a fatal kidney disease. Only your blood is of the right type to save him. So, your circulatory system is plugged into his, cleansing his blood and allowing his kidneys to recover. You are, as it were, turned into a human dialysis machine. But only for nine months, because at the end of that time the violinist's kidneys will have returned to normal and you can be disconnected. Should you go along with this and allow yourself to be confined against your will for nine months? Thomson thinks this 'outrageous'. Why should the violinist's right to life outweigh your right to control your body?

The case is analogous to that of pregnancy by rape, but it might be extended. Suppose you wander carelessly into the wrong ward of the hospital: you intend to visit your sick grandmother but you find yourself, through negligence, in the ward labelled 'Volunteer Human Dialysis'. The doctors innocently think you are a volunteer, and next thing you know you are plugged into an ailing trombone player. This seems analogous to pregnancy through carelessness. Maybe it can be extended further, say to ignorance that is not your fault. You volunteer as a human dialysis machine thinking it will not be all that inconvenient, perhaps taking up a few hours a day, with the rest of the time your own. Maybe the doctors did not explain the situation clearly enough. Two weeks after being plugged into an ailing harpsichordist, you find that it is far more inconvenient than you imagined. This looks similar to intentional pregnancy in the case of, say, a young woman badly informed about things such as morning sickness, weight gain, varicose veins, migraines, physical immobility and loss of libido. Perhaps the analogy can be extended to cases where you are fully responsible for your actions and know all the consequences: you volunteer to be plugged in, knowing the inconvenience, but then an emergency crops up – your mother is dying and wants you at her beside. Now, you volunteered as a human dialysis machine out of the goodness of your heart, but surely if a personal emergency arises you should be allowed to change your mind – after all, family comes before strangers, even if they are world-renowned musicians. This looks a bit like intentional pregnancy, where a good social reason comes up for changing your mind, like that all-important promotion which will give you the income to send your other children to the school they deserve. May you not change your mind and 'terminate the pregnancy'?

It seems, then, that if the thought experiment works it can be extended to cover many, perhaps a majority of cases of pregnancy. Whether it is the mother's fault that she became pregnant does not seem to have anything to do with it either: it just looks like a high price to pay for one's momentary carelessness that one ends up inconveniently plugged into another human being for nine months. And if one is ignorant through no fault of one's own, or has overly optimistic ideas about what pregnancy involves, then the plugging-in might begin to look like a veritable punishment of the innocent woman.

According to Thomson, the violinist has no more right to the use of your kidneys than a fanatical cinema-goer has the right to force her favourite film star to come over from Hollywood and heal her with a touch of his cool hand on her fevered brow. The same, it is implied, goes for the unborn child making use of the mother's hospitable environment. Could it be objected that the film star has, by virtue of being in the public eye, forfeited his right not to be harassed by fans who think he has the healing touch? Have you forfeited the right not to be plugged into an ailing violinist by virtue of being even within 50 miles of a hospital where human dialysis takes place? Surely not, any more than a woman has forfeited control of her body to another human being by virtue of being fertile, having sex, mixing in the company of men, and the like. What is she supposed to do – lock herself in her house?

Such is Thomson's argument. Note that, as far as the position being defended here goes, *even if* fault were relevant in some cases – 'you've made your bed, so lie in it', so to speak – the fact that there is obviously no fault in other cases, such as rape, would mean that an anti-abortion position based on fault would have to concede the permissibility of abortion in just such cases. It would, then, not really be an anti-abortion position at all, but a compromise stance that allowed abortion in some cases but not others. So let us concentrate on the original violinist case, analogous to pregnancy by rape, where there is no question of bringing in the fault of the woman in order to defend the right to life of the foetus.

It might be thought that while the fault of the woman is not relevant, the fault of the other party is. It is tempting for the anti-abortionist to say that the cinema-goer case is not analogous to the violinist case because the cinema-goer, misguided as she may be about the healing powers of her favourite star, intentionally seeks to force him to 'heal' her, and can rightfully be resisted. This, it might be thought, would be an unjust assault on the star's bodily integrity, which he is allowed to resist by force. The violinist, on the other hand, being an innocent pawn in the hands of the well-meaning Society of Music Lovers, may not be resisted because he has not intentionally encroached on anyone's rights. I think this is mistaken. Even if the cinema-goer were involuntarily brainwashed into believing her favourite star could heal her, and hypnotised into flying over to Hollywood in search of him, she could legitimately be resisted by force. The point here is that the right of self-defence is available only against aggression that is *not just*. Writers on this subject usually speak of *unjust aggression*, which may be thought to mean that only a conscious, knowingly wrongful assault may be resisted, but this interpretation is incorrect. The point about the injustice of the aggression is to distinguish cases where it would be *wrong* to act in self-defence – such as resisting a police officer in the lawful pursuit of his duties (even if the person he is arresting is in fact innocent) – from others. Now, in those other cases there may indeed be a deliberately wrongful assault, but equally the assault may be by someone stupefied by drink or drugs, or otherwise not in their right mind. (Some philosophers call such an aggression a 'materially unjust' as opposed to a 'formally unjust' intentional attack.) In *both* kinds of case, self-defence is available and so may be used.

Suppose, for example, that a mad scientist has drugged sleeping Fred with a chemical that will cause him, in an hour's time, to wake up, hunt me down, tie me up and play me endless recordings of Vivaldi's *Four Seasons* – Fred has been turned into a psycho music torturer with me as his only target. What action am I entitled to take against him? To be sure, he is innocent, a victim of the mad scientist – but I may resist him. If he lunges at me with a ghetto blaster, I am entitled to use force to make him back off. I am entitled to plug my ears. I am allowed to put as much distance between me and him as I like. There are many things I am allowed to do in defence of my bodily or mental well-being. The question is: am I allowed to kill him? Could I kill him in his sleep? One would have thought not. Am I allowed to shoot him in the head as he lunges at me with his portable CD player? Again, one would have thought not. The inconvenience has not yet begun, but then neither has it begun when you wake up and find yourself plugged into the violinist. It is not a question of whether the inconvenience has begun, but rather of whether the action leading to the inconvenience has begun. Once you, the 'human dialysis machine', wake up and see what is in store for you, you have a decision to make: What can you do to restore your bodily integrity? Does it include homicide?

Thomson's intuition is that it does, but the intuition is contestable. Suppose you walk into the Human Dialysis ward out of curiosity, knowing roughly what goes on there. You are suddenly confronted by a team of doctors and the violinist on his stretcher: they are chasing after you with a plastic tube pointed in your direction. What are you allowed to do? You can run, of course. But then you are backed into a corner. You can reach for the nearest can of sleeping gas and spray them all, if one is near to hand. If you have a gun, you may even shoot over their heads, or perhaps at their legs. But are you allowed to shoot the violinist in the head and then say, 'Well, your problem is solved'? No more, I would suggest, than you are allowed to shoot to kill any of the doctors. Is this just pedantic hair-splitting? Not at all: it is the sort of thing courts examine every day of the week in order to see whether someone has exceeded their legitimate right of self-defence. The exact circumstances need to be discovered, but the general principle is clear: it is wrong to kill someone in order to escape physical inconvenience, whether that inconvenience lasts for a day or for nine months.

Now imagine the following case. Carol was kidnapped, drugged and raped as a young woman. Not only that, but in order to make sure she had no memory of what happened, her crazed assailants kept her locked up for the nine months she carried her child, drugged and unconscious, in a kind of coma. She delivered the child, it was taken away, she was woken up and sent out into the street. Carol returns to her normal life and becomes a moderately successful businesswoman. Twenty years later she meets a young man who announces himself as her long-lost child, which is indeed what he is. Carol does not know a thing about him, but he declares that, as her child, he intends to invoke a state law that compels any parent, no matter what the circumstances, to feed, clothe, house and generally support any biological offspring up to the age of thirty. This would mean a severe encroachment on Carol's whole life, her bodily and mental integrity, her property, her lifestyle. Everything would change. What is she allowed to do in response? Morality would, I suggest, entitle her to refuse all but the most basic assistance. If the young man broke into her house and started raiding the cupboards, she could treat him as a common burglar. But could she kill him? If he were a diabetic, could she hide his insulin? Rightly, we would say no. But the question now is: if Carol is not allowed to kill him then, why should she be allowed to kill him before he is born, if she knew she were carrying him? Wouldn't such an act look like a case of making him pay for the crime of another? The point here is not that whether an aggressor is innocent or not makes a difference to one's right of self-defence, but that it sometimes looks as though what is being advocated in certain cases is *not* self-defence at all but a kind of sublimated punishment of a third party for an offence someone else has committed. And as a matter of psychological fact this is often what happens in the case of rape: the woman, rightly feeling outraged at the violation of her body, and wanting to punish the rapist, takes her anger out on the child. However understandable such anger may be, at least two serious ethical mistakes are being made. First, it is not up to the woman to punish her assailant, it is the obligation of the state; second, her anger is directed at the wrong person altogether. Again, it must be emphasised that *this* is what opponents of abortion should mean when they say the victim of rape must not punish the innocent third party, namely the child; *not* that it is wrong to kill an 'innocent aggressor' because he is innocent. It is wrong to kill an 'innocent aggressor' who threatens you with physical inconvenience because it is a wholly disproportionate form of self-defence. (Recall the remarks on collision of rights in chapter 2 of *Moral Theory*: the less urgent right – here bodily integrity – must give way to the more urgent – the right to life.) The same goes for an aggressor who is guilty, who knows exactly what she is doing, such as the misguided cinema-goer in search of the star who can 'heal' her. The real point about innocence is this: if the victim of rape wants to be angry, she should be angry at her assailant, not her child, who did not ask to come into existence. As far as the *action* she may take against the child is concerned, however – the child *qua* threat to her bodily integrity – there are limits. She may not kill it, but she may well be permitted to give it up for adoption.

Thomson's violinist case, then, rests upon an intuition that is eminently contestable. It is not at all obvious that your plight, being plugged into the violinist, allows you to kill him.

But, it might be objected, there is an equivocation on the meaning of 'kill' in my response to Thomson. Sure, it would be wrong of you to stab the violinist in the heart; but what about merely disconnecting the tube? You are not, you protest, trying to kill him, only to free yourself; and if he dies, that is an unfortunate side effect. It is here that the Principle of Double Effect (PDE) comes into play. Recall from chapter 3 of *Moral Theory* that one of the clauses of PDE is that where a morally indifferent act (disconnecting a tube) has two effects, one good and the other bad, there must be a *proportionality* between the good and bad effects for the initial act to be permissible. In the violinist case the good effect is your being released from nine months' inconvenience, and the bad effect is the death of the violinist. Is there a proportionality here? Evidently not. Hence you are not permitted to disconnect the tube, unpleasant though the prospect of your confinement must be – and this is really just an explanation of why your self-defensive acts must always be proportionate; in other words, the bad effects of your acts must always be proportionate to the good you are seeking to defend.

This is not to say that the situation can never be subtle and complicated. In particular, it is when your life is at stake that the question of self-defence can become fraught with difficulty. We have seen that physical and mental inconvenience would not justify disconnection of the tube. But suppose now that, as the violinist is brought back to health by the use of your kidneys, your own body is slowly being poisoned by his infected blood, and within nine months you will be dead. Now what should you do? Again, you may not grab a knife and stab the violinist through the heart: the right of self-defence is precisely what it says, a right of *defence*, not a right of intentional homicide. If you are attacked by a knife-wielding mugger and you have a gun, you may surely use it, but not to shoot him through the head, at least intentionally (you may do it by accident in the confusion of the attack, but that is another matter). If your life is genuinely under threat, or you at least reasonably believe it to be, you may use whatever force is necessary *to repel the attack*, even if it means maiming your assailant (because there is a clear proportionality between your life's being saved and the mugger's suffering grievous harm), and even if it means *knowingly but unintentionally* causing his death (because there is a proportionality between your life and his).

In the life-threatening violinist case, however, your options are limited. Disconnect the tube, and he surely dies. Keep it connected, and you surely die. Consider now the case of a pregnant woman whose child poses a threat to her life. Such cases were once common but are much rarer now, thanks to medical advances. But they still occur: for example, the position of the foetus may threaten a rupture of the mother's internal organs, or a massive haemorrhage. What can be done? Is the doctor allowed, say, to crush the head of the child (craniotomy) in order to allow it to pass through the birth canal? But this means the certain death of the child. On the other hand, suppose a woman is diagnosed with uterine cancer, and when operated on is discovered to be pregnant. Can the doctor go ahead and remove the woman's uterus, even though the child will again surely die? In this latter case, the initial act is removal of the uterus, an act not wrong in itself: its effects are the saving of the life of the mother, and the death of the child. The application of PDE suggests there is indeed a proportionality between the two – life as against life. Crucially, there is no *intention* to kill the child, only to save the mother: the child's death is not a *means* to the saving of the mother, otherwise it would be a case of killing one innocent person to save another, which is every bit as wrong as a judge's condemning one innocent man to death in order to save other innocent men from homicide by a rioting mob. The cancerous womb case is not the same as that of a woman who goes to hospital for a hysterectomy to lessen the risk of her developing uterine cancer in later life (a practice recommended, dubiously, by surgeons allegedly zealous for the welfare of post-menopausal women), and who is discovered to be pregnant. May the doctor go ahead and remove the uterus, with the child dying as a result? Here the requisite proportionality is not present: the child will certainly die, but the mother will merely have a *smaller risk* of a *possibly fatal* disease she may never in fact get.

Let us return to the craniotomy case. Should we group it with the cancerous womb case, or with the case of stabbing the violinist in the heart when you are being poisoned to death by his blood? Does the doctor in the craniotomy case intend the death of the child? It is hard to see how he does not. Recall from chapter 3 of *Moral Theory* the case of the person who chops off another person's head and says in his defence, 'I didn't intend to kill, only to decapitate. I knew he would almost certainly die, but I didn't mean this to happen.' It was said that the decapitator could *conceivably* not have intended death, but that the circumstances would have to be extraordinary, and the state of the accused's mind would have to be assessed very carefully were he to plead such a defence. Craniotomy, it appears, is in a similar category. A surgeon may well have developed a technique for piecing together crushed skulls and so keeping alive a child on whom he performs craniotomy – clear evidence of an intention not to kill. But in the absence of exculpatory evidence such as this, the mere expression of regret over the death of the child, or the verbal protestation 'I did not intend to kill', has little probative weight, whether at the tribunal of law or of morality. In the current state of medicine, if the intentional crushing of a child's skull is not also an intentional killing, it is hard to know what would be.

It does not, on the face of it, appear that disconnecting the tube in the life-threatening violinist case is similarly to be counted as an obvious instance of direct, intentional homicide. Remember that the agent's state of mind is crucial in assessing what he intends. Do we really want to say that the tube disconnection inevitably points to a homicidal intent in the same way that a decapitation or a head-crushing does? Viewed *from the standpoint of the agent*, the violinist case is so out of the ordinary that one could easily imagine your disconnecting the tube without paying the least attention to its effect on the violinist. Or if you did, it is difficult to imagine your thinking, 'I am now killing him', unless perhaps you discovered he was your longstanding enemy whom you were gleeful about having the opportunity to dispatch. Can we imagine the doctor in the craniotomy case thinking, 'I am crushing the child's skull but I am not killing him, though he will in fact die'? Does this ring true? It *might*. As was said in chapter 3 of *Moral Theory*, we are not talking about metaphysical necessity, but about the contingent circumstances of the case. Yet we can see a big difference between the craniotomy and cancerous womb cases. It is perfectly easy to imagine the doctor in the second case thinking, 'I am removing the womb, and the baby will die, but I am not deliberately killing it.' This is all the more easy to believe nowadays, when premature babies can be kept alive at ever earlier ages (presently around 22 weeks), thus providing extra evidence (albeit defeasible, and assuming he was aware of and prepared to use the available technology) that a doctor who removes a cancerous womb is not an intentional killer. Clearly there are difficulties of factual interpretation to which ethicists are bound to be sensitive. But the principles themselves, it has been argued, are clear enough.

All of this, it has been objected again and again, seems like so much hair-splitting. How can doctors make fine distinctions between types of threat to the mother's life? Aren't they bound to save her life no matter what, instead of engaging in pedantic philosophising about the Principle of Double Effect? Such protestations miss the whole point. It is *not* just the life of the mother that is at stake. Any judgement that the mother's life must be saved no matter what, however well intentioned, must involve at least an *implicit* judgement that somehow, for reasons most of which have already been dismissed, that the life of an unborn child counts *less* than the life of an adult – that it is *less* human, *less* worthy of protection. If that does not amount to a kind of unjust discrimination, it is difficult to see what does. And if anguished life-or-death situations, thankfully more rare in obstetrics than they used to be, do not bear enough importance in a person's life to call for as much philosophising as necessary to *make the right judgement of how to act*, without sacrificing the possibility of acting altogether by sinking into Hamlet-like deliberations, then again it is hard to see just where philosophising *is* called for.

The resulting position may seem harsh. For all that Judith Jarvis Thomson has performed a service by calling attention to the importance of rights with her brilliant analyses (one of the more important contributions to recent moral philosophy), she has not shown that a right to abortion can be grounded in a woman's right over her own body. Consideration of her argument has led to the position that abortion is not justifiable even in cases of rape (or, by parity of reasoning, incest), or when the mother's life is at stake. A doctor may indeed do all that he can to save the mother's life, *short of deliberately killing her child in order to do so*. The saving of one innocent life does not justify the taking of another. And if this is how abortion is to be regarded in such extreme and painful cases, how much more should it be regarded as wrong in the 99 per cent of situations where abortion is carried out to spare the mother inconvenience, financial hardship, difficulties with the father of the child, and so on? In all such cases PDE does not even begin to apply, not only because the disproportionality is obvious, but because the death of the child is directly and deliberately intended. No attempt is made by mother, doctor or abortion clinic to save such babies.

1.6   The Foetus, the Person and the *Person*

We saw in chapter 4 of *Moral Theory* that the *personism* espoused by so many philosophers in discussing the value of human life has serious flaws. It takes an important aspect of moral evaluation – the centrality of rationality and self-consciousness to a correct metaphysical account of what a human being is – and asserts that only beings, whether human or not, that *have* those characteristics *actually*, as opposed to *potentially*, deserve the highest form of protection that morality can offer. We saw that this leads Peter Singer, for instance, into making a complicated formulation of his position designed to ensure that the drugged and the sleeping (among others) come out as *persons*. But the problem does not go away by making the definition of *personhood* more complex.

For the *personist*, what matters are the actual psychological characteristics of a human being. This does not mean that a human being ('person' in the normal sense) has to have, here and now, certain beliefs, desires or other mental states to qualify as a *person*; rather, he has to have certain *capacities*. Michael Tooley puts it very broadly at one point, saying that 'an entity cannot be a person [that is, *person*, in my terminology] unless it has developed to the point where it is capable of at least some sort of mental life'.[18] This will not do, however, since the capacity to feel pain and pleasure is a mental one and yet not all sentient animals, for the *personist*, are *persons* (such as cats – Tooley's example is kittens – dogs, birds, aardvarks . . .). Tooley toys with the idea that there are *necessary* and *sufficient* conditions for *personhood* and provides a list of likely characteristics, but the ones he and other *personists* such as Singer focus on are (to use Tooley's words): 'the capacity for self-consciousness', 'the capacity for rational thought', 'the capacity to envisage a future for oneself', 'the capacity to remember a past involving oneself' and 'the capacity for being a subject of non-momentary interests'.[19]

Now, Tooley's own argument is complex and not a little obscure, and there is no room to consider it in detail here. We can, however, look at whether the general *personist* position espoused by him, Singer and others is tenable in respect of the foetus. Perhaps the best way to do so is to see how *personism* deals with the position of human beings who are asleep, drugged or otherwise temporarily unconscious. Are they *persons* while in the unconscious state? If not – as *personism* does appear to imply – it would seem to be permissible, on this theory, to kill them for any reasons that would justify killing a foetus, for example if the existence of the unconscious person was in some way a burden on other people responsible for him, an inconvenience for them, or unwanted for some reason or other parallel to the reasons why the vast majority of pro-abortionists believe abortion is justified. Although it may sound bizarre, it follows from *personism* that if Brenda's husband Charles is preventing her from making some important choice in her life, say, to take on a career, and she despises him for this and wants to be rid of him, from the *moral* point of view it would be best for her to wait until he was in a state of non-*personhood*, say asleep, and inject him with a fatal poison.

One need not labour the repugnance of such a consequence. If a moral theory allows that sort of behaviour, then that is a *reductio ad absurdum* of the theory. Needless to say, *personists* deny that any such consequence follows from their theory. How so? Speaking with approval of Michael Tooley's position, Singer says:

> To have a right to life [Tooley believes in rights; Singer thinks it is sometimes 'convenient' to use the term, although there are no such things], one must have, or at least one time have had, the concept of having a continued existence. Note that this formulation avoids any problems in dealing with sleeping or unconscious people; it is enough that they have had, at one time, the concept of continued existence for us to be able to say that continued life may be in their interests. This makes sense: my desire to continue living – or to complete the book I am writing, or to travel around the world next year – does not cease whenever I am not consciously thinking about these things. We often desire things without the desire being at the forefront of our minds. The fact that we have the desire is apparent if we are reminded of it, or suddenly confronted with a situation in which we must choose between two courses of action, one of which makes the fulfilment of the desire less likely. In a similar way, when we go to sleep our desires for the future have not ceased to exist. They will still be there, when we wake. As the desires are still part of us, so, too, our interest in continued life remains part of us while we are asleep or unconscious.[20]

When discussing the fact that so many people, including many disabled, have protested publicly at his lectures, even causing the cancellation of conferences at which he was due to appear, Singer says:

> I pointed out [to handicapped people who had criticised him in a magazine article] that I was advocating euthanasia not for anyone like themselves, but for severely disabled newborn infants, and that it was crucial to my defense of euthanasia that these infants would never have been capable of grasping that they are living beings with a past and a future. Hence my views cannot be a threat to anyone who is capable of wanting to go on living, or even of understanding that his or her life might be threatened.[21]

Euthanasia will be discussed in the next chapter; the relevance in the present context of the words just quoted is what they tell us about how *personists* handle the case of the unconscious human being. Later in the article in which the second passage appears, Singer modifies his claim, possibly in reaction to the 'capable of wanting to go on living' criterion – for it might be argued that the sleeping are incapable of wanting to go on living, *while they are asleep*. So he says: '[M]y views in no way threaten anyone who is, or ever has been, even minimally aware of the fact that he or she has a possible future life that could be threatened.'[22] Now, it seems, the criterion is 'present or past awareness of a possible future life'. What secures the lives of the sleeping, then, is that even if they are incapable, while asleep, of wanting to go on living, they *once* were so capable, or at the very least 'minimally aware' that they had a 'possible future life'. (Recall the remarks made about the last two quotations in chapter 4 of *Moral Theory*.)

But we can dismiss the 'present or past awareness' criterion immediately. It is a central part of the position of Singer, Tooley and other *personists* that someone diagnosed as being in an 'irreversible coma' may be killed or allowed to die. Yet the irreversibly comatose human being was *once* aware that he had a possible future life. So past awareness does not matter in the slightest to the *personist*. What, then, saves the sleeping person from being a possible victim of supposedly justified homicide? In the first passage quoted, Singer claims that a desire to go on living does not 'cease to exist' when someone falls asleep. In the second, he lays stress on the 'capability' to want to go on living. Tooley, in the list cited above of markers of *personhood*, mentions 'capacity' again and again. Now it is not right to say that when someone is asleep or drugged he *wants* things, or *believes* things, or *knows* things or is *aware* of things in the same way as when he is fully conscious. Otherwise a person who, say, killed another while under the influence of drugs, or while sleepwalking, would be as guilty of homicide as someone who did it with full awareness. But it is a simple fact that a person's mind can be so impaired, or influenced in one way or another, that he does not have beliefs and desires in the same way as if he were in a condition of normal awareness. Further, even when we are in a state of normal awareness we do not have all our beliefs and desires in the same conscious fashion. As I type these words, there are many things I believe which I have not thought about for a long time and am not thinking about now. But I can bring them to the forefront of my mind and so be aware of them: for instance, when I think about it I am aware that I believe the earth is round, that seven plus twenty is twenty-seven, that Quito is the capital of Ecuador. I have these beliefs, but until I think about them they are only *potentially* conscious. But what does it mean to have an unconscious belief or desire? Singer says a desire I have when awake does not 'cease to exist' when I am asleep, but he does not tell us in what sense, precisely, the desire continues to exist. Now to explore this matter would take us too far into vexed topics in the philosophy of mind. For instance, some philosophers of a physicalist bent say that unconscious mental states are somehow 'coded' in a part of the brain during unconsciousness, and so literally exist somewhere in space. Others more inclined to behaviourism say that the only sense in which the desire continues to exist is that if the person is restored to consciousness and prompted with certain questions, he will give certain responses.

It is not necessary, however, to delve into such issues here. For whatever the ultimate explanation of unconscious mental states, the point is that *potential* must be a crucial ingredient in the explanation. There must be *something* true of the sleeping person such that, when restored to consciousness, he will acknowledge having, and having had *even* when unconscious, certain beliefs, desires, and so on. A sleeping person is, for Singer and Tooley, a potential *person*. On Singer's definition, a *person* is 'rational and self-conscious'. But a person in a drunken stupor might hardly be rational, and when asleep hardly self-conscious. So he is not a *person*. But something is true of him such that his *personhood* can be made to 'return' to him. Tooley speaks of 'capacity', Singer of 'capability'. Whatever the term, the fundamental *personist* way of dealing with the sleeping, the drunk, the drugged, and so on, is to say that they are not under threat from the *personist* stance on killing because they are potential *persons*.

Once potentiality is introduced into the equation, though, there can be no backtracking. This means that to deny its applicability to the case of the foetus would be arbitrary, for there is no significant way in which, metaphysically speaking, the potentiality of the foetus *differs* from that of the drugged or sleeping man. They are all in a state in which there is *latent mental functioning* of the kind the *personist* uses as the ground for calling anything a *person*. There are differences between the cases, of course: the sleeping man is mature and fully developed, the foetus is immature and developing; the drugged man has not lost all consciousness, whereas the sleeping person has, and the foetus has not yet *reached* consciousness but will surely do so (barring injury or malformation) if it is, quite simply, *allowed* to do so. But it is hard to see how these distinctions make a metaphysical difference of the kind which supports a moral distinction. All of these beings are in some state of dormancy, that is, their normal functions are in some way suppressed or not fully realised, and for that suppression to be lifted each needs to be roused from its dormancy in some way: the sleeping person needs to be woken up; the drunk needs to get sober; the drugged man needs to wait for the drugs to wear off; and a foetus needs food, warmth and a generally hospitable environment. If these requirements are fulfilled in every case, each one of these creatures will *do what comes naturally*, and bring or restore himself to a state of normal and full functioning, which includes rationality, self-consciousness and all the other operations that go to make up the human being.

We can see, then, that the *personist* is quite correct to insist on the importance of mentality in the definition of what counts as the most important being for ethical purposes: the fact that human beings are rational and self-conscious is not accidental to the consideration of their moral status. He is also correct to assert, at least *officially*, that what matters are mental capacities or capabilities. But the *personist* strays from the right path in almost every other respect. In particular, the *personist* errs in asserting that those features of the mind have to be both present *and operative* for a being to possess the value that it has. If that really were the case, then not only would the drunk, the drugged and the sleeping *ipso facto* not possess moral value, but neither would any *person* who lost his *personhood* whenever he had a momentary blackout. But surely this is not the result the *personist* wants. To get off this absurd track he needs to appeal, as we said, to potentiality. Once he does so, then not only do the sleeping, drugged, and so on, come back within the ambit of serious moral concern (Singer), or of the right to life (Tooley), or of the right to life understood as absolutely inviolable (traditional morality), but so does the human being at every stage of development, from zygote to adult. Indeed, the fact that *personists* regularly speak of capacities and capabilities about as much as they speak of actual desires and states of awareness shows that they do, at least implicitly, recognise the crucial role of potentiality in ascribing *personhood*, since a capacity just *is* the potentiality for exercising a given function.

But the ambit of moral value does not stretch further back. It does not embrace the sperm or ovum as such (whatever else our duties may be in respect of sperm and ova) because, as already argued, what a sperm or ovum has to do to give rise to an adult human being and what a foetus has to do are *radically different*. The sperm and ovum must *cease to exist* before bringing about the existence of any human being, adult included;

the zygote, embryo and foetus do not have to cease to exist – on the contrary, they must continue to exist and to grow and develop. The sperm or ovum is no more a potential *person* than an egg is a potential cake. Nor are sperm and ovum taken together a potential *person* any more than eggs, flour, water, and so on, are a potential cake (as opposed to being potential *ingredients* of a cake), or a mass of nuts, bolts, fuses, cables, wheels, and so on, a potential car. Or, to put it another way, you can *if you like* speak of a given amount of eggs, flour, water, and so on, as a potential cake, but only so long as you mean no more than that they have the potential to *give rise to* a cake. There are different *grades* of potentiality, and what is being argued here is that as far as possessing the right to life is concerned, the potentiality that matters is the kind that inheres in an entity such that all that is required for the potentiality to be realised is that the entity itself continue or resume *normal functioning*. And as we saw in chapter 4 of *Moral Theory*, the concept of normal functioning simply cannot be understood without considering the *kind* of thing an entity belongs to, in this case the species *human being*.

To see how easy it is to be cavalier about one's use of the term 'potentiality', consider the sorts of example Tooley thinks of as supposedly showing the absurd consequences of attributing rights to foetuses. First, he argues, if there is such a thing as a biological entity that is a potential *person* (zygote, embryo, foetus, young child – since Tooley thinks even young children are non-*persons*), we can at least imagine there to be an electronic potential *person*, an electronic device that 'was so programmed that it would alter its own circuitry in such a way that it would come to have those . . . properties that make something a person' (where by 'person' he means what we are calling *person*). If, then, it was wrong to kill a biological potential *person* (as we have been arguing) it would also be wrong to kill its electronic counterpart. And the same for a counterpart that was mechanical. So far, so good. Now, he continues, there is no reason to restrict the right to life to *persons* who are spatially connected, or whose parts are of the same general type (biological, electronic, or mechanical): 'It is logically possible for a person's body to be a whole that is unified causally, rather than spatially, and for its parts to be of different general types.' Hence: 'If it is wrong to destroy potential persons of a biologically unified sort or of an electronically unified sort, must it not be equally wrong to destroy potential persons that involve either different types or parts, or parts that are spatially separated, but causally connected, or both?'

Tooley then goes on to describe a mythical machine 'that will bring together a human sperm cell and an ovum, and then sustain the life of the resulting organism until it becomes capable of independent existence'. Such a system, he argues, 'has the potential of giving rise to a person. Indeed, it has a totally active potentiality in this respect, in contrast to that possessed by a human zygote. The zygote requires external assistance – the provision of nutrients and warmth, and the disposal of waste – whereas the system requires nothing beyond the absence of interference.' Suppose, then, that you damage the system in some way, say by cutting the conveyor belt carrying the sperm cell to the ovum, so the two cells die rather than unite to form a new organism. 'Is such an action seriously wrong, in the way that killing a normal adult human being is wrong? I suggest that very few people indeed would accept this view.' But if the idea is that potentiality is relevant to the question of the right to life in a way that 'has consequences that are inconsistent with almost everyone's moral views', we should give up this idea and hence the premise according to which it is wrong to destroy a biological potential *person*.[23]

Tooley's elaborate argument does not, in fact, advance the *personist* case beyond the standard (and as we saw misplaced) objection that the collection of sperm + egg is a potential *person* and so destroying a sperm or egg should, if potentiality matters, be every bit as bad as destroying a zygote. The fact that Tooley has described a system with a 'totally active potentiality' that requires nothing more than the absence of interference is irrelevant. (It should be said, though, that he conveniently forgets that machines need an energy supply, and the right temperature, and the means to give off heat and other by-products, just as much as a human zygote, so how he works out that the system possesses greater total potentiality than a zygote is difficult to understand.) Where Tooley's thought experiment is flawed is in his assumption, which he also attributes to the anti-*personist*, that 'if it is wrong to destroy biologically unified potential persons, what reason can there be other than that it is wrong to destroy a certain sort of potentiality?'

To see the absurdity of Tooley's case, based as I believe on a cavalier use of the concept of potentiality, consider the following analogy. No one would deny that there exist in the world potential Oscar winners. Many good actors out there fall into this category, and Tom Blanks is one of them. Suppose Tom Blanks is on the set of his latest film, directed by the great Steven Spiegelman. Blanks's role is the greatest of his career, and he is a sure bet to win an Oscar. Being a fan of the rival actor Mel Gibbard, however, I want nothing more than for my hero to win the Oscar. So I calmly walk on to the set of the Spiegelman film and shoot Tom Blanks dead. Would anyone deny that I have murdered a potential Oscar winner? But now suppose I am in court, having been convicted of murder, and the judge is considering whether to sentence me to 199 or 723 years in jail (we're in an American court). One of the facts he holds against me is that I have killed a great actor, a potential Oscar winner, no less. In my defence, which is based on a careful reading of Michael Tooley's theory of potentiality, I say:

> How can it be seriously wrong to kill a potential Oscar winner? After all, when you think of it, the total potentiality to produce an Oscar winner resided not just in Tom Blanks himself, but in the entire film set, with all its lights, cameras, props and everything else. Quoting Tooley with appropriate modifications I say, your Honour, that the total system has the potential of giving rise to an Oscar winner. Indeed, it has a totally active potentiality in this respect, in contrast to that possessed by Mr Blanks. He requires external assistance – not only the provision of nutrients and warmth, and the disposal of waste, but also good lighting, expert make-up, a script, and so on – whereas the entire film set, considered as a system, requires nothing beyond the absence of interference. But if I had, say, burned all the scripts on the set, or cut a cable to the lights, thereby – let us suppose – permanently halting production of the film, I would also have destroyed a potential Oscar winner. I am not talking about the film itself, which may *also* have been a potential Oscar winner – I admit I would have destroyed that. But I also would have compromised the system itself that had the potentiality to produce the Oscar winner Tom Blanks. Would such an action have been murder? It would have been wrong on other grounds, such as criminal damage to property, but no one in their right mind would say that I had murdered a potential Oscar winner. From which I conclude, your Honour, that the fact that Mr Blanks was a potential Oscar winner is morally and legally irrelevant to the question of what sentence I should receive.

If this scenario is absurd, it is absurd for the very same reason as Tooley's. The potentiality of a system to *produce* a *person* in no way equates to the potentiality of an organism to *develop into* a *person*. What is wrong about destroying a potential *person* is not merely that 'it is wrong to destroy a certain sort of potentiality'. There may indeed be things wrong with destroying certain sorts of potentiality – cutting the cable carrying the sperm in Tooley's system, or cutting the cable to the lighting on the set of Tom Blanks's movie – but whatever is wrong with such acts, it will not be that one has destroyed an individual that *itself* has the capacity to realise or manifest certain characteristics that are morally important. We can perhaps call one kind of potentiality or capacity *productive* and the other *developmental*, though in this context the notion of development does not *necessarily* include the notion of passing from an immature stage to a mature one. What the *personist* sees in the wrongness of killing a sleeping man is not a productive capacity but a developmental one, the capacity to waken and resume conscious behaviour. With this we can safely agree, while noting that what this implies is something true of human beings *as such*, even immature ones, or ones whose developmental capacity is stunted by injury or malformation. (How can we even begin to understand what injury *means*, or what malformation *means*, unless we assume the *prior* existence of a capacity that is injured or malformed?)

Potentialities are not free-floating things that can reside equally and in the same way in individuals, systems, groups and collections. One has to look at each *type* of entity to decide precisely what kinds of potentiality it has, how they exist in the entity, how they are realised, how they can be damaged, and so on. The *personist* at least implicitly sees, as much as his opponent, that when it comes to the right to life it is the developmental capacities of individual organisms that are central to the debate, not other kinds of capacity belonging to systems, or collections, or whatever.

Where does this leave us as far as potentiality is concerned? We have seen that the *personist* relies on this concept just as much as the humanist. This reliance, even if the *personist* does not admit it, also embraces the zygote, the embryo and the foetus. But to point out that they are potential *persons* is just to say that they are *human beings*, since every human being has the capacity for the kind of mental life characteristic of the *person*, even if the human being is at an immature stage, or the capacity is damaged, or both. If the destruction of a potential *person* is seriously wrong, this is equivalent to saying that the destruction of a human being is seriously wrong. The term *person*, therefore, drops out of the picture, and we are left with the proposition that it is the *human being* who has a right to life, in virtue of being the *kind of thing* which, in virtue of a special capacity, typically exercises certain functions of rationality and self-consciousness which are rightly considered to be of the highest moral importance.

1.7 Abortion, the Law and the Public Good – A Concluding Note

A discussion of the thorny issues concerning abortion and public policy would require a chapter in itself. We could not see how law and politics interact with the abortion question without considering the way they interact with morality in general. This topic was touched on in the abstract in *Moral Theory*, and will be broached again as we progress, but a full-scale analysis must be left for another day. For the moment, I want to consider very briefly two objections to the idea that abortion should be illegal, for no other reason than that they come up in the abortion debate so frequently that to omit mentioning them altogether would leave our discussion incomplete. As a preliminary, consider the following claim:

1.7.1 'I personally disapprove of abortion but would not impose my opinion on other people'

This is an assertion heard again and again, and it seems to give the speaker the best of both worlds, combining evidence of a sense of right and wrong with an admirable tolerance for other people's divergent views on such a sensitive and controversial subject. Is it, then, a view one should cultivate?

It is essential first to distinguish the view from the *legitimate* idea that a person might not be *sure* whether a certain action was right or wrong and so not be convinced other people should have any particular position on the matter. For instance, you might not be sure whether you have an obligation to pay a certain tax, say because it may go to an unjust cause. In such a state of uncertainty you would be rash to prescribe that others should think payment was or was not a duty. But in the abortion case what I have in mind is the person who is personally sure abortion is wrong (or at least *says* he is sure) but insists his view should not be imposed on others.

Consider the same sort of opinion with the word 'abortion' replaced by the word 'rape': 'I personally disapprove of rape but would not impose my opinion on other people.' Or 'burning down the homes of black men': 'I personally disapprove of burning down the homes of black men but would not impose my opinion on other people.' It does not have the same sort of ring to it, does it? This is because we have become so conditioned to accept that as far as abortion goes it is perfectly respectable to have such a view, that we can no longer see how ridiculous it really is, *on the assumption that abortion is wrong, and seriously wrong at that.* One can of course see why, socially speaking, such a view is common – nearly everyone agrees that rape and burning down the houses of black men are serious wrongs, but abortion is still, at least in some countries, so controversial that to have a more 'dogmatic' view of the matter (as pro-abortionists see it) is positively to invite conflict.

The function of morality, however, is not simply to preserve social harmony. We should all get along as much as possible, but not if it means sacrificing either rationality or one's commitment to fundamental principles of right and wrong. As far as rape goes, how many people would fail to speak up against it if they were confronted by someone who maintained that it was permissible, maybe even *necessary* in some circumstances? How many people would not risk an argument, would not risk losing a friendship, or upsetting someone else, by speaking out against rape? If so for rape, or for burning down the houses of black people, why not for abortion?

As far as rationality goes, the question here is what you mean by 'impose'. There is nothing irrational about having a strong view on a moral matter and yet refusing to browbeat others into agreement, or to threaten them with ostracism, or violence, or some other bad consequence, if they do not agree with you. Indeed, that sort of behaviour is nearly always wrong itself. Far less, then, should anyone try to *coerce* another into agreeing with him. Everyone is free to have their own private beliefs, at least in the sense that they have a right not to be coerced into believing something, and in all except grave circumstances should be free from any sort of interference whatsoever. This does not, however, mean people have a *right to believe whatever they like*, because freedom in the sense of a right to non-interference is not the same as freedom in the sense of a right to act, whether the act is mental or physical. For instance, I have the 'right to believe' that the moon is made of cheese and that two and two make five *in the sense* than no one can legitimately coerce me into believing otherwise; but I have no right *as such* to believe these absurdities. I have no right as such to believe *anything* false, even if I have a right to non-interference with my belief. This follows from what was said in *Moral Theory* about rights, that they are primarily forms of protection governing a person's pursuit of the good. Now truth is a good, falsehood is not; therefore there can be no genuine right to pursue falsehood, hence no right to believe what is false. In fact we need to be more precise: I might believe what is false *thinking it is true*, and so I would still be pursuing the good of truth. But then I would not believe a falsehood *qua falsehood*, but *qua purported truth*, and I would change my belief when shown that it was false. But once I am shown the reasons why a certain belief of mine is false, I have no right to continue believing it; furthermore, if I have any substantial *doubt* whether it is true, I must immediately *suspend* belief and make inquiry until I get to the truth. Perhaps there are few people who believe what is false in the face of flagrant evidence to the contrary – though the number is, I would suggest, much larger than you think – but there are many who persist in believing what they know is at least doubtful, and long after they have been put on inquiry. To say they have a right to go on believing what they have more than fleeting doubts about is to fly in the face of the fundamental point that the right to believe something is meaningful only in the context of the good of truth.

So if 'impose' means 'coerce', it is quite rational to disapprove of something while acknowledging everyone's right to peaceful disagreement. But if by 'impose' you mean 'persuade or try to convince', then it would be a sacrifice of rationality both to disapprove of something and to think it was wrong to try to persuade others that they too should disapprove. 'I would not impose my opinions on others' sometimes means no more than 'For the sake of peace and quiet I would not ever try to argue with someone about it', but far too often what people mean is that arguing and trying to convince are in themselves wrong, some kind of 'imposition on the sincerely held values of others'. Again, I ask: would you say the same about, say, theft or child abuse? Would you say: 'I disapprove of child abuse but I would never try to convince someone else to abandon their sincerely held belief that it was all right'? Would you try to convince a notorious paedophile who waxed lyrical about how much fun he had abusing young boys and girls? If so, why would you limit applying your persuasive powers to people who were openly engaged in the practice you disapproved of? Isn't it right that the mere having of a belief that child abuse is legitimate creates a moral climate in which it is more likely to be accepted and acted upon than if everyone disapproved of it and voiced their disapproval strongly when necessary? If so, why is abortion any different?

1.7.2   'It is not the business of the law to interfere with such a difficult decision'

Should people be free to make mistakes? When the abortion issue leapt to the forefront of public policy debate in the 1960s and 1970s[24] many politicians, in the USA for instance, were still opposed to it on moral grounds. In order to square their ethical views with what they believed – rightly or wrongly – was a massive swing of public opinion in favour of legalisation, they devised (with a little help from 'policy advisers') a formula they thought would satisfy everyone. Abortion was wrong, they said, but the state should not interfere. This was the formula adopted by would-be congressmen and presidents who still at least publicly maintained that they personally disapproved of abortion – and it has been used by politicians ever since. The position is based in part on the view we have just examined about the 'imposition' of one's ethical opinions on others, but also on a view of the role of the state and of the law.

Now, on the assumption – undoubtedly true – that for many people the decision to abort their child is enormously difficult, fraught with psychological and emotional turmoil, did the politicians have a point? Consider the civil rights movement in America, which was also at the centre of social activism and policy debate *at the very same time* as abortion. What should we have thought of a politician who said:

> The granting of civil rights to black people is a decision fraught with difficulties. So many people oppose it, and for them it would be psychologically tumultuous to have to come to terms with the civil equality of black people. To grant civil rights would be to throw many communities into turmoil. It would have ramifications we can only begin to grasp. As a policy-maker, I cannot see how the function of the state should be to interfere with privileges so many white people have enjoyed for so long. Whatever I personally think about civil rights for blacks – and I do believe they should have them – I have a duty to the whole community, and so I will not use the legislature to interfere in such a controversial and difficult area.

Is this a position you would feel comfortable with? What if the politician had been speaking in the nineteenth century about slavery? Liberating slaves was every bit as controversial then as abortion is now and yet we do not, looking back, have much regard for politicians who thought the state had no right to outlaw what so many people thought was a fundamental right of slave-ownership. Even if every single slave-owner had had enough of a conscience for his ownership of slaves to weigh heavily on it every day of his life, would that have been enough of a reason for the state not to act? If not, why is abortion different?

To say that the state has no right to stop seriously immoral actions, however controversial they be and however difficult it may be for people to refrain from carrying them out, is tantamount to saying the state really is not the guardian of the common good. It is to say the state does not have the function of protecting fundamental rights, such as the right to life. Certain theorists, namely libertarians, do indeed believe the state has very little to do with public morality at all. Although there are various degrees of libertarianism, all adherents believe the state has a minimal role in securing the common good, and that people have the inalienable right to commit a wide range of immoral actions, to make their own 'moral mistakes' and to take the consequences. Such a position is pernicious and absurd, and does not stand up to a moment's scrutiny. (Can you think of the reasons why?) Should the state outlaw theft? arson? assault? rape? slavery? child abuse? cruelty to animals? incest? counterfeiting? perjury? subornation of perjury? obstruction of justice? corruption in public office? drug-dealing? If abortion *really does* involve the taking of innocent human life, how is it any different?

1.7.3   The 'backstreet' objection

One of the most common objections to the prohibition of abortion is the claim that it would place women back in the position they used to be in, of having to undergo highly dangerous 'backstreet' abortions. It would place the woman in the hands of people who were semi-trained or maybe had no training at all in terminating a pregnancy. They might not have any medical qualifications. And the fact is that in every society in which abortion is illegal women die from backstreet abortions, or suffer physical harm such as infection, haemorrhaging and infertility. (The numbers in the USA have been, however, grossly exaggerated; and all these consequences happen in the case of legal abortions as well.)

Is this a reason, then, for taking abortion away from the backstreet and into professionally run clinics regulated by the state? Many people think so, but it is hard to see why. What would you think of a politician who said:

I am disturbed by the number of backstreet contract killings being carried out by members of the Mafia and other gangland organisations. These murders are often bloody and excruciating. Some victims survive and are maimed for life. Unscrupulous operators, often untrained or at least semi-trained in the art of killing, receive thousands of dollars for their acts. A whole black market in contract killing has arisen. I propose to solve the problem by taking contract killing out of the backstreet and into the hands of the state. I will lobby for the introduction of state-run contract killing centres furnished with expert killers and the latest hi-tech equipment. Every January, leaders of the major gangland organisations will be able to nominate up to three opponents they would like eliminated. A specially-trained police force will then round up the nominated victims and take them to a state-run centre, where they will be painlessly killed, and with a minimum of fuss, by one of our experts. All nominations will be dealt with on a first-come, first-served basis. The state will charge the person making the nomination a set fee determined by an appointed regulator. There will no longer be any need for backstreet contract killings.

Has the politician convinced you of the need to eliminate backstreet gangland murders by putting them into the hands of the state? Or do you still think contract killing should be illegal and that the state should make every effort to stamp out such activities? The 'backstreet' objection can, in fact, be used as a purported argument for the legalisation and state regulation of a vast number of acts that are now illegal and immoral. (Can you think of examples? What about drug dealing or child abuse?) If the objection does not work in the case of contract killing, for example, how could it work in the case of abortion? Why is abortion any different?

1.8   Conclusion

It would be silly to pretend that much of what has been said in this chapter will not upset and offend a lot of people. (They may want to stop reading the book at this point, because it doesn't get any better.) It would be silly to pretend that abortion does not arouse the strongest emotions in people. It is very, very hard to have a rational debate about it. (I try to avoid the subject, just like everyone else!) And yet these cannot be reasons for not trying to consider the issues logically, and for not taking the argument where it leads. Many people will find, especially when reading the last section, that their ethical views are, to put it plainly, inconsistent. Inconsistency is a bad thing, as much in ethics as in any other branch of human thought. It should be banished completely from one's view of the world. If, on reading the last section, someone does find that they are inconsistent, they must eliminate the inconsistency. This can lead to intellectual disturbance, if not turmoil, for it is hard indeed for people to revise their beliefs to make them fit together into a coherent whole. And yet they must.

It is often said that every child should be a wanted child. This is something with which it is hard to disagree. The thought of a child coming into the world unwanted, unloved, neglected, is painful to say the least. Everyone has the duty to look after their children in the best way they can, maintaining them in body and soul, instructing them, watching over them, disciplining them where necessary, setting a good example. Above all, children must be loved. If a child faces the prospect of coming into the world unloved, however, does it follow that he should be killed? Does 'every child a wanted child' entail 'every unwanted child should be killed'? What is the logic behind the entailment? Perhaps the foregoing discussion has cast some doubt on whether there is any logic there at all.

2

Euthanasia

2.1 Introduction

We saw in *Moral Theory* that the principle of the unconditional protection of innocent human life is at the centre of morality. No moral philosophy that qualifies or demotes this principle, or that removes it from decision-making in ethics, can hope to call itself humane and therefore to command the respect of right-thinking people.

In no matter is the urgency of respecting this principle more apparent than that of so-called 'euthanasia' or 'mercy killing'. Coming from the Greek for 'good death', the term 'euthanasia' has come to be applied specifically in the medical field to the intentional killing of a human being for the purpose of ending his suffering or of removing some burden. Note, however, that it should be construed broadly so as to cover circumstances such as an accident, where an injured person asks a passer-by to end his suffering by killing him, or a wounded soldier asks his comrade to be 'put out of his misery'. The central moral considerations are the same whether or not the setting is professional or institutional (such as in a hospital), though the medical case does raise specific questions of its own, such as what the role of a doctor should be. While the purpose of euthanasia, namely the ending of suffering or removal of a burden, is the one explicitly stated by most organisations that support legalisation of the practice, we will see that other objectives are involved, and that these too need to be evaluated in the light of the philosophical ideas used to justify them.

Euthanasia in various forms is no new practice in civilisation. In ancient Sparta, those regarded as physically unfit for some purpose, or as incurably ill, or as useless to the state, were killed or allowed to die. In ancient Greece and Rome, the evidence suggests that deformed babies were 'exposed' or left to die. (Sometimes children were killed simply because they were unwanted, such as girls – as happens now in China. So we can see how it is to some extent arbitrary whether certain kinds of killing, especially infanticide, are discussed in the context of abortion or euthanasia.) The practice reached heights hitherto unthinkable in Nazi Germany and various of the Communist countries. It has most probably always been present in one or another part of the world. But the fact that a social practice is common, or even prevalent throughout the world, does not make it morally legitimate. Indeed, the revelation of the atrocities that took place as part of Hitler's 'euthanasia' programme caused many of the nations of the world, particularly in the West, to recoil from the thought that it may be permissible for anyone, especially doctors or other health-care workers, to kill or assist in the killing of an innocent person either because it was thought to be in that person's interests or in the interests of anyone else, including society as a whole.

The resistance by society to the legalisation of euthanasia, however, resting as it does partly on its express prohibition by an unbroken Jewish and Christian moral tradition thought by many people now no longer to have anything to teach us, is slowly breaking down – just as it has in the case of abortion. The practice is now accepted *de facto* in many countries, though the laws say otherwise, and legalisation is but a short step away.

The breaking down of this resistance can be attributed to several factors apart from the general rejection of the West's moral and religious tradition. One that must be mentioned is the staggering advance in medical technology over the last few decades, which has made it increasingly easy for doctors to keep patients alive in circumstances that once would have been dismissed as hopeless. This ability consists among other things of artificial means of feeding, watering and respirating patients in various states of incapacity such as paralysis, coma, or what might be called the 'persistent non-responsive state'. It also includes the availability of an ever-increasing variety of drugs capable of fighting diseases that once would have overwhelmed vulnerable people such as premature babies and the elderly. And it also includes the provision of the highest possible medical services, at least in the affluent West, to more and more people who once would have been excluded from even basic health care.

All of these developments are to be welcomed and encouraged. Nevertheless they have, in the minds of some, led to situations where people are enabled to stay alive in circumstances in which it is thought that their 'quality of life' is too diminished to make that life 'worth living'. This might, it is said, be due to extreme pain or discomfort, or to a dependence on others thought to be degrading or undignified, or to a person's living a life that is or will become seriously unfulfilling due to his decreased capacity, for example, 'to respond to an environment, to respond to challenges, to give and receive affection in relationships'.[1]

It is for these and other reasons that supporters of euthanasia urge its legalisation. Our main concern here, as we have seen, is not the current or proposed future state of the law; rather, it is with the ethical issues at the centre of practical problems, and so these are what I shall be discussing. The ethical issues are, of course, more important either than the state of the law or of medical practice: this is because medical practice must follow the law, and the law must follow ethics, not the reverse. Once the ethical position is clarified the law must be adapted to it, and medical practice must then conform to the law. Thus the conclusions that should be reached about the morality of euthanasia will in most cases have fairly obvious and direct relevance for proposals concerning both law and practice.

2.2   Varieties of Euthanasia

Various distinctions have to be considered when evaluating euthanasia. The first concerns consent – whether the patient agreed to be killed or requested it. If there is such a request or agreement the euthanasia is called voluntary, and if not, either non-voluntary or involuntary. Some important points should be noted in respect of voluntary euthanasia. One is purely factual, namely that it is the subject of greatest public controversy, being lobbied for heavily by various organisations such as the Voluntary Euthanasia Society in Britain and the Hemlock Society in the United States. The media regularly air programmes supporting voluntary euthanasia, almost always concentrating on the suffering of the person who wants to be killed, and rarely raising the level of argument higher than the mere slogan 'death with dignity'. There is thus a clear and unmistakable push for its legalisation, and the example of the Netherlands is unfailingly presented as a favourable precedent, although in that country euthanasia is (at the time of writing) still officially illegal, doctors hardly ever being prosecuted.[2] I mention this factual point partly because it is philosophically suggestive. Those who support killing by request are variously mute or vague about their attitude to killing that is not by request, or else support it equally strongly (in certain cases, at least) but do not lobby for it as vigorously. The thought then arises that this is because they believe it easier to make out a *prima facie* case for killing when it is asked for than when it is not. The voluntariness component thus assumes a central role in the case for euthanasia. If they are correct about this, and I think they are, it follows that if in the end the case for voluntary killing *cannot* be made out, then it is likely that no case can be made out for euthanasia of *any* sort. It should be added, however, that the voluntariness component is ultimately a philosophical 'red herring': supporters of euthanasia, whether it be voluntary or not, in the end base their reasoning on the same considerations, as we will see.

A further point about voluntary euthanasia is that the consent must be *actual*, that is, there must be an express request for death, though the request need not be made immediately before being carried out. It could be expressed in a so-called 'advance directive' or 'living will', much discussed of late, in which a person stipulates what is to happen to him if he is in a condition in which he is no longer able to request or agree to death; further, the person must not have said or implied anything since the framing of the directive to contradict its terms. There are notorious problems with advance directives, such as the possibility that a given directive does not advert to the precise circumstances in which the person now finds himself, or is no longer applicable because of technological advances not known about when the directive was framed, or is otherwise vague or difficult to construe. It can be assumed for present purposes, however, that a directive *might* not suffer from these or other defects, and so could constitute a clear request for death even if in practice such directives never do so.

The consent involved in voluntary euthanasia must be completely free. It will not be completely free if given under conditions of ignorance, fraud or fear. The requirement of complete freedom reflects the idea that a request for death has the form of an *abandonment* of the right to life, and an abandonment cannot be partial. The analogy with property, which will be discussed at length later, is instructive. A person who throws away a jewel, having been told it is a worthless trinket (or merely erroneously thinking this to be the case), has not freely abandoned his property; nor has he done so if pressured into throwing it away. As will be seen, the analogy with property is flawed when used to support voluntary euthanasia, since the right to life cannot be abandoned, but the point here is that even if an abandonment is impossible, the *attempt* can be made under conditions of complete freedom. (One can freely intend the impossible, such as an escape from an escape-proof prison, at least if one believes it to be possible.) Again, an analogy with contracts supports this idea. A person who contracts marriage with someone distinct from the person she *believes* she is contracting marriage with is properly said, both in morality and at law, not to have freely consented to the marriage. Now it might be argued, with some propriety, that *no* request for death can be completely free, as there is always some pressure, whether subtle or not so subtle, or some error about one's condition, and so on; but let us assume for the sake of argument that a person might make a completely free request to be killed, even if no one has ever done so.

Euthanasia that is not voluntary can be non-voluntary or involuntary. It is involuntary where the person killed refuses or otherwise actively withholds consent (again, whether this be at the time of the killing or in an advance directive), or where the person *could* have been asked whether he consented, but was not. Less time will be spent discussing this, but not for the reasons usually given by those who write about euthanasia. Typically, involuntary euthanasia is regarded as obviously wrong in a way that its voluntary counterpart is not. This is because ethical weight is given to *autonomy*: just as a person's consent to be killed is said to legitimise the killing, so his withholding of consent (or the ignoring of his wishes when he could have been consulted) illegitimises the killing. As will be shown, however, the concept of autonomy as construed by supporters of euthanasia is ethically irrelevant to the debate, and moreover this is implicitly *agreed* by both sides. The *real* reasons for supporting euthanasia have nothing whatsoever to do with autonomy and are common to euthanasia in all its forms. Less time will be spent on the involuntary kind, then, because the invalidation of those reasons in respect of the other two kinds will suffice to show this kind to be impermissible as well. A further reason involuntary killing is seldom discussed at length is that it is assumed to be rare and so of less pressing ethical concern. That this is false, however, is shown by the report of the Remmelink Committee, which carried out a thorough and detailed survey of euthanasia in the Netherlands. The report showed that in 1990 well over one thousand people (perhaps even five thousand or more, judging by the less than transparent wording of the report) were killed by doctors without explicit request (though they could have been consulted). (A similar figure was reported again in 1995. In both 1990 and 1995 well over 50 per cent of doctors interviewed said they either had or would be prepared to end the life of a patient without their explicit request, the clear implication being that this included cases where the patient was or would be capable of being consulted.) Sometimes it is said that involuntary euthanasia must be rare, since there could be no conceivable reason why a person who could have been consulted was not (Peter Singer suggests this). But the assertion is specious since there could well be one of a number of reasons: for instance, a doctor might worry that, were he explicitly to ask the patient whether he wanted to be killed, the latter, even if he agreed, would tell his relatives, who would cause a furore; such a scenario is hardly inconceivable. It should also be noted that not all writers regard involuntary euthanasia as obviously wrong, and in the honesty of their reasoning show why voluntariness is an irrelevance, whatever its *apparent* importance. Jonathan Glover, for instance, suggests that it is not obviously wrong that someone going to a Nazi concentration camp, ignorant of their terrible fate, should be killed without their request before they arrive at the camp, in order to spare them the ordeal.[3] And although Peter Singer does not officially wish to justify involuntary euthanasia, he also says that 'if we are preference utilitarians, we must allow that a desire to go on living can be outweighed by other desires'.[4] By its very nature, then, preference utilitarianism, as with all forms of consequentialism, must allow involuntary euthanasia as more than a mere logical possibility.

Non-voluntary euthanasia is the killing of someone who is not capable of being consulted as to his wishes. There are various reasons why this might be the case. The most commonly discussed ones involve babies and infants, and adults who are in a coma, or in what is usually called a 'persistent vegetative state' but which is more properly called a 'persistent non-responsive state'. A coma can be exhibited in a variety of ways, ranging from the case of a person all of whose vital functions, such as eating, drinking, excretion and breathing, need to be maintained artificially, to that of someone needing very little attention except perhaps food and drink. There might be, according to current testing procedures, almost total cessation of brain function, or there might only be damage to some of the neo-cortex, which is thought to support 'higher' mental functions such as thought and speech. In general there is little if any response to stimuli, and no locomotion. Here voluntariness (in the absence of an advance directive) is not an issue, and supporters of euthanasia will advert explicitly to 'quality of life' criteria in assessing whether a given patient should (or could) be killed. Such criteria also extend logically to patients who are terminally ill, and in such pain that they need medication so strong that it renders them unconscious and so 'incompetent' to make a decision about whether to be killed; or even to elderly people suffering senile dementia. Again, 'quality of life' criteria are applied to newborn babies suffering some handicap; it is not a rarity for babies with a disability as mild as Down's Syndrome to be left to die (most are aborted), and the more serious the handicap, spina bifida being the one usually cited, the more likely it is that, in a typical Western hospital, the child will be treated 'conservatively', that is, not at all, with or without the parents' consent. Indeed, in a much-publicised case in New Zealand in 1998, a severely handicapped baby was allowed to die (deprived of life support) even though the parents explicitly wanted their child to be kept alive, even putting pictures of the baby on the Internet in the hope of gaining public support. The court in New Zealand permitted the doctors to withdraw treatment.[5]

2.3 Voluntary Euthanasia and Autonomy

Having laid some of the groundwork for assessing the ethics of euthanasia, we can move on to the assessment itself, bearing in mind the principles already laid down in chapter 4 of *Moral Theory* concerning the right to life.

Consider some of the following remarks: 'I'm not giving up . . . but everyone has the right to say they don't want to continue'; 'I've always had control over my life . . . I just want to have control over my own death'; 'I want you to do something for me so that if I decide I want to die, I can do it on my own terms and exactly when I choose.'[6] These are all expressions of the right to *autonomy* in one's actions, or to self-determination in respect of what a person does with his life, including ending it. The voluntary euthanasia campaigner Derek Humphry puts it thus: 'The quintessence of voluntary euthanasia is personal choice and self-control, with sometimes a little help from one's friends.'[7] The point is put more formally by Singer, who states: '[T]he principle of respect for autonomy tells us to allow rational agents to live their own lives according to their own autonomous decisions, free from coercion or interference; but if rational agents should autonomously choose to die, then respect for autonomy will lead us to assist them to do as they choose.'[8]

The idea here is that the right to life is *alienable*, or capable of waiver. This is the principal argument for voluntary euthanasia: *All rights are alienable; there is a right to life; therefore, the right to life is alienable.* If a person of sound mind, thinking rationally, assessing his own situation as carefully as he can, with all relevant information made available to him, makes a deliberate decision to die, which decision is unencumbered by duress or undue influence, and expressed clearly and persistently, then we should, it is argued, take this to be an alienation by him of his right to life. From which it is claimed to follow that other agents are duty-bound to respect that person's autonomous choice and provide him with whatever assistance is necessary to carry out his decision. If he is capable of taking his own life, we should provide him with the equipment necessary to do so. If he is too frightened to do it himself, or is physically incapable, we are permitted, if not bound in conscience, to do for him what he would otherwise have done for himself.

The problem with the argument set out above is that, though valid, the first premise is not true. The principle of respect for autonomy is entrenched in current moral thinking and derives essentially from Kantian ethics. Its current expression, however, is not something Kant himself would have recognised. For Kant, the autonomy of a rational being was subject to the precepts of morality. Thus he famously claimed that suicide was immoral, arguing that there was an incoherence in the idea that a rational being could somehow will his non-existence. Equally famously, however, the paucity of his conception of the Moral Law left him with few substantive arguments as to *why* there was an incoherence here. Current thinking, however, influenced as it has been by existentialist, libertarian and relativist theories, sees autonomy as equivalent to self-determination, or the decision by a free being to decide for himself, on whatever grounds are meaningful *to him*, to live and to die as he wishes.

Further consideration, however, shows that there can be no truth to the idea that all rights are alienable.[9] The principal analogy drawn by the euthanasia supporter is with property rights. Surely, it is argued, property rights are alienable, so why isn't the right to life? A premise usually found in this argument is that the right to life just *is* a species of property right, since we own our bodies. (Some readers may recall the 1980s play supporting suicide and euthanasia, *Whose Life is it Anyway?*) One response is that the right to life is not a property right vested in us; theists sometimes argue that it is God who owns our lives or our bodies, not us – we have them on trust, as it were, to use correctly. (Let us, for simplicity, assume that if we own our bodies we own our lives, and vice versa.) Some writers, theistic or not, argue that our bodies are not the sorts of thing we can own anyway. Whatever the merits of such claims, let us put them to one side for the purpose of the argument. The problem for the friend of the life – property analogy, nevertheless, is that there are *still* relevant dissimilarities between the rights to life and property, and any similarities *support* the inalienability of the right to life.

The hallmark of property is that it is alienable. So if I happily stand by watching while you take apples from my orchard, or say 'Sure, take as many as you like', you do me no wrong. And of course property can be sold, given away or bequeathed. The disanalogy with life, however, is that while you can certainly alienate your right to this or that property, for example, your apples, you cannot alienate your right to property *in general*, considered apart from any particular piece of property. You cannot validly say, 'I renounce my right as a human being to own property.' Alienating your right to this or that property does not entail alienating your right to property in general, and is thus compatible with retaining that right. On the other hand, a purported alienation of your right to your particular life entails a purported alienation of your right to life in general, it being impossible to have more than one life. So, whereas the alienation of the right to this or that property says nothing about the right to property in general, the purported alienation of your particular life does say something about what you are trying to do with your right to life in general. There is thus an important disanalogy showing why particular property can be alienated in a way that a particular life cannot. Any *similarity* between the two cases only supports the inalienability of the right to life, since the right to property in general does seem inalienable.

It might be said that even the right to property in general is alienable. What about someone who renounces her right to property in general when, say, she enters a commune where there is no private property? Here it seems there would be nothing unjust about the leader of the commune's depriving the new member of her secretly acquired clock-radio. But there are at least two possible interpretations of such a case which point to its dissimilarity with the right to life. They are mutually exclusive, but either one will block the analogy, and anyway they might have separate applications to different cases – so we can leave open which interpretation is correct. One is that there is no alienation of the right to property in general, only a consent to abide by the laws of the commune, which may forbid private property. Once the new member ceases to be a member by leaving, and hence ceases to be subject to the laws of the commune, she is free to exercise her right to own property again, a right that never left her. Another interpretation is that there is an alienation but it is only temporary, and the right is reassumed once the member ceases to be a member. In neither case is there a permanent renunciation of the right to property, which is evidenced by the fact that the leader of the commune would be acting manifestly unjustly if he chased after the former member, acknowledging that she had left but still trying to stop her owning any property! In the case of a request for death, however, the intention is permanently to renounce the right to life – once killed, the right could hardly be reassumed. Supporters of the 'right to die' cannot buttress their position by appeal to a case such as this.

Reflection on other cases shows that there is nothing absurd in the concept of an inalienable right, and, moreover, that there are a variety of such rights. Nevertheless, examples that would once have commanded universal assent may not do so now, even if they are plausible. This is because the conception of autonomy which Kant understood, and which itself is embedded in traditional morality, has mutated, under the influences mentioned earlier, into what might be called a doctrine of the *paramountcy of the will* – the idea that the will must be allowed to range freely over whatever ends a person deliberately chooses as integral to his 'personal fulfilment', perhaps in one of the variety of utility-maximizing ways proposed by consequentialists, the utility being, however, solely personal. Perhaps this can be seen in the current attitude to bodily integrity. People once thought there was an inalienable right to bodily integrity: you simply could not cede your right not to have your bodily integrity assaulted. Of course you could consent to an infringement in some cases, such as a surgical operation, but this was not a *cession*, merely an agreement to a limited, well-defined infringement for the explicit purpose of *promoting* bodily integrity. Indeed, apart from therapeutic or socially necessary cases, for example, bumping into people in a crowded room, it was thought you could not consent to any old assault on your bodily integrity, since this was a good you were morally bound to promote. So any purported abandonment of the right to bodily integrity was considered null and void. If a person were to say, 'Here's my body; do what you will with it', and moreover to say that this permission had effect *in perpetuity*, that is, was a genuine renunciation, he would have been considered irrational or subject to unwholesome influences. Now, however, it seems that many people do not find anything irrational in a similar statement by someone who was such an inveterate masochist that he allowed any and every assault on his bodily integrity. But reflection on less arcane cases shows that the contemporary attitude is not so firm. Perhaps you would think more carefully if someone came up to you holding a syringe and assorted paraphernalia, and asked you to inject him with heroin because he had not tried it before and was keen to get addicted. (Perhaps he asks you because he is too nervous to do it himself, or is physically incapable.) Now, even viewing this as a purported permission to infringe, surely you would think twice, if not refuse the request outright. But if you would baulk at it as a purported permission to infringe, how much more would you think twice if you were told by the person that he had abandoned any right he had to be healthy, and one of the first things he wanted to do after such an abandonment was to get addicted to heroin? Wouldn't your reluctance properly be said to stem from the belief that the right to bodily integrity is not the sort of thing a person can simply renounce?

Consider another example, say someone desperate to stay hooked for the rest of his life on smoking or drinking. He knows that every so often he will have second thoughts and want to reform his ways, but it is precisely at those times, he tells you, that you must make sure he has a plentiful supply of alcohol or tobacco at hand so as to ensure he stays addicted. Would you agree to such a request? Suppose, when you question him on his motive for wanting to stay addicted, he claims that he has, quite simply, given up his right to be healthy, for whatever reason. Again, it is fair to say that most of us would find the doctrine of the paramountcy of the will coming under extreme pressure here. There are some things, we would say, that you just cannot give up on. If this is so, then perhaps those who agree with the proposed way of dealing with these cases ought to go back and re-examine their intuitions about cases where they *disagree* about alienability; and the right to life ought to be one of those cases.

I have said that the moral importance of autonomy is not equivalent to the paramountcy of the will, though this is how it is currently understood. A proper understanding, however, sees autonomy as always and everywhere subject to human good. Autonomy is not the moral capacity to do whatever you like (even if what you seek to do is primarily 'self-regarding', in John Stuart Mill's terminology); this is accepted on all sides of the euthanasia debate, except by the most extreme libertarians or relativists with flawed moral theories of their own. Nor, however, is it the moral capacity to do whatever you *believe* to contribute to your 'fulfilment' or even to be *good* for you. Since morality is objective – there exist *truths* about what is good for a person – someone might, quite simply, have false beliefs about what is good for him. Of course a person might be incapable of making a mistake about what he *wants* to do, or about what he thinks will make him *feel* good or otherwise contribute to his well-being as understood by him. But to claim that such facts – about what a person *believes* is good for him – exhaust the moral questions to which they are relevant is unambiguously to work with a subjectivist conception of morality, which was rejected in chapter 1 of *Moral Theory*. The possibility of false beliefs about what is good for a person entails that autonomy must be limited – limited, that is, by the very human goods that it is proper, *qua* human being, to pursue. The will can have various degrees of freedom in, say, the means chosen to pursue some good, but it still must be directed at the pursuit of the good. And since human life is indeed a good, and the fundamental good, since it is the source of all human dignity and well-being (see chapter 4 of *Moral Theory*), autonomy cannot be exercised with a view to abandoning it. The same goes for human dignity itself. A person can live in an undignified way, but he cannot abandon his basic right to live in a dignified way, a right that he is indeed bound to exercise within the limits of circumstance.

When autonomy is construed in this way, there can be seen to be no conflict between it and the good of life. Autonomy does not include the right to kill, or the right to be killed, any more than it includes supposed rights to act against any other good, such as that of human dignity. Rather, autonomy is constrained by and ranges over all *morally legitimate* options, and in the pursuit of such options the moral agent has, and must be accorded, the right to exercise free will. Such a constraint is *truly* liberating, in that it provides a structure within which the agent can recognise his worth as a human being, and outside of which he becomes the prisoner of a way of thinking that is in its way seductive but ultimately destructive.

It should be noted too that what has been said about voluntary euthanasia applies equally to 'physician-assisted suicide', which has also been the subject of much recent lobbying and media discussion (virtually all of it supportive of the practice). What it would be wrong for someone to do to another at his request, it would be wrong for the person making the request to do to himself. This is because the mere availability or lack of means to carry out an illegitimate choice makes no difference to its wrongness. There will, in the case of assisted suicide, be a slightly different account of the distribution of moral responsibility, but the wrongness of the end pursued means that those who procure or co-operate in the act are still liable to the extent of their participation. The person who commits suicide will have committed a wrong act as well as having wrongly asked for the participation of another in that act; and the latter, while not guilty of having killed anyone, will have blameworthily co-operated in a killing in the same way that anyone is to be blamed for co-operating in an immoral act.

In the light of these considerations, we can see that there is no right to voluntary euthanasia *qua* voluntary. I also suggested, however, that the voluntariness requirement, given so much support by those who ultimately wish to see the legalisation of euthanasia in all its forms, is quite simply an ethical 'red herring'. Just as you would, it is hoped, baulk at injecting someone with heroin on request, so you would, it is hoped, baulk at any old request to be killed. If a person in no pain, in no distress, perhaps with no more than a bout of influenza, were to ask for death, no doctor (perhaps not even the infamous Dr Kevorkian) would accede to the request. Why? If the request is genuine, that is, a sincere attempt at alienating the right to life, why *shouldn't* the doctor accede to the request? Why does an evaluation of the patient's reasons *matter*? The fact that the reasons *do* matter itself indicates that it is not the voluntariness component that is morally relevant, but the reason for infringement. Thus it seems that most, if not all, parties to the debate will agree that there simply is no right to do with one's life whatever one wishes. The real disagreement, protestations by some supporters of voluntary euthanasia to the contrary, is over whether there can be good reasons to act on a request to infringe someone's right to life other than the mere fact of the request itself. It is here that so-called 'quality of life' judgements enter powerfully into the debate, and it is to this matter that we must now turn.

2.4 Non-Voluntary Euthanasia and 'Quality of Life'

There are various sorts of case appealed to by supporters of non-voluntary euthanasia. Recall that non-voluntariness amounts to the lack of an explicit request either to be killed or not to be killed, by someone who is not capable of making such a request. Recall that any request need not be contemporaneous with the decision to kill or not to kill: an 'advance directive' against killing, by a person currently incapable of making a re-

quest, would render the killing of that person an act of involuntary euthanasia. Also, if he were capable of making a request, but not consulted,
then the killing would be involuntary. Cases of non-voluntariness, then,
centre on the lack of capacity to make a request by someone who has
either always lacked the capacity, or once had it but now does not, and
never expressed a desire regarding death relevant to the circumstances he
is currently in. The former situation is usually illustrated by the case of a
handicapped baby, say with spina bifida, or anencephaly (where most of
the brain is missing, though enough is present for the baby to maintain its
vital functions for some period of time), or some severe physical or mental disability, or even a mild disability such as Down's Syndrome or cer-
ebral palsy. The latter situation is usually illustrated by cases of coma,
such as a patient wholly unconscious, that is, in a constant deep sleep, or
by a patient in a persistent non-responsive state, where there might be
periods of waking and sleeping, though no response to stimuli according
to current medical tests. Or sometimes it is exemplified by the case of a
patient with a 'locked-in' syndrome, say after a severe stroke, where he is
alert and conscious, but virtually unable to respond or communicate except perhaps by eye movement – he might be almost completely paralysed. Other discussed cases include elderly people with severe dementia
or otherwise almost totally incapacitated and dependent on others for
food and daily care: they are conscious, but perhaps 'incompetent', that
is, unable to make express requests about how they are to be treated. In
all of these and similar cases, the patient, whether child or adult, may to
some degree require artificial life support, such as respiration, or tube
feeding, or intravenous drugs to support vital organ function. Or he may
require no more basic care than feeding by hand, as well as warmth and
hygiene, with his vital functions being otherwise self-supporting. All types
of combination may arise, and consideration of the particular facts of a
situation is always essential in deciding how to treat a person in a given
condition. But there are certain broad themes applying to the cases mentioned that enable us to outline a wholly general approach. It is impossible, however, to elaborate appropriate principles and guidelines without
discussing flaws in the arguments *for* euthanasia in any or all of these
cases.

Supporters of euthanasia who espouse a consequentialist ethical theory
are inclined to try to forge a distinction between babies and adult human
beings. Although consequentialists do not believe in *rights*, they sometimes give a passing nod to the concept by claiming that babies do not

have the characteristics that make them subjects of rights, which in consequentialist terms means that they do not meet some threshold requirement for being subjects it would *of itself* be wrong to kill, all things being equal. So, it might be said they lack, in the words of Peter Singer, 'characteristics like rationality, autonomy and self-consciousness', in which case '[k]illing them, therefore, cannot be equated with killing normal human beings', the implication being that babies are not normal human beings. The absurdity of such a claim is apparent from the very stating of it, and recalls the consequentialist stipulation that killing people is not wrong *per se*, only *persons* understood in the technical philosophical sense (always italicised here and in *Moral Theory*) of beings 'capable of seeing themselves as distinct entities, existing over time', which is possible for '[n]o infant – disabled or not', who thus lack 'as strong a claim to life' as *persons*.[10] The thought, then, is that babies, simply by *being* babies – disabled or not – do not even reach the first rung of the consequentialist ladder of moral importance: perhaps the capacity to feel pain gets them some of the way, but the 'all things being equal' clause renders sentience of minor significance. The concept of *personhood* has already been discussed and criticised at length (in the previous chapter and in chapter 4 of the companion volume), but it is worth making some further brief remarks relevant to the present context. We must always bear in mind the *personist* emphasis on *occurrent* mental states as crucial to moral status. As was shown in the last chapter, the *personist* in fact relies on potentiality (indicated by such terms as 'capacity' – Tooley – and 'capability' – Singer) as much as his opponent, but the official position is that a being is not a *person* unless it is actually in a state of awareness of itself, of its past and/or future, actually desires to live, and so on. It has to have a *present* sense of itself, to be engaged in ongoing 'personal projects', to behave in a way indicative of its awareness.

For the *personist*, then, the proposition that man is a rational animal (to quote Aristotle) is not strictly true; what *is* true is that *persons* are rational. On the traditional view, babies are as rational as any human, whether or not they can currently (or ever will) engage in certain types of behaviour, display certain kinds of awareness, or be in any state of actual know-ledge of themselves as beings with a past and/or a future in which they have an interest. On the *personist* view, only certain kinds of human being, in certain circumstances, can be called rational: indeed they may be rational at one time in their lives and not rational at another: rationality can come and go like health or hunger. But it has been my contention that rationality as a component of humanity never leaves an individual any more than his humanity itself leaves him. Further, the sense of oneself *as* doing such-and-such, say existing over time, covers a multitude of distinct characteristics. Is it bare awareness of mortality that matters? Or the actual making of choices that evidence a sense of oneself as having an ongoing 'project' for one's life? Or is it the having of sensations that matters? Or feelings? Or emotions? Or desires? Or preferences? Or 'interests'? Are the relevant interests simply the ones *stipulated* by the *personist* theory? If so, the theory begs the question. Or is there another sense of 'interest' that captures what the consequentialist wants to say? (Recall the 'shopping list' of indicators of *personhood* offered by Tooley and mentioned in the previous chapter.)

The point of raising these questions in this context is to show that there is no *one* property or set of properties that *personists* agree upon as providing the threshold that a baby, or indeed an adult suffering one or other medical condition such as those mentioned above, must meet in order to have moral importance. But it is still the common *personist* conviction that even a normal, healthy baby, let alone a disabled one, has very little claim on life, since its does not fit into a technical category of importance about whose contents *personists* are hazy. In a notorious example, Singer goes so far as to place newborn babies in the same moral category as *snails* as far as killing is concerned: 'Killing a snail or a day-old infant does not thwart any desires of this kind [for the future], because snails and newborn infants are incapable of having such desires.'[11] Indeed, the *personist* uncertainty over just what makes a *person* is usually 'compensated' for by the 'all things being equal' clause favoured by consequentialists, or what are sometimes called 'extrinsic considerations'. Thus, it is the 'effect the killing will have on its parents'[12] that makes the killing of a baby undesirable, it is sometimes said. On the other hand, if parents 're-gret that a disabled child was ever born',[13] this might be a reason *for* killing it. Further, acceptance by many consequentialists of the notorious 'replaceability thesis' means that, if parents had a child with a comparatively mild disability such as haemophilia (Singer's example), and wanted to have another child who (almost certainly?) would *not* have this condition, they would be well advised to kill the first child and replace it with another. Indeed, the importance of whether they *want* to do so is unclear in consequentialist writings: they may simply be *obliged* to, on a common view, though 'adverse effect[s] on others' need to be considered. If the consequentialist calculation shows that the killing and replacement would have a greater net 'benefit' than any other action, it is hard to see why it would be anything other than a *duty*.[14]

The theory I have been defending, however, differs greatly from any version of *personism* (whether or not supplemented by consequentialism – which it usually is) in its attitude to babies, handicapped or not. The right to life attaches to *all* innocent human beings, at every stage of development. Theorists such as Singer and Tooley correctly point out the logical implications of the *personist* approach: not only does it make abortion permissible, but consistency requires its extension to *infanticide*. It is proper to think, however, that any theory that leads to the permissibility of infanticide has gone wrong very early. For morality requires, above all, the *protection* of the most vulnerable members of society, of which babies are a prime example. If morality is not about this, then it is about nothing. And there can be no argument here that parents have a right to decide whether their baby lives or dies, for they *have* no such right: the power to choose the life or death of their child does not sit alongside the power to decide their child's education, or how it is to be brought up. And before we move from *personism* to the question of a 'life worth living', it is worth delving a little further into the issues just raised.

The fundamental idea on which the traditional moral attitude to killing the innocent is based is well put by a recent critic of consequentialism in applied ethics, Jacqueline Laing: 'It is a part of the very concept of innocence that it is not susceptible to variation by the desires or consent of others. On the contrary, desires of third parties, to be morally relevant, must conform to the standard of reasonableness.'[15] And yet, as was mentioned in chapter 4 of *Moral Theory*, it is not clear whether, for the consequentialist, preferences must always be taken at face value (as long as they are not incoherent) or can sometimes be omitted from calculation on the ground of unreasonableness. Singer, for one, equivocates on the point, as Laing notes. He says, for instance, that '[p]arents may, *with good reason*, regret that a disabled child was ever born. In that event the death of the child will have on its parents can be a reason for, rather than against killing it' (my emphasis).[16] Is Singer saying that the disabled child's life is objectively regrettable? If so, the preference of the parents is taken into account because it is allegedly a reasonable response to the child's disability. If so, one might wonder whether the preferences of a Chinese couple are reasonable if they regret having produced a girl when what they and their culture most value is a boy. Would it be reasonable for them to kill her and replace her with a boy? You might have thought not, but for the consequentialist it is not just the health or disability of the child that matters, but the overall effect of its existence on the family and society generally. If, as Singer believes, 'adverse effects on others' must be taken into account, he can hardly dismiss as unreasonable the Chinese parents for whom there is a great social stigma (say, in their village) and financial burden in having a girl. If Singer does in fact want to distinguish here between the disabled child and the burdensome female, he needs to give an account of the rationality of preferences which is *consistent with the consequentialist way of deciding moral questions*, something neither he nor any other prominent consequentialist appears to have done. On the other hand, if the preference utilitarian is true to the pluralism and preference-neutrality of consequentialism (emphasised by Bernard Williams), he will not concern himself too much with the reasonableness or otherwise of the parents' preferences: if the parents of the disabled child want it to die, then they may kill it. And the same for the Chinese parents of the female child, even if their regret is merely personal and not based on anything more than a sense of shame which may not be objectively justified, given the actual attitudes of others. (Needless to say, if there is an objectively adverse social effect this will merely cement the overall calculation in favour of the death of the girl. If the society at large wants the girl to live, the calculation will lead to her life being spared, whatever the parents may think; in any case, the child's living or dying will be a decidedly precarious affair.)

The contrast with traditional morality could not be clearer. For the traditionalist, the very innocence of a person, child or adult, *requires* that other people respond reasonably to its existence and condition. Innocence demands protection, and disability, however severe, demands care. Singer himself believes that there is such a thing as 'the basic attitude of care and protection of infants [that] we must not imperil'.[17] He invokes it when tackling the question of whether it is legitimate to grow human beings with deliberately damaged brains for use as spare parts in transplant surgery. So again he seems to be suggesting that there are certain attitudes which it is reasonable to have towards our children. And yet invoking the 'attitude of care and protection' is surely curious, given that the consequentialist already approves of killing, when maximisation requires it, the unborn, the immature, the comatose, the severely disabled, the senile and the terminally ill. (Usually, though not always, they will not be *persons*; sometimes they will have asked to be killed, for example, the terminally ill.) Why does killing people in such categories *not* imperil our 'basic attitude of care and protection' to human beings in such situations? If it does, it seems Singer at least ought to have second thoughts about what he recommends. If not, it is hard to see why 'baby-farming' would be any more of a problem. In any case, just think of all the needy patients whose lives could be saved by the extra supply of organs: wouldn't the potential diminishing of our 'basic attitude of care and protection' towards infants be more than compensated for by the enhancement of our attitude of care and protection towards needy patients?

For the consequentialist, then, there appears to be a trilemma: (1) take third-party preferences at face value, and make the innocent person's living or dying depend contingently upon the attitudes of others; (2) insist as well that preferences abide by a reasonableness constraint that is also consistent with consequentialist procedure, which (a) requires the spelling out of the constraint, something not done yet and unlikely to prove easy, and (b) must still lead to judgements, in *some* cases, that make an innocent person's living or dying contingent upon the attitudes of others; (3) insist on a reasonableness constraint that entails giving up consequentialism. Needless to say, the consequentialist is unlikely to be impressed by this trilemma, given his generally divergent intuitions about what is or is not morally repugnant.

Returning now from the question of preferences, we have seen that one of the central arguments against non-voluntary euthanasia is based on the falsehood of *personism* (criticised at length in chapter 4 of *Moral Theory*). We saw in the previous chapter that the *personist* can only fix his definition so as to include the drugged, the sleeping, and so on, at the cost of bringing in every other human being, which entails *personism*'s collapse into humanism. Another argument, directed not just against non-voluntary euthanasia but against any kind of euthanasia – when the voluntariness element is seen as the irrelevance it ultimately is for all parties – concerns the concept of a 'life worth living'. It is simply impossible to give a non-arbitrary account of the category into which a human being must fall for him to have a life that is *not* 'worth living'. Supporters of euthanasia can and do appeal to a multitude of 'morally relevant characteristics' as ingredients in the recipe for a being who is or is not 'worthy of life'. It is no accident that they do so, since various combinations give results that are not obviously nonsensical, no matter how immoral they may be, but that differ greatly as to who is admitted to the special category of beings deserving of some moral consideration. In every case, however, the category will be one that excludes certain people, whether they be young, old, incapacitated or otherwise presently, or inherently, unable to exhibit the full range of behaviour typical of a healthy adult human being. Such categories, therefore, fly in the face of the fundamental idea that all human beings, at whatever stage of development, whether 'normal' or not, have equal dignity and deserve whatever protection they need from the aggression of those more powerful than they are.

One reason why supporters of euthanasia rely on 'quality of life' judgements is that they confuse intrinsic and instrumental value. Suppose you believe that the sole point of being alive is that it gives you the means to do other things that are fulfilling, or enjoyable, or valued by your society, or whatever. Faced with a person in a deep coma, unable to do anything for himself except perhaps breathe (though even this may need artificial support), you may tend to think that the quality of this person's life is virtually zero, since it is not being put to any of the uses that give life its sole point. It will then be a short step to conclude that a variety of extrinsic considerations, such as the financial cost to the state, or the distress of the patient's family, tip the balance in favour of killing him. A view of the importance of life, however, which sees it as having intrinsic as well as instrumental value, countenances a different approach. Now it would be perverse for anyone to say that the comatose patient was *flourishing*, or exercising his humanity to the fullest – clearly he is not. But then neither do *any* of us flourish in an undiminished way, and it is impossible to see how the person in a comatose state is qualitatively different from any of us in that respect; it is only the *degree* of diminished flourishing that is different. But the question of whether and to what extent the person is flourishing is irrelevant to a consideration of whether the *last remaining* good he pursues, namely bare life itself, should be eliminated as well. His life may no longer have instrumental value, but its intrinsic value remains untouched by illness or incapacity, no matter how severe. Recall that in chapter 4 of *Moral Theory* I said it was the pursuability of goods *in general* that made life intrinsically valuable. In other words, it is not that a particular person's life has a point if *he* is capable of pursuing other things of value. *His* life has a point even if this is not the case, because human life *in general* has the characteristic of involving the pursuit of goods, which makes human beings the sorts of beings who are subject to moral evaluation. Since this pursuit is conceptually inseparable from life itself, life must be seen as the fundamental element among a number of elements that constitute a moral existence, which is an existence of intrinsic dignity. Further, I distinguished between the claim that life has value if goods are pursuable, and the claim that life has value *only* if goods are pursuable. Supporters of euthanasia usually conflate these two claims, but it is only the second that enables them to argue (leaving aside the general/particular point just made) that if goods are not pursuable by some individual, that individual's life loses value. Yet it is this second claim that is unjustifiable, because it ignores the status of life as a basic good in its own right. An analogy here with the value of art is helpful, though imperfect.[18] Charles may possess a beautiful work of art and yet it may for one reason or another (say, the cost of insuring it, or having to look at it day after day) cease to give him the pleasure it once did. The work of art will thus cease to have instrumental value for him; but it would be wrong to conclude that he was free to destroy it. This is not because someone *else* might derive pleasure from it – suppose the work of art, though beautiful, pleases no one because its style has gone out of fashion. Still, Charles would not be free to set it on fire, and again not because one day, *perhaps*, someone might derive pleasure from it. Since it is a beautiful work of art, it retains its beauty even if it pleases no one and serves no useful purpose. (Recall the discussion at the beginning of chapter 4 of *Moral Theory*.) As with many works of art currently in existence, its fate might lie in a dusty attic. Destroying it, however, would be a different matter – an act of cultural vandalism, we might say. But if this is the right attitude to art, how much more should it be the right attitude to life?

One argument often proposed in support of euthanasia is that 'we would not treat a dog like that', so why should human beings be left in a state of total incapacitation, which may involve severe pain? If we are prepared to 'put out of its misery' a suffering animal, why not a human being? There are two possible responses to this line of thought: they may be mutually exclusive, but since our concern here is with euthanasia, all that needs to be shown is that despite its intuitive appeal, the argument carries little weight and can be handled in a variety of ways. (In fact, as the next chapter will suggest, it is the second response we should prefer.) The first will appeal to believers in animal rights, namely that perhaps we ought to re-examine the idea that it is acceptable to kill an animal merely because we presume to judge that its suffering makes its life 'not worth living'. It is a familiar idea among believers in animal rights that we ought critically to examine our intuitions about what is acceptable treatment of animals. We cannot, then, simply take it as given that the euthanasia of animals is permissible. A more plausible account of such an action, it might be said, is that it is not the suffering of the animal that we cannot bear, but our own discomfiture at having to deal with the animal, knowing that we are limited in what we can do to ease its distress.

Another response to the argument is to question the blithe drawing of analogies between our treatment of animals and our treatment of each other. We regard it as acceptable, for instance, to keep animals as pets, to curtail their freedom of movement for our own pleasure, to train them to respond to our every command, to breed them when and how we see fit; not to mention the obvious facts of our eating animals and wearing their skin, and various other forms of exploitation. We rightly regard it as unacceptable to treat each other in a similar fashion: if the fight against slavery was against anything, it was against such forms of treatment. We have an attitude to animals, then, that is quite different to our attitude to each other as human beings. A believer in animal rights will say that such attitudes are inconsistent, and that 'putting an animal out of its misery' is just one example of treating animals as less than full objects of moral respect. On the other hand, a person who believes that the difference in attitude is justifiable will require far more in support of the euthanasia of people than a mere gesture at a familiar slogan.

A further problem with the case for euthanasia lies in a subtle confusion of ideas found in the writings of its supporters. Surely, it is argued, we *do* recognise that some lives are not 'worth living', as can be seen in our attitude to drugs which cause birth defects. When the link is discovered, the drug is withdrawn and compensation is paid to the victims. We do not simply regard the lives of children disabled by a drug taken during pregnancy as 'different' from those of healthy children; we regard the disability as tragic, and 'the life of a disabled person as likely to be . . . worse than that of a normal person'.[19] The problem here, however, is the confusion between the idea of a life that is worse than another, and one that is not 'worth living' pure and simple. The life of a child disabled by a drug may indeed be scarred by a great evil, the effect of the drug undesirable, the drug itself dangerous and compensation payable. Indeed, the life of a disabled person may, if the disability is severe, be *worse* than that of a normal, healthy person. But 'worse' does not mean 'worthless'. It is one thing to acknowledge that one life may be worse than another because the condition or circumstances of the first are worse than those of the second, and quite another to say that the life of the second is not 'worth living'. There is a vast argumentative gap between claiming that we can *compare* lives according to how well they are going and claiming that there is a *threshold* below which a life possesses 'negative value'. The appeal to the facts just mentioned, then, has no force.

Supporters of euthanasia often remark that the plausibility of their case is seen when more attention is paid to the 'mercy' in 'mercy killing'. Euthanasia, it is said, is driven by a motive of benevolence towards the suffering, and this exculpates the person who carries it out. Once this motive is given its due importance, it can be seen that euthanasia is far from murder, as its opponents portray it. There are several problems with this line of argument. First, to say that the motive of the 'mercy killer' is praiseworthy is to beg the question of whether the motive even *makes sense*. A person may protest that he acts out of benevolence without *in fact* doing so, if his motive is incoherent. And it is incoherent to suppose that the death of a human being can be good *for him*. On the contrary, if an action is good for a person, it improves his condition, or makes his life go better than it would have had the action not been performed. Setting someone's broken leg is good for him, as is curing someone's disease. But you can never cure a person by killing him – death is not, as it were, the ultimate medicine. Which is why R. M. Hare, the most influential consequentialist thinker of recent times (and regarded by many as one of the century's most important moral philosophers), was dangerously confused when he wrote, in support of Singer, to a German bioethicist: 'Singer's position no more involves discrimination against cripples than does the setting of broken legs. One sets fractures because one thinks that it is better to have whole legs than broken ones; but this does not imply any contempt for cripples who for some reason did not get their legs restored to normal.'[20] (Recall the discussion in chapter 4 of *Moral Theory* of whether a person can benefit materially after his death.)

Second, there is far more to the motives of the 'mercy' killer than the admittedly incoherent desire to do good for a person by killing him. At least on a consequentialist view 'extrinsic considerations' come into play, and if there is any value to be found in the life of a disabled baby, or of a senile adult, that value can be outweighed by the burden on the parents of that baby (who might want to have another, healthy child) or on the family of the adult, or on the state, of caring for the person concerned. The 'family as a whole', it has been claimed by Singer, can decide if it is in *their* own best interests to kill their child.[21] Jonathan Glover says: 'Some senile old people and some children born with gross abnormalities may be such an emotional burden on their families that, thinking purely of side-effects, it would arguably be better if they were dead.'[22] Once motives connected with such considerations come into play, it becomes clear that 'mercy killing', if it is about mercy at all, is often about being merciful to everyone but the patient. If someone kills another out of the motive to prevent him from being a burden to the killer or to other people, that motive is better described as 'sinister' than as 'benevolent'. Third, even if it were possible to have saintly motives when killing another, that would not justify the act. Suppose a person murdered his grandmother with the motive of benefiting under her will and thereby being able to feed his poor, starving family. This would hardly relieve the killer of guilt. And finally, on a consequentialist view of action, *all* motives are irrelevant: only consequences count morally.

So no consequentialist can appeal to the motive of mercy in the justification of euthanasia. All he is allowed to appeal to is the magic ingredient X that the consequentialist seeks to maximise. Whether someone's life is 'worth living' will depend on the extent to which X is maximised in his case. For a preference utilitarian such as Singer, what matters in the first instance is whether the individual wants to live; and whatever the answer to that question (the question is of course irrelevant if the potential victim is not competent), the decision whether he ultimately lives or dies depends on what *other* people want: the individual's family and friends, the medical personnel caring for him (for whom a large and probably the principal consideration will be the bearing of the financial and logistical burden of having the individual 'on their books'), the state as a whole, and anyone with some sort of interest in the individual's life or death. Now if, as was argued in *Moral Theory*, the whole idea of 'maximisation' by a consequentialist calculus is mistaken, there can be no calculation of whether someone's life is 'worth living'. The supporter of euthanasia, if not relying on some such chimerical, pseudo-mathematical concept of a life 'worth living', will tend to use the term as a catch-all category loaded with subjectivity and personal preference. In neither case does the concept rest on plausible objective principles.

2.5 Active and Passive Euthanasia

Two broad types of killing have traditionally been recognised by both morality and law: killing by commission and killing by omission. The former involves a positive act that brings about death and the latter involves a failure to act that brings about death. Just as not every act causes a death, so not every omission causes a death. As you sit reading this book, there are many things you are omitting to do, such as going for a walk, that do not cause a death. Also, as you read this book people are dying from disease in the Gobi desert: but your not flying there to help, even if you *knew* they were dying, and even if you *could* fly there (you had the time and the money, and so on), does not bring about the deaths of those people.

Some omissions, however, do bring about deaths. An omission that does so, all things being equal, is as morally culpable as a positive act that brings about death. A mother who starved her child to death would be as guilty of murder as if she had beaten it to death, assuming no peculiarity of circumstance to differentiate the cases (suppose the starving and the beating are deliberate and wanton). The primary feature of an omission that is as morally culpable as a commission in similar circumstances is that there is a *prior duty to act*. A duty to act can arise in various ways: it can arise from a promise; or from a legally binding contract (which creates a moral as well as a legal duty to honour it); or from a condition of responsibility for another's behaviour (an employer, for instance, has a duty to prevent crime by his employees in the course of their work, and a teacher has a duty to ensure, within the limits of his capability, that his students do well at school); or from a condition of responsibility for public welfare (the state is duty-bound to keep law and order); or in numerous other situations. In particular, there is a duty to take care of those for whose care we are responsible. The responsibility arises from a relationship of proximity, not merely geographic but based on the structure of a society, its laws, customs and institutions. Typical relationships of proximity involving a duty of care are parent – child (the duty of care being reciprocal, since the child has the duty to care for its parents when necessary), guardian – ward, teacher – pupil (the teacher being duty-bound to provide a safe environment at school), employer – employee, and doctor – patient.

It is common practice now, however, for doctors to 'treat selectively' certain patients. This means that patients who would otherwise have been cared for are left to die, such as babies born with certain disabilities, or terminally ill patients who contract minor ailments, such as infections, that could shorten their lives if left untreated. Thus some doctors, for whose patients they have a duty of care, now practise killing by omission in certain situations. Since killing by omission, where there is a prior duty to protect life, is morally as culpable as a positive act to bring about or hasten death, such failures to act come within the ambit of principles governing euthanasia. Usually, they are called cases of passive euthanasia, and a positive intervention to end life is called active euthanasia. Morality, however, recognises no difference between a failure to cure an infection in a terminally ill patient, even if his death were imminent, where the failure involves the intention that the patient should die, and a lethal injection to hasten the death of such a patient.

Supporters of euthanasia often appeal to the widespread practice of 'selective non-treatment' as an argument for active intervention to bring about death. First, they say that the acceptance of death by omission amongst the medical profession shows that it is part of normal medical procedure based on expert judgement, and is thus morally justified. Second, they ask: 'if it is right to allow infants to die, why is it wrong to kill them?'[23] After all, allowing a baby (or other patient) to die can lead to a protracted and painful death, especially if the doctor simply refrains from attending to the patient's vital needs, such as food and drink. Would a quick, painless injection not be more humane?

As to the first point, there is a difference between what is accepted at a given time as standard medical practice and what is a morally *acceptable* practice. Morality in medicine is not defined by what doctors typically do. Rather, as was said earlier, practice follows morality and is therefore dictated by what is morally acceptable. In various societies and at various times in history (and even now) the medical profession has actively co-operated in unacceptable behaviour, such as forced sterilisation and abortion (even pro-abortionists baulk at the thought of *coercion*), eugenics, torture, and medical experiments on 'undesirables', be they physically disabled or politically dangerous. Of course, morality needs to take account of expert medical judgement, since it is impossible to frame ethical directives for specific cases in the absence of detailed knowledge of current medical techniques, methods of diagnosis, assessment of the risk of certain procedures, and so on. But ethical directives are about the *ethical* treatment of patients, not just about what is technically possible, or expedient, or cost-effective. Principles of ethical treatment must therefore follow ethical guidelines, and the actual practice of the medical profession must abide by those principles.

As to the second point about 'selective non-treatment', the conditional assertion on which it is based presupposes an answer we have already seen to be unacceptable. The assertion is that if allowing a patient to die is right, so is active killing; indeed, active killing might be *preferable*, if it

involves less pain and trauma for all concerned. But whereas the supporter of euthanasia asserts the antecedent of the conditional, that it is
right to allow death, the opponent denies the consequent, that active killing is ever right. Since active killing is never right, neither is allowing a
patient to die. Killing by omission, then, is morally as culpable as killing
by commission. The crucial qualification, however, is that the kind of
killing by omission that is as culpable as a killing by commission is where
the intention of the omission is to *end life*. That the intention is relevant is
precisely the point of the comparison for both supporters and opponents
of euthanasia. What the supporter countenances is *intentional* active killing in some cases, just because it would be 'better for all concerned' than
the widespread intentional *passive* killing ('selective non-treatment') that
occurs at present. But in order to become clear about what is and is not an
intentional killing by omission we need to make some distinctions between different kinds of case.

Various confusions have undermined the proper understanding of the
active/passive distinction. Sometimes, supporters of euthanasia talk as if
any withdrawal of treatment is *ipso facto* a justifiable omission. This,
they claim, is because when treatment is withdrawn, say for an infection,
'nature is allowed to take its course', and the patient dies not from this
but from the underlying disease. There are at least two problems with
such reasoning. The first is that to the extent that the appeal to nature's
taking its course is used as an implicit justification for at least the permissibility of an omission that has this result, it is spurious. Suppose a child is
prescribed antibiotics for a serious infection, and the parent begins giving
them but stops the treatment after a week, and the child dies. Can she
evade responsibility as the *agent* of death by pleading that nature took its
course and the child ultimately died of the infection? The parent is not
responsible for the initial illness, but her *specific duty* to take care of the
child in her charge makes her responsible for the death of that child if she
withdraws treatment. The responsibility is both moral and causal: the
active withdrawal of treatment *prevents* recovery and *hastens* death. Thus
her omission to continue with the antibiotics is murder, as is the failure of
a doctor to continue giving antibiotics to a terminally ill patient who develops an infection. It is hard to see how the fact that the patient is going
to die anyway (aren't we all?) makes a moral difference.

The second problem is the confusion of factual situations that are importantly different. The withdrawal of treatment may have the complexion of an omission or a commission, depending on circumstances. The

failure by doctors to give treatment to newborn disabled babies is a clear *withholding* of treatment, and so an omission. The failure to continue antibiotic treatment already begun looks like an omission by *withdrawal*, since treatment has commenced, that is, the doctor is intervening positively, but then stops intervening, or ceases to act. On the other hand, the disconnecting of the air supply of a comatose patient connected to a ventilator looks much more like a *commission* by withdrawal, as does the turning off of an intravenous drip. Here what gives the behaviour the complexion of a commission is that it is a positive intervention in a continuous life-sustaining process, no different to the doctor's placing a pillow over a patient's mouth to stop his breathing; whereas the decision not to continue with antibiotics involves no intervention, just a failure to do what the doctor had previously been doing. Perhaps a conflicting intuition is generated by the thought that if a total stranger walked into the hospital and switched off the ventilator, it would self-evidently be a killing by commission, whereas if done by the doctor who began the ventilation in the first place, we would be less inclined to call it a commission. On the other hand, it is hard to see how the facts about who started the treatment make a difference. Fortunately, however, this attempt at classification, interesting though it is, is also relatively unimportant ethically since, as has been said, a killing by omission is morally as bad as a killing by commission, where the intention is to end life. Two practical consequences of a correct classification, however, are that first, those who are more impressed by the wrongness of commissions than omissions, even if the impression is unjustified, should recognise that some types of behaviour they regard as instances of the former are really instances of the latter; and second, since culpable omissions arise in the context of duties to act, there might be a temptation to treat all types of behaviour leading to death by those with duties to act in given situations (such as doctors) as omissions, which is wrong. Those capable of culpable omission are equally capable of active killing.

Another confusion involves the bringing in of a different distinction to the active/passive one: that between intention and foresight. Sometimes it is said that there is an ethical inconsistency in claiming that a doctor does no wrong if he omits to give a disabled child antibiotics, 'knowing full well that without antibiotics the child will die',[24] but does do wrong if he gives the child a lethal injection. Here the question of knowledge is brought in and it muddies the waters, so it is important to recapitulate some of the points made in chapter 3 of *Moral Theory* about the importance of the intention/foresight distinction. The distinction, as we saw, is encapsulated in the famous Principle of Double Effect (PDE), which has come under enormous attack in recent years, mainly from consequentialists. The principle has been criticised in a wholly *ad hominem* way as essentially religious, and also as mysterious or obscure. In fact, PDE is none of these things. It is a simple and easily grasped codification of the intention/foresight distinction, a distinction essential to any moral theory worthy of the name. This does not mean that its *application* in a given factual situation might not be difficult and complex.

You will recall that PDE follows our common-sense understanding of morality by giving a central place to *intentional* action in moral evaluation. Intention is central because morality is about ends and objectives, what an agent *tries to achieve* with his actions. This may also be, and usually is, what he *wants* to achieve, and what he *believes* or *knows* he can achieve, but intention is not mere desire, belief or knowledge. Intention concerns *purpose*. Thus, a doctor who gives a patient a lethal injection, say an overdose of painkiller, because he *intends* to kill the patient, commits a straightforward intentional killing. If he injects the patient with a saline solution, thinking it is a lethal dose of painkiller and intending to kill, then again, although the patient does not die, the doctor's *intent* is to kill. If, on the other hand, he gives a non-lethal dose of painkiller with the objective of eliminating the pain and not the patient, he does not intend to kill, even if the patient suffers a severe reaction and dies. Further, if he gives a dose he believes is likely to be lethal, but does so with the intention to dull the pain, which may be so severe it requires a high dose, and the patient dies, he does not intentionally kill. And if his intention is the same but this time he is virtually *certain* the patient will die, he still does not intentionally kill, since this simply was not his purpose.

The distinction between what an agent intends, and what he believes or knows, is always portrayed by consequentialist writers as at best a mere semantic distinction of no moral relevance. After all, if the consequences or effect of actions are what matter, how can a mere difference in state of mind be relevant? The reply to this criticism is that, on the contrary, there is a *world* of difference between intention and foresight (where by the latter we include cognitive states such as belief and knowledge). Far from being a mere semantic difference, it is a profound difference rooted in the nature of things that completely alters the complexion of an action. Indeed, it alters the very *identity* of the action, because the very characterisation of what the agent *does* depends on what he *intends*. Is the doctor trying to kill the patient's pain? Or is he trying to kill the patient? What does he *intend*? There cannot be a more fundamental difference relevant to the problem of evaluating the doctor's behaviour.

It would be wrong, however, to infer from the central importance of intention to moral evaluation that where an agent performs an action and merely foresees a certain result rather than intending it, he avoids responsibility altogether. Consider a doctor who, in order to treat a patient with a minor illness, say a common infection, prescribes a highly dangerous drug that he foresees may well cure the infection but is also likely to provoke a cardiac arrest. Can he avoid responsibility for the bad effect by saying that he did not *intend* to cause a cardiac arrest, merely to cure the infection? Of course we would say he cannot. He may not be guilty of an intentional killing if the patient dies, but he will at least have been grossly negligent, and at most subjectively reckless in his disregard for the serious side effect, which brings with it a high degree of culpability. The reason for this is that the condition he tries to cure simply is not grave enough to warrant a treatment that risks serious side effects. More abstractly, he does not have a *sufficiently weighty reason* for allowing the risk of a bad effect flowing from his action. Hence we must recognise extra elements in the intention/foresight distinction that give the distinction its proper ethical role. We can say that it is permissible to perform an action of which an evil effect is foreseen only when certain conditions obtain. (They were stated more precisely, and discussed in depth, in chapter 3 of *Moral Theory*.) First, the action must not be intrinsically wrong (prescribing a drug to cure an illness is not intrinsically wrong). Second, something good must flow from the act (such as the curing of the infection, or a strong chance of its being cured), and it must not be caused by the evil effect, since an axiom of morality is that the ends do not justify the means (the risk of cardiac arrest is not a *means* the doctor employs to cure the infection, rather it is an independent side effect). Third, the agent must intend only the good effect (the curing of the cold), since it is wrong to intend an evil effect (the risk of cardiac arrest, which in this case is foreseen). Finally, the agent must have, in the good which he intends, a sufficiently weighty reason for permitting the evil effect that also flows from his act, since it is wrong even to *permit* an evil without such a reason. In this case, the doctor does not have a sufficiently weighty reason to allow the risk of cardiac arrest, and he would certainly be acting wrongly if he prescribed a drug carrying that risk for no ulterior purpose whatsoever, except perhaps curiosity as to its effects.

So, to return to the earlier case of a doctor who omits to give a disabled child antibiotics, knowing full well it will die without them, further matters need to be settled before responsibility can be assessed. Suppose that the antibiotics carried a high risk of causing brain damage. The doctor might then omit to give them with the express intention of avoiding this effect, while foreseeing but not intending probable death. Is this a sufficiently weighty reason for the omission? It would be foolish to think that such questions are always easily answered, but two important points need to be kept in mind. First, death is rarely if ever a physically certain effect of a given therapy. Rather, certain therapies hasten death, or increase its likelihood, or make the likelihood very high, and the question is then whether the *risk* of death is permissible, given the therapeutic objective. Indeed, death is rarely if ever a physically certain effect of *anything* that we do in the pursuit of some good objective. A parent who rushes her desperately ill child to hospital, in the process going through every red light in heavy traffic, creates a substantial risk of death in pursuit of a good objective. Normally such behaviour is permissible if there is no alternative, if the aim is sufficiently praiseworthy and directed at the good of an individual or the common good. On the other hand, if getting the child to hospital means running over a pedestrian as a virtually certain but intended effect of driving, our judgement would be different. Similarly, if a certain fatal poison was discovered to have marvellous pain-killing properties, it would be unacceptable to use it. This is primarily because the unintended effect *defeats the therapeutic purpose* for which it is used, which is to keep the living patient in as good a condition as possible. Thus one needs to balance the degree of likelihood of the effect, its severity, the importance of the therapeutic objective, its achievability, and the availability of alternatives. Perhaps no objective can outweigh the physical certainty of death, but a high risk might be worth running for relief of unbearable pain, just as it is worth running in a dangerous operation aimed at relieving someone of a grave condition. It is these risks that must be assessed in clinical situations.

Second, consequentialists who see no point in the intention/foresight distinction invariably portray such an assessment as a 'covert quality of life judgement'. If, say, relieving severe pain is permitted at the cost of a high risk of death, this, they say, will be because we have made a prior judgement that the patient's quality of life will be so poor without treatment that we allow it to take precedence over saving life. This is a gross misrepresentation of the reasoning involved. A patient in severe, persistent pain is of course suffering from an evil which the doctor should, if possible, try to eliminate or minimise. Such a judgement is *nothing like* the judgement that the patient's 'quality of life' will be so poor as not to be 'worth living' without treatment, or that he is 'better off dead' than in pain, thus legitimising any and every attempt to relieve pain no matter what the attendant risks. Nor indeed is the judgement that the doctor is *permitted* to take drastic measures the same as the judgement that he is *obliged* to. The consequentialist will always say that since the patient is better off dead than in such pain, death is *preferable* to such pain. On a utility calculation, he will say, the doctor is *morally obliged* to give the high-risk treatment since it involves the good consequences of a chance of pain relief and a high risk of death, which together outweigh a life in such pain. *No such calculation* is made on a non-consequentialist view such as that being defended here. The death of an innocent person is always a grave evil, it never factors into a moral equation as something desirable by comparison to the alternative of a life of diminished flourishing, and so a doctor would, I contend, be within his rights to refuse to administer the high-risk treatment even if he had a sufficiently weighty reason for giving it. In other words, the reason makes the treatment morally lawful, but never obligatory. Indeed, this is a current medical practice which should be maintained: doctors frequently refuse to administer dangerous therapies even if there are serious benefits to be obtained, though they may be obliged to refer the patient to a doctor who would be inclined to act. Further, the moral judgement does *not* involve anything like a consequentialist sliding scale of pains, pleasures, desires or preferences, the wishes of people other than the patient are not given the equal importance they are on that scale, and there is no threshold below which a patient's life ceases to be 'worth living' according to a specious quality of life judgement. The intention/foresight distinction and its various qualifications involve quite a different way of thinking, and the consequentialist misrepresents it by claiming otherwise.

Further, the consequentialist claims that for a supporter of the distinction, it follows that we can 'avoid responsibility simply by directing our intention to one effect rather than another'.[25] We have already seen that an agent cannot simply plead 'I foresaw the effect but did not intend it' in order to avoid responsibility: all of the conditions attached to the distinction need to be considered, such as whether there was a sufficiently weighty objective involved in taking the action he did. But it must also be emphasised that talk of 'simply directing our intention to one effect rather than another' is a caricature of human action. (See further chapter 3 of *Moral Theory*.) The doctor who omits to give the disabled child antibiotics and pleads that he merely foresaw death but did not intend it, needs, like any person whose actions are under scrutiny, to be asked certain questions. Was he trying to achieve something else? If he says he was trying to avoid causing brain damage, and there is evidence that this is an effect of the drug, and his behaviour at the relevant time supports this interpretation, we can take his plea to be a faithful reflection of his state of mind. But if he does not have any other objective to produce – he simply withheld the drug – or he admits to proposing euthanasia to the parents just prior to the decision not to act, or he says his objective was 'to spare the child a miserable life', or various other pieces of evidence are produced to show that his aim or purpose – what he was trying to *achieve* by not acting – was the child's death, then any plea to the effect that he 'merely foresaw' death must fall on deaf ears. Courts of law are, and have for centuries been, adequately equipped to deal with such cases and to evaluate evidence of a person's state of mind. Far from an agent's being able 'at the drop of a hat' to direct his intentions one way rather than another, the distinction between what he intends and what he foresees, what his purpose was and what it was not, reflects *a fundamental difference of psychological attitude*, which can be judged by innumerable pieces of evidence concerning behaviour, words spoken, known or previously expressed opinions, and so on. Far from being a superficial semantic distinction, the difference between intention and foresight lies at the heart of our interpretation of the behaviour of others, doctors included.

2.6 Ordinary and Extraordinary Means

In 1989, a terrible disaster at Hillsborough football stadium in England claimed the lives of 96 people. One of the injured was Tony Bland, whose brain was starved of oxygen in the accident. He lapsed into a persistent non-responsive state (called a 'persistent vegetative state' by the medical profession), in which it seems most (but by no means all) brain function ceased. For four years he lay in hospital. Throughout that time he breathed spontaneously, his eyes were open most of the time, but he did not communicate with anyone, as far as could be determined. Nor could he swallow, so he needed to be fed through a tube. In 1993, after a lengthy court battle, his family and doctors won the right, via a declaration of the House of Lords, to withdraw the tube feeding him and giving him fluids. He died soon afterwards.[26]

A major issue in the case was whether artificial feeding constituted 'medical treatment', since the court considered that in some circumstances treatment, as opposed to basic, non-medical care, could be withdrawn. The circumstances in this case, it held, were that Mr Bland's continued life was a source of 'humiliation' and 'indignity' to him, and a violation of 'how he would want to be remembered'. We have already looked at the issue of quality of life judgements and pointed out their arbitrariness and their failure to respect the dignity of every human being. Whereas the court saw Tony Bland's life as undignified, its proper response should have been to recognise that there is nothing whatsoever undignified in living with disability or even total incapacity, but that true indignity lies in the thinly disguised contempt with which some human beings regard others.

Our main concern here, however, is with the issue of medical treatment. The court was gesturing at a traditional ethical distinction between types of means used to care for and prolong the life of the sick. According to the distinction, there is no obligation to maintain the last vestiges of life at all costs, no matter what the burden. This might appear to conflict with the unconditional value of human life: after all, if life has ultimate value, is any act too burdensome to perform in promotion or protection of life? The conflict is illusory, however. For there is a tight connection between what we are obliged to do and what we *can* do: our duties cannot extend beyond our physical and mental capacities. Heroic action is rightly praised, but it is never imposed. Rather, morality requires action in conformity with the normal abilities of a person given his situation in life, his pre-existing duties, his expertise, and so on.

The distinction, then, is between what are usually called *ordinary* and *extraordinary* actions. In the case of actions related to the prolongation of life, ordinariness consists in the maintenance, by oneself or by others for oneself, of normal, everyday means of sustenance. These include things such as food, drink, shelter and warmth. To refuse any of these when to do so would hasten or bring about death is tantamount to suicide, or culpable homicide if denied to one person by another where there is a responsibility of the latter for the former. On the other hand, extraordinary actions are ones that are overly burdensome, futile, or involve serious dangers to the person treated or others. An individual has the right to refuse extraordinary treatment for one or all of these reasons, the common thread being that such treatment would test his capacities beyond what he can reasonably be expected to bear. Similarly, a doctor is permitted to refuse to administer extraordinary treatment because of such an effect on his patient, or because it tests the doctor's own capacities beyond what he, *as a doctor*, can reasonably be expected to do. A typical case would be a patient brought into emergency, haemorrhaging severely, all of whose vital functions barely register on the monitors, and who goes into persistent cardiac arrest. Such a person would be on a headlong rush towards death, and there are, given the laws of nature and the limits of medicine, bounds to what a doctor in such a situation can and should do. Of course, resuscitation should be attempted, along with the usual emergency-room procedures for restoring cardiac and other bodily functions. But the patient may recover, only to go into arrest again, and this may happen several times. After a while, the doctor will simply give up, having done all he can, within his physical and technological limits, to keep the patient alive. After that, the underlying condition will prevail and the patient may well die. This is a typical case in which a doctor is permitted to cease treatment, where to carry on would be futile.

In current writing on euthanasia, however, and as reflected in the judgement on Tony Bland, 'extraordinary' is interpreted to cover virtually any intervention, simply because it is artificial, or assisted by technology, or provided by professionals. Food and drink are the most basic and ordinary means of sustaining life, yet the court decided that because they were being provided through a tube they constituted 'treatment', and since they were treatment they were also by implication extraordinary, involving artificial intervention in natural processes. Thus they held that Tony Bland could be starved to death. Although an inquest after his death found he died from the injuries suffered in the original accident, this flew in the face of reality, since he had been alive for four years after the accident, breathed on his own, and simply needed help to eat and drink, along with other basic maintenance. Far from dying from the original injuries, he uncoincidentally died soon after the court ruled that his feeding tube could be withdrawn.

It is wrong, however, to regard the provision of basic care as medical treatment. Doctors have duties both as members of their profession and as ordinary human beings, and they can be responsible for the care of a person in both capacities, especially where basic care is involved. The mere fact that food is provided using artificial equipment by someone wearing a badge or carrying a stethoscope does not mean that the feeding, which is the common duty of *any* person who has the maintenance of another in his hands, comes within the province of special or professional care, even if professional skills assist in providing that care. This is no different to the case of a doctor who bandages the gash of someone he sees lying bleeding in the road: if he is carrying his black bag he might be able to do a better job than a non-professional using a torn shirtsleeve, but he is exercising a duty of common humanity by which any of us would be bound in similar circumstances.

Second, basic care aside, medical treatment is not extraordinary simply by virtue of involving machinery or electronics, or requiring round-the-clock attention, nor simply by virtue of being expensive. The issue of classification becomes more difficult as new, specialist technologies come into question, and there is no room for a detailed discussion. Several points can be made, however. One is that the ordinary/extraordinary distinction is not fixed. Several centuries ago, the amputation of a leg to save a life would have been extraordinary because it was intensely painful and distressing, but now the operation, while still a drastic measure, is easily and painlessly performed. There is nothing mysterious or incomprehensible about the fluidity of the distinction: procedures that were once beyond the capacity of a patient to bear or a doctor to perform competently are now routine; as expertise develops, so human capacities improve. Again, the distinction varies at a given time across circumstances. The use of cardiac resuscitation is extraordinary where arrest is continuous and persistent, and ordinary where the heart responds well and regains its normal function (of course, this is not known by the doctor in advance, so assessment of probabilities is involved). Antibiotics are ordinary treatment for an elderly patient with Alzheimer's disease who contracts pneumonia (pneumonia might be the 'old person's friend', but this does not mean doctors can help it along by not treating it where there is hope of recovery); but extraordinary for a person likely to suffer a severe allergic reaction to them.

A further point is that, contrary to its misrepresentation by consequentialist writers, there is no 'covert quality of life judgement' involved in deeming some means extraordinary relative to the circumstances. The use of a respirator on someone in a coma from which there is little hope of recovery is not extraordinary by virtue of that fact. It would be if it still failed to provide proper oxygenation due to some chronic bodily breakdown, but not simply because the patient may not recover. The confusion centres on the meaning of 'futile'. It does *not* mean 'incapable of restoring an adequate quality of life', but 'incapable of fulfilling its designated function'. A respirator on its own will not repair severe brain damage, nor cure paralysis. But it is not meant to. Its function is to enable someone to breathe, and if it does that it is anything but futile. The same applies to food, drink and warmth.

The problem of high-risk treatment is already covered by the intention/ foresight distinction. If a given treatment runs such a high risk of serious harm that it would defeat the purpose of the treatment, which is to restore health, then it could be deemed extraordinary and may be withheld by a doctor, or indeed withdrawn once commenced (say, if the risk increases substantially during administration), as long as the intention of the doctor is not to bring about death. (A doctor might protest: 'How do I know what I intend in these sorts of complicated and dangerous situations? I just *act* as the situation demands.' The response is (a) that this begs the question of what the situation *does* demand, including morally; and (b) that if a doctor does not know what he intends when he carries out a procedure, perhaps he should cease practising as a doctor and spend more time getting to know himself.) As for burdensomeness, this is a difficult matter requiring careful consideration of cases in the light of principle. Again, it does not involve a simple consequentialist calculation. The mere fact that a treatment is expensive does not make it extraordinary. Nor does the fact that it could be used with greater success on another patient. As long as it is not *futile* to use it on one patient, that patient should not be abandoned in favour of another simply because the probability of success is higher. Nor does the fact that the cost of the treatment is better put towards other medical resources to achieve a greater overall 'good'. One cannot simply trade off a respirator for a comatose patient against five X-ray machines. Nor can one balance a comatose bank clerk against a Nobel Prize-winning economist who might recover from brain damage if resources were diverted from the former person. Once such calculations are made based on 'quality of life' judgements and opinions about who deserves treatment, who will make a 'greater contribution' to society, who is more 'productive', and so on, the whole point of medicine is defeated and patients cease to be human beings with equal dignity, but rather units in a production line. Burdensomeness *does* involve questions of cost and distribution of resources, and certainly prior decision-making about how to allocate funds must be informed by questions such as: How can as many people as possible have access to as much overall care as possible? How great is the *need* for respirators compared to the need for, say, CAT scanners? What alternative means of treatment are available? What preventive measures against certain conditions are in place? But such decision-making must not be informed by a judgement to the effect that comatose patients, for instance, simply do not deserve treatment because they are 'less than human', or have no further 'contribution' to make to society.

In a given case, a patient must not be treated in such a way as to give the impression: that his treatment is a gift; that it will be used on him unless and until the doctor judges his life not to be 'worth living'; that when this judgement is made, he will be left to die and the equipment will be moved on to someone else. Rather, the burdensomeness of a treatment is related to whether it is doing what it is supposed to do, whether it carries unacceptable risks, and whether and to what degree it taxes the capacities of doctor or patient. In particular, doctors have duties to more than one person. If a treatment requires such ongoing involvement that a doctor is at serious risk of neglecting his duties to other patients, the treatment can be deemed extraordinary, but again a careful consideration of cases is required.

There is much more that could be said about the ordinary/extraordinary distinction. But I hope that it has at least been shown what the distinction is *not*; that the true distinction is a necessary element of bioethical thinking; and what are some of the principles and applications for which the distinction is appropriate.

2.7   Euthanasia, Death and 'Brain Death'

It is an analytic truth that euthanasia cannot be performed on someone who is already dead. The question is, when is a person dead? It is easily asked, but more difficult to answer. Although it would take us too far into metaphysics to defend it, there is at least a case for saying that death itself is not something that can be observed. This might seem a startling claim: after all, don't doctors observe death all the time? I would say that what they or anyone else observes is *the moment of death* – they observe a person's dying, but they do not observe *what actually happens* which *constitutes* the death of that person. To take an analogy, we cannot directly observe each other's thoughts, in the sense of seeing what actually goes on inside a person's mind when he thinks something – no amount of looking inside the brain will locate a thought. But we can observe each other in the *act* of thinking. (Let us leave aside whether it is possible directly to read someone's mind. Even if a human being could perform such an unlikely feat, his having direct *knowledge* of the thoughts of another would not mean he actually saw what was going on in the other's mind.)

For practical purposes, not being able to observe the actual event or events that constitute death makes the *determination* of when a person has died more difficult than it otherwise would have been, because we have to rely on *evidence* of death, *signs* or *indicators* of death. This is all we have to go on. But what are the indicators of death? This too is a difficult matter, as witnessed by the way criteria have changed over the years. Something like the irreversible cessation of circulation and respiration has been the traditional definition of death (in the sense of *certain indicator* of death). But how do we know when these processes are irreversible? When the person is dead? But that would be circular. The fact is, throughout the whole of human history up to the last few decades, and in virtually every civilisation that has left us records of the way they treated the dead, the *irreversibility* of breathing and circulation have themselves been determined by something like *the onset of putrefaction* (or the *withering* of the whole body, especially in warmer and drier climates, where putrefaction takes a long time if it happens at all.) If you want to be really sure someone is dead, you need to wait for his whole body to begin to decay. (Since the *onset* of putrefaction can be confused with a disease such as gangrene, even this indicator is liable to lead to misdiagnosis in rare cases; waiting for the signs of decay in the *whole* body cancels out this possibility.) In most cultures bodies have traditionally been left exposed ('in state') for several days, both to allow a proper process of grieving and to make it quite clear to all and sundry that the person is indeed dead and in at least the initial stages of decay.

The onset of putrefaction as an indicator of death is now seen by virtually everyone in the medical profession, and in medical ethics, as preposterous – not because it is not certain enough, but because it is *too* certain! After all, there is not much you can do with a putrefying body other than bury it. You cannot 'harvest' its organs – its heart, lungs, corneas, kidneys, liver, pancreas, and so on. Now the 1950s and 1960s brought great advances in medical technology, allowing patients to be kept alive for longer than ever imagined, even indefinitely, through artificial respiration, tube feeding, and various instruments for keeping the blood circulating, the body warm and the other life processes intact. Although this should have been seen as cause for rejoicing that life could be maintained beyond the bounds of what was thought possible, doctors soon began to see 'ethical problems' on the horizon. Uncoincidentally, within months of the famous (and unsuccessful, since the patient died 18 days later) heart transplant by Dr Barnard in 1967 in South Africa, Harvard Medical School, seeing the possibilities opening up for organ transplantation, set up a committee to 'redefine' the concept of death. As the committee's chairman Henry Beecher told the Dean of the medical school, 'the time has come for a further consideration of the definition of death. Every major hospital has patients stacked up waiting for donors.'[27]

As subsequent events revealed, the entire procedure of the Harvard Brain Death Committee, as it came to be known, was governed by political motives. Organ transplant operations were increasing in number and success; doctors wanted fresh, healthy organs; patients needed them; so the committee redefined death to open up the market. The committee did not even pretend to enter into metaphysical and impartial scientific discussion of what death *is*. When it published its findings in 1968, its motives were clear: (1) organs were needed; (2) people were being kept alive by technology even though they had 'permanent loss of intellect' and were a 'burden . . . on their families, on the hospitals, and on those in need of hospital beds already occupied by these comatose patients'.[28]

The Harvard committee's new definition – 'whole brain death' – won the day, was confirmed by a presidential commission in 1981, and is still the definition that commands an overwhelming consensus among doctors, other health-care workers, scientists working in the field, and medical ethicists. 'Whole brain death' was defined to mean various things: 'permanent loss of intellect'; 'no discernible central nervous system activity'; 'irreversible loss of all brain function'; and even 'irreversible coma as a result of permanent brain damage'. The last definition, however, covers even those patients in a 'persistent vegetative state', who sometimes breathe spontaneously (without help), blink their eyes and have other reflex actions. But the Harvard committee did not want to go so far as to count such people as dead. (As Singer comments: 'To call for the undertakers to bury a "dead" patient who is still breathing would be a bit too much for anyone to swallow.'[29]) Nor have most 'experts', until the last decade or so. In 1993, as I mentioned earlier, the House of Lords allowed Tony Bland to be starved to death, even though he was in a persistent nonresponsive state and so definitely was not suffering from 'whole brain death'. The Law Lords were somewhat vague as to whether Mr Bland was dead. Lord Hoffmann stated that 'his body is alive, but he has no life', a curious contradiction he immediately qualified by saying that he had no life 'in the sense that even the most pitifully handicapped but conscious human being has a life'.[30] The general view was that Mr Bland was in a state 'with no prospect of recovery', and 'of no benefit'[31] to him – as though being alive were not beneficial.

We are now in a position where people such as Tony Bland – whose brains are still partially functioning, who are breathing, vomiting, dribbling, sleeping and waking, twitching their muscles or even moving their eyes – are, throughout the world, having their food withdrawn, being denied continuing medical treatment, in short, being 'allowed to die'. Often their organs are 'harvested', and the relatives of such patients regularly report having pressure exerted on them to agree to their loved one's becoming an 'organ donor'.

Why the shift from 'whole brain death' to something less? The need for organs has been mentioned. So has the belief that a person who is diagnosed as whole brain dead might be a 'burden' on others, from which it follows that someone who is *less* than whole brain dead is also conceivably a burden, since there is little difference between the cases as far as the strain on the family and the health-care system is concerned. But at the bottom of the further 'redefinition' of death to cover breathing people such as Tony Bland is, once again, *personism*: unless the person is conscious he is not a *person*. If he is not conscious he can 'have no life', as Lord Hoffmann said in the Bland case. In the end, the extent to which the brain is damaged – part or whole, brainstem (supporting breathing, circulation and other basic body functions) or cortex (supporting higher mental functions) – is not *of itself* the proper focus of attention. This notion is reinforced by the fact, as Singer points out, that recent experience has shown that the brains of people suffering from apparent whole brain death – as diagnosed by standardly accepted procedures such as testing for spontaneous eye movement and reactions to various stimuli – still carry out certain functions, such as supplying hormones to the rest of the body. Neurophysiologists now realise that there is far more to the brain than electrical activity, hormonal activity being equally important, if not more so.[32] 'Whole brain dead' patients who are cut open for their organs sometimes show an immediate rise in blood pressure and the quickening of their heartbeat, both of which are brain-regulated. There are two things to note about these startling facts. First, they have not stopped doctors from continuing to take organs from patients diagnosed as 'whole brain dead', which shows that they do not take the criterion seriously them-selves. Second, they are consistent with the fact that the person having his organs taken out *is feeling pain*.

That he is not feeling a thing, however, is asserted by doctors time and again. These are only reflex responses, they claim. How do they know? Well, they cannot answer 'Because the brain is dead', since we have just seen that when a person is diagnosed as 'whole brain dead' his brain may still be functioning – indeed, given the poor state of our knowledge of the brain, it is fair to conjecture that virtually every single person who has ever been diagnosed as having 'permanent and total loss of brain func-tion' has had a brain that was, in some respects, still functioning. And yet they insist that these bodily responses are merely reflex, like the twitching of a frog's leg after it has been cut off.

Do they, then, insist that the patient whose heart jumps when he is cut open for his kidneys is really dead after all? Some do, but as Singer shows, most do not. Nor do many relatives who are asked whether they would agree to the removal of their loved one's organs for transplant. Indeed, as Singer shows, the diagnosis of death involves not a small amount of hy-pocrisy in the medical profession. Some doctors *say* the patient is dead but do not believe it. Some say he is 'technically alive' but 'clinically dead', 'as good as dead', 'dead enough', or 'about as dead as you can get'. (These phrases are not all taken from Singer, but are readily heard in conversa-tions with doctors and in reports that reach the media.) In fact, as Singer accepts, all such patients are, quite simply, *alive*. But *that* should not stop their becoming organ 'donors', he continues, because what mattered all along, even to the authors of the Harvard report on brain death, and what matters to just about everyone now, is whether the person is (a) conscious, and (b) capable of ever regaining consciousness. In other words, is the person concerned a *person*?

Once we turn back from the blind alley we are taken down by debates about brain death, says Singer, and we focus on *personhood*, we will then see that Tony Bland, every bit as much as a patient whose brainstem itself is severely damaged so that he needs almost total artificial life support, can from the ethical point of view be regarded as a potential source of organs for transplantation. The same goes for a baby born with hardly any brain, or one born with a severely damaged brain. They are all un-equivocally alive, but then who said being alive as such counted for any-thing? Remember that I claimed earlier that the only sure sign of death is putrefaction, long after a person's organs have ceased to be of any use to anyone. Singer agrees. He says: 'If we choose to mark death at any moment before the body goes stiff and cold (or to be really on the safe side, before it begins to rot) *we are making an ethical judgement*' (my emphasis).[33] In other words, when we disconnect the life-support system of a person whose heart is still beating, or we take the food away from a person who is still breathing, we are indeed killing him, but we are more importantly making an ethical – in other words, for Singer, utilitarian – judgement about, for instance, the benefit that patient's death can confer on others by the supply of his organs. We are, as traditional morality puts it, sacrificing the life of an innocent person to save others, as surely as the judge who condemns an innocent man to death to quell the rioting mob.

Perhaps you are not yet convinced that the thousands of people around the world today with various levels of severe brain damage, who are used as organ 'donors', are really alive. If so, consider the following. Charles is on a respirator; he is fed through a tube, but does not appear to move, and his eyes are always closed. He responds to no stimulus whatsoever, not even the most painful. Nothing can be done to rouse him. The doctor declares him dead, and asks for permission to disconnect life support and take out his organs, to which Charles's family agrees. When he is cut open, the doctor sees his heart is beating. The body is disconnected from every artificial device, and the heart still beats. The blood pressure fluctuates, maybe the heart quickens. It takes an hour to remove the required organs, and during the entire period the heart continues to beat. Is Charles dead? The doctor believes Charles is a 'beating-heart cadaver', as the technical term goes. Does such a term make sense?

It is a fact that these sorts of operation occur throughout the world on a regular basis. The surgeon prefers the heart to beat while he removes the organs, so that he has a constant supply of blood for as long as possible, keeping them fresh and more likely to work in the subsequent transplants. Sometimes, however, the disconnection is made and the doctors and family wait for the heart to stop beating. It can, in fact, beat for an hour after disconnection. Is the body a 'beating-heart cadaver' during that time? Would you be happy for it to be buried while its heart is still beating? Or cremated? If not, why would you be happy for its organs to be removed?

As Martyn Evans points out, not only ought we to be decidedly uneasy about burying someone whose heart is still beating, but the fact that heartbeat does not influence advocates of 'whole brain death' as the criterion of genuine death means that logically they should not be swayed either from diagnosing as dead someone who is still breathing, as Tony Bland was: 'there is no convincing reason', Evans asserts, 'why those who accept the idea of "brainstem death" [that is, usually death of the whole brain, including brainstem] can distinguish – as they do – between the moral significance of persistent heartbeat and the moral significance of persistent breathing'.[34] If it is permissible to 'harvest' the organs of someone whose heart is still beating, it should be permissible to do so even while he is still breathing. What is the difference? To say that breathing requires the brain in a way that heartbeat does not, and moreover in a way that somehow makes a *moral* difference, is beside the point. Even if we *knew* – which we do not – exactly whether and how either heartbeat or circulation depend on brain activity, the question is why the brain *as such* matters at all to someone who believes the organs can legitimately be taken from a person with a persistent heartbeat. To reply 'Because breathing shows the brainstem is still functioning' does not help, because why does the brainstem matter? To say 'Because it regulates breathing' is circular. To say 'Because breathing is important' is again not to say *why*. After all, not only has heartbeat already been dismissed, but a patient might fail most if not all of the other selected criteria for brainstem function and still breathe spontaneously – 'brainstem' death has never been taken to mean 'total loss of brainstem function', as Evans points out, not least because no one knows how to *measure* total loss of brainstem function. And even if breathing were made the *only* criterion of brainstem function, or the most important, we still need to know why. No appeal to the social, cultural or emotional centrality of breathing to our understanding of life can be a good reason, since the same applies equally, if not more, to a persistent heartbeat.

As we saw earlier, to the vast majority of doctors and medical ethicists the only reason why brain activity is more important than heart or lung activity is that the brain supports consciousness. Heartbeat is increasingly being disregarded, as is breathing, which as a matter of logic is only proper. As has been argued, it is hard to see how the regulatory role of the brain in either heart or lung function can be non-trivially shown as crucial to the determination of death or to the moral assessment of how a person should be treated. Furthermore, lung function can be maintained by a respirator, and even cardiac function by an artificial heart (the technology of which is improving in leaps and bounds). Why does the existence of such maintenance mean that the patient either is dead or can be treated as if dead? No doctor would say this of a fully conscious paralysed child who needed spoon-feeding, so the fact that a person's bodily functions need assistance cannot be the answer. The answer is that for most doctors and medical ethicists it is consciousness, not life, that matters. The same applies to advocates of euthanasia for the purpose of removing organs (as well as removing a 'burden' on the family and the state). And yet we would baulk at burying someone who had a beating heart, or who was still breathing. Perhaps, as *personists* become more and more explicit about the consequences of their theory, they will advocate the sweeping away of that taboo as well?

It follows from what has been argued that virtually every case in which a person's organs are removed for transplantation is a case of homicide, whether intentional or negligent. So little is known about the nature of death and its relation to physiology that even in, say, the case of a car accident where the victim is pronounced dead on arrival at casualty, and has his organs immediately removed, he is probably still alive. And I briefly mentioned the common phenomenon of rising blood pressure and quickening heartbeat when a 'brain-dead' person is opened up for his organs. This looks for all the world like a reaction to pain. Is it? It would take us too far afield to explore the area, but there are good reasons for the claim that *even on the personist criterion of consciousness* some, perhaps most, organ donors are being wronged, in the sense that they can feel pain and are fully aware of their bodies' being cut open without anaesthetic, an experience whose horror it is difficult to imagine. It is also quite possible, if not probable, that Tony Bland felt the agony of starving to death. In evidence I offer first a story and then a piece of research.

In 1996 it was reported that a Mr Gary Dockery, aged 39, awoke from being in a coma for 7½ years. A policeman, he had been wounded in 1988 by a shot in the head, and had been in a coma ever since. His family never gave up hope, and when he developed pneumonia they maintained a bedside vigil. (Many such patients, as well as senile elderly people with pneumonia, are not treated and allowed to 'slip away'.) Mr Dockery suddenly awoke and began talking. Soon he was telling jokes and talking to relatives on the telephone. His sister Lisa, according to a family friend, said 'it was like flipping on a light switch'. The friend added, 'All of a sudden, Gary started mumbling. She [Lisa] started talking to him and he started saying words.' He asked for his sons, whom he had not seen since they were aged 5 and 12. When they came into the room, now aged 12 and 20, their father still recognised them. According to the report, 'While amazed and encouraged by Mr. Dockery's consciousness, doctors cautioned the family it could be temporary. The brain works to repair itself from injury, but how long it can keep Mr. Dockery alert is unknown.' It turned out that Mr Dockery 'talked, joked and reminisced for eighteen hours'. According to his police partner Kenneth Cox, 'he was afraid to go to sleep. He wanted to just keep talking and listening.' Soon, however, he had to have an emergency operation on his lungs and 'spoke rarely after the surgery'. His doctors said he could still 'read, recognize numbers and say hello or good morning', but he was 'partially paralyzed and could not feed himself or walk'. Mr Dockery died from a pulmonary embolism in April 1997.[35]

The empirical research concerns two studies. The first was conducted in 1996, and involved an examination of the records of 40 patients admitted to a brain damage rehabilitation unit between 1992 and 1995 and who had been diagnosed as being in a 'persistent vegetative state' (the same state as Tony Bland, whom the House of Lords declared could be deprived of food). It was found that 17 of the patients (43 per cent) had been *misdiagnosed*, and were able to communicate effectively using eye-pointing or a touch-sensitive buzzer. What the authors mean by 'misdiagnosis', of course, is that the patients were every bit as conscious as you or I, though diagnosed as 'vegetables'. Indeed, the study suggests that the very idea of a 'persistent vegetative state' is to say the least dubious, and that the best one can say is that some people enter a persistent *non-responsive* state. Most of them do not receive nearly enough of the therapy they need, as was revealed in a recent television documentary on the brilliant results obtained at a special institute in Hungary. Patients whom their families had just about 'given up for dead', who looked as though they could not move a muscle or respond to a single stimulus, when given appropriate therapy and the right sort of equipment (such as buzzers and other instruments sensitive to the slightest muscle or eye movement), were able to communicate as normally as anyone else.[36]

The second study appeared in a different journal but in the same week as the first. It concerned a survey of over one thousand British neurophysiologists, neurosurgeons, rehabilitation therapists and other doctors, asking them about their attitude to the management of patients in a 'persistent vegetative state'. Of the doctors, 90 per cent said that it could be appropriate not to treat acute infections (such as pneumonia) and other life-threatening conditions, and 65 per cent said that the withdrawal of 'artificial nutrition and hydration' – that is, food and water – could be appropriate.[37]

2.8   Euthanasia and Nazism

In 1949, Dr Leo Alexander, an American-Jewish psychiatrist who was a consultant to the US Secretary of War at the Nuremberg war crimes trials, wrote:

> Whatever proportions (Nazi) crimes finally assumed, it became evident to all who investigated them that they had started from small beginnings. The beginnings at first were merely a subtle shift in emphasis in the basic attitude of the physicians. It started with the acceptance of the attitude, basic in the euthanasia movement, that there is such a thing as life not worthy to be lived. This attitude in its early stages concerned itself merely with the severely handicapped and chronically sick. Gradually the sphere of those to be included in this category was enlarged to encompass the socially unproductive, the ideologically unwanted, the racially unwanted and finally all non-Germans. But, it is important to realise that the infinitely small wedged-in lever from which this entire trend of mind received its impetus was the attitude toward the non-rehabilitable sick.[38]

In recent years there have been protests all around the world at speeches and lectures given by supporters of euthanasia. In Germany, Switzerland and Austria conferences have been disturbed or forced to be abandoned. The protests have come from the disabled, from religious groups, and from people with a painful memory of what happened under Nazism, in which tens of thousands of people deemed to have 'lives unworthy of life' were systematically exterminated. The 1941 film *Ich klage an*, about a doctor who kills his wife when she is diagnosed as having multiple sclerosis, was seen by 15.3 million Germans. By then euthanasia propaganda had convinced many if not most people that it was acceptable if formally 'legal' and discreetly carried out. Indeed, relatively few of the officials in the Nazi euthanasia programme were seriously punished by the Allies, itself a disturbing fact. As far back as the 1920s, a poll in Saxony found that 73 per cent of parents responded positively to the following question: 'Would you agree to the painless curtailment of the life of your child if experts had established that it was suffering from incurable idiocy?' Some parents even petitioned Hitler to allow their disabled children to be killed, to which he readily agreed.

It is no coincidence that people in countries that suffered under Nazism have been at the forefront of demonstrations against public advocates of 'mercy' killing. After all, many of them have direct or indirect knowledge of the very programmes now being advocated. Is it surprising that many of them, convinced of the evil inherent in such policies, demand that their advocates not be allowed to spread such propaganda?

Professor R. M. Hare, one of the 'fathers' of modern consequentialist bioethics, has written: 'It [current writing in support of euthanasia] does not support anything like Nazi practices, which involved the killing of children on questionable scientific grounds without the consent of their parents.'[39] Further, he adds, modern writers appeal to the 'balance of advantage' for everyone in allowing such killing.

As anyone with even a superficial knowledge of the Nazi programme is aware,[40] it is precisely the 'balance of advantage' that the Nazis invoked in their support: advantage for the parents, for the doctors, for the rest of the family, and of course for the state, for whom only the 'socially productive' had moral value. Further, while the killing was often without parental consent, it often *was*. In any case, as we have seen, parents have no right to decide whether their child lives or dies and, moreover, even if they have *some* say in the matter, according to contemporary writers, it is not decisive, and the consequentialist calculation might *require* that their child be sacrificed to the advantage of the health-care bureaucracy or of the state in general, not least because they might be able later to produce a healthy child who would be less of a drain on public resources. Current advocates of euthanasia do not base their opinions on racial grounds, but nor, as we have seen, did the Nazis. They *extended* their policies to include racial and ideological undesirables, but the policy of destroying 'lives unworthy of life' (*lebensunwerten Lebens*), based on criteria of social and financial burden to others, never wavered. As for 'questionable scientific grounds', nothing is more questionable than the pseudo-scientific concept of a Quality Assisted Life Year, or QALY, so much in use by medical professionals and others as a slide rule in the calculation of whether a human being has the prospect of a life above a certain arbitrary threshold, in which he will be a 'productive' member of society.

It is, therefore, a mistake to claim that we are at the edge of a slippery slope to mass murder. We are *on* that slope, one that has already been traversed by other societies.[41] This time, however, we have technology and expertise far in advance of anything available to the Nazis. We are able to maintain the lives of people for longer and longer periods and to harvest their organs when we deem fit, to be used for other units on the medical production line. Doctors, equipped with ever-improving technology and burdened by increasing demands for economic productivity, are becoming servants of the state hired to maximise utility.[42] And, in many ways, the state and the judicial system, which give implicit and progressively explicit support to euthanasia, have far greater powers, both to persuade and to execute policy, than those possessed by the Nazi state. Given these considerations, it is hard to see why advocates of euthanasia are horrified at the suggestion that there is any significant parallel between what they support – which is increasingly less a matter of abstract proposals than of everyday concrete reality – and what the Nazis themselves carried out.

3

Animals

3.1 The Problem

Just as the conflict over abortion has raged since the 1960s, so too the problem of our treatment of animals has taken a prominent place in moral debate. In fact the 'animals issue' has its roots in the nineteenth century, when in Britain, the USA and elsewhere, parliaments passed various kinds of anti-cruelty legislation and charitable bodies were formed to protect animals from harsh or neglectful treatment, rescue strays, promote public understanding of animal welfare, and so on.

In the past few decades, however, what used to be a generally accepted movement for the humane treatment of animals has turned into, or been enlarged by, other currents of thinking that have led to the animals issue becoming perhaps second to abortion in the passions and divisions it arouses. Just as pro-abortion and pro-life supporters have engaged in stormy protests and even outright violence, so there have been clashes between different sections of society over the question of animals: 'animal liberationists' attack scientific establishments and farms, releasing captive animals into the wild; 'animal rights' supporters block the transport of sheep and cattle for slaughter in other countries; farmers and scientists in turn accuse their critics of ignorance and stupidity; in Britain in 1998 several hundred thousand farmers and their supporters marched through the streets of London to protest the erosion of their way of life partly because of the animal rights movement – the march included supporters of fox hunting who defended their pastime against strident criticism in the media and its proposed prohibition by law. Animal experimentation, hunting, the eating of meat, the existence of zoos and circuses, the destruction of habitats, even the keeping of pets: all of these and other practices involving animals have come under intense scrutiny. They have led to bitter divisions between those who wish to see animals protected as much as possible from human exploitation and those who, in one way or another, rely on the use of animals either for their own benefit or to confer, as they believe, a benefit on society at large. Clearly, what began as a movement for the humane treatment of animals has become a more ideological, hardline grouping, which has in turn hardened the stance of its opponents. Even the traditional animal welfare and humane societies, which have tried to insulate themselves from the ideological conflict over animal liberation and animal rights, have been drawn into the argument, and their leadership challenged by more hardline animal supporters for what is thought to be an unacceptable compromise over the treatment of animals by humans.

In this chapter we will look at the animals issue from the perspective of the traditional ethical theory that has already been sketched at some length and applied to concrete problems concerning the morality of taking human life. Should the right to life, which I have argued belongs to every human being, be extended to non-human animals? (The single term 'animal' will be used to cover non-human animals in general.) If not, in what way does moral consideration extend to the animal kingdom?

3.2   The Conditions for Rights – What They Are Not

In order to answer these questions, we need to explore further the nature of a right, or better the conditions (necessary and sufficient) for the possession of a right. If animals satisfy those conditions, then they have rights, and if they lack any of them they do not. But this is where the debate immediately becomes complicated by the fact that supporters of animal rights differ among themselves over just why it is that animals have them. In other words, they offer differing theories about what is required for a being to possess rights. The first part of our discussion, then, will be negative, and will involve sifting through the most important theories. Some but not all of them find explicit presentation in the literature; others are theories that are commonly heard in public discussion. In all cases I have tried to single out the prominent features of each theory and to focus on them. It will be argued that none of these theories gives a proper grounding for rights. The second part will be positive, in which a more plausible theory of the conditions for being a rights-holder will be presented. I will then argue that no animal satisfies these conditions. The discussion will then move on to a brief account of how animals do, nevertheless, come in a certain way within the scope of our proper moral consideration.

3.2.1 Consciousness

Perhaps the most common argument for animal rights is based on the claim that animals have consciousness. Although stated in this general way, what proponents of the view must mean is that *some* animals have rights because *some* animals are conscious. Only advocates of a kind of *mentalist* theory, according to which *every* living thing is conscious, would say, for instance, that ants or scallops possessed consciousness. And yet they are no more conscious than trees, even though they are in other crucial respects entirely different kinds of organism from any plant. Of course one might object, 'How do you *know* ants aren't conscious?', but I leave it to entomologists to provide the evidence, none of which is at present available. A minimal feature of consciousness is the ability to feel pain and pleasure, and there is no evidence that ants feel either: there is no 'sizism' behind this opinion – one should not deny consciousness to ants because they are very small. It is just that their bodies are not, as far as anyone knows, *built* to support feelings of pain or pleasure or any other kind of subjective awareness, even though they clearly receive and process information.

At this point it is worth mentioning the relevance of *behaviour* to the question of consciousness. Behaviour is one of the most important kinds of evidence we have for consciousness on the part of other creatures (even human beings other than ourselves!), but we cannot argue in any straightforward way from behaviour to consciousness. We cannot say, for instance, 'An ant immersed in water and then removed will spend several minutes rubbing the water off its antennae in a way that looks for all the world like the manner in which I dry myself off after a shower, so it must be feeling the water on its body.' The fact is that a machine could be made out of Lego to do exactly the same thing. A Venus flytrap closes its 'jaws' around a fly in a manner that looks quite similar to the way I close my jaws around a piece of chocolate, but the plant does not taste the fly. The inference from behaviour to consciousness is fraught with difficulty, not least because we have to be careful not to describe a piece of behaviour in a way that *presupposes* the existence of the consciousness we are trying to prove! Suppose I tell you that yesterday I picked up a living being, skinned it alive, cut it into pieces, and slowly burned it over a fire, while its vital fluids seeped out, its flesh sizzled and it even seemed to emit what sounded like tiny squeals as it roasted away. It sounds gruesome, but you wouldn't be too fussed if I told you I had been roasting a potato. How much more, then, must we be careful about descriptions when talking about animal behaviour. We say that the plant *wants* a good watering, that it *drank up* the water, that bees *love* to make honey, that I made the wasp *angry* by brushing it away. There is nothing wrong with using *anthropomorphising* terminology, that is, words that apply properly to human beings but only *metaphorically* to plants and animals, so long as we do not try to prove anything by such usage. To understand properly the relation between consciousness and behaviour, we need to look into the way in which a given species of animal is *constituted*, what kind of physiological structure it has, and whether that structure looks as though it is capable of supporting consciousness analogously to the way human physiology (in particular neurophysiology) supports consciousness. But even then we may not get very far, because we know precious little about how it is that *we humans* have consciousness!

Not all animals are conscious, that is, not all animals have subjective awareness of their environment, where that awareness amounts to the ability to *feel* or *have the experience* that their environment has such-and-such features. By 'environment' I include a creature's own *body*, which for any conscious being, us included, can be considered in a way as part of that creature's external world. (I have a certain kind of experience when I see a bright blue sky; I have another when I feel pain in my arm; they are both, in a sense, experiences of the world around me, even though my arm is intimately connected to me in a way the sky is not.) Some animals, however, are most definitely conscious. Dogs can feel pain; but how do we know they do? The answer, again, is a complex one, but it does involve a consideration of the kind of behaviour they manifest and of their innate physiology. First, they behave in ways that are identical to the ways we typically behave when we are in pain: they yelp (we scream or say 'ouch'); they recoil (so do we); they lick their wounds (we typically rub ours; their act of licking seems to be more than a mere attempt to *repair* the wound in the way, for instance, that an ant will fiddle with a broken antenna); they behave for all the world as if they are angry – they bare their teeth (so do we, if the pain is severe enough) and become aggressive (as we do). There is, then, a relatively finely-based parallel between the behaviour of a wounded dog and of a wounded person: though the dog's set of pain responses is a *subset* of ours, since there are kinds of things we do (such as cry, grumble, and maybe look for a lawyer) that have no canine counterpart. Nevertheless, the dog's pain responses just listed could in theory be reproduced by an unconscious machine. This is why we must look also to physiology, to the way behaviour is linked to phenomena such as hormonal response, blood pressure, respiration, circulation, body temperature, and of course neurophysiological response. These are not things that can be mechanically reproduced, though they can be *simulated*. As we said, there is so much we do not know about the physiology of pain and how it is related to behaviour, but we know enough to say that a dog can feel pain. Moreover, we do not need to have personal and detailed physiological knowledge to make a highly probable judgement that this is so. People knew that dogs felt pain in ancient Greece, though there was barely any technical knowledge of the subject. They simply went by things such as the fact that dogs are warm-blooded, and have a body plan that is close enough to the human one, and behave in ways that are closely enough related to human behaviour, for it to be a reasonable judgement that dogs were sentient.

So consciousness as a criterion of rights will not allow rights to be ascribed to all animals. Will it allow rights to be ascribed to those animals that are conscious? It is hard to see how mere sentience would be enough. Why should a being be said to have rights merely because it can feel pleasure and pain? One answer might be that pleasure is good for a creature and pain is bad for it (on the whole). This means that if an animal is at least conscious enough to feel pleasure and pain, there are *ipso facto* ways in which its life can go well or badly for it. Since rights confer moral protection on a being in its living of the good life (see chapter 2 of *Moral Theory*), animals should also be seen to have rights. This will not do. If what sentience is supposed to contribute to the conditions under which a being possesses rights is that things go well or badly for it, the same could be said for any living thing, sentient or not. Plants thrive with adequate water, food and light; otherwise they wither and die. Bacteria also die without nourishment and an appropriate environment. For every single living being, there are conditions for it to live well and conditions for it to live badly. The same is not true of sticks, stones and sandcastles. Hence consciousness of pain and pleasure does not add anything to the argument for animal rights. The question is, how does *consciousness* add something? An animal can live well or badly without being conscious.

A more elaborate account, then, is needed to show what it is about consciousness that confers rights on animals. Tom Regan presents perhaps the most careful and persuasive defence of animal rights using this concept.[1] For him, the sort of consciousness that matters is the consciousness that makes an animal a 'subject-of-a-life'. To be a subject-of-a-life is not merely to be sentient, or to have bare awareness of one's environment:

> To be the subject-of-a-life is to be an individual whose life is characterized by [the having of] beliefs and desires; perception, memory, and a sense of the future, including their own future; an emotional life together with feelings of pleasure and pain; preference- and welfare-interests; the ability to initiate action in pursuit of their desires and goals; a psychophysical identity over time; and an individual welfare in the sense that their experiential life fares well or ill for them, logically independently of their utility for others and logically independently of their being the object of anyone else's interests. Those who satisfy the subject-of-a-life criterion themselves have a distinctive kind of value – inherent value – and are not to be viewed or treated as mere receptacles.[2]

Regan's theory is a detailed one and there is no room to look at all its aspects or subtleties. Instead, I shall take it as representative of a significant strand of thinking about animal rights and consider as we go along the parts of it relevant to the present discussion. The first thing to note is that Regan has produced an impressive list of characteristics of a 'subject-of-a-life'. He claims to have produced a *sufficient* condition of having rights – any animal that possessed all of the above characteristics would be a subject-of-a-life and so have rights, in particular the rights to life, to respectful treatment, to being allowed to fulfil its nature undisturbed – but not a necessary one. In other words, he does not say explicitly that an animal must have *all* of these features to be a subject-of-a-life. He at least allows the possibility that a merely sentient creature was a subject-of-a-life; but he also goes on immediately to say that 'it is radically unclear how the attribution of inherent value to these individuals can be made intelligible and non-arbitrary'.[3] The same, he says, goes for a human being in a permanent coma.

Which animals does Regan think are subjects-of-a-life? All mammals, he believes, though he expresses uncertainty about newly born or other very young ones. As for birds, fish and other non-mammals, he does not consider them to have inherent value because they are not subjects-of-a-life, but condemns killing them 'in the name of sport or in pursuit of a profit. Even assuming birds and fish are not subjects-of-a-life, to allow their recreational or economic exploitation is to encourage the formation of habits and practices that lead to the violation of the rights of animals who are subjects-of-a-life.'4 The implication is that killing birds and fish purely for food, or to prevent disease spreading to other animals, for example, would be permissible, at least if it did not involve undue pain and suffering (birds, if not fish, are sentient and must have their sentience respected all the same).

Regan's criterion of a subject-of-a-life is still consciousness-based, only the sort of consciousness he considers relevant is richer and more complex than mere sensation or feeling. Memory, emotion, beliefs and desires, preference-interests (by which Regan means *being interested in* certain things, whether good or bad for one), a sense of the future, a sense of *one's own* future – these all appear to involve a kind of conscious awareness, one with which we are all familiar to some degree. Recall James Rachels's remarks about the difference between being alive and *having a life*, which were discussed in chapter 4 of *Moral Theory*. What Regan is doing is putting forward the idea that (some) non-human animals *have a life* and so are worthy of the gravest moral respect. (This does not mean, however, that he means by 'having a life' exactly what Rachels means, though there is a substantial overlap.) But is Regan's criterion convincing?

Let us put to one side the characteristic of having a sense of one's own future, since that brings in self-consciousness, which I want to consider separately. What about the other characteristics? For a start, perception and memory do not seem to take us much beyond pleasure and pain. Why should a creature have rights because, among other things, it perceives and remembers? What is the conceptual connectxion with rights? Regan does not tell us, but instead claims simply that these features are ingredients in a complex mental life sufficient to give its possessor inherent value. Perception and memory indicate the presence of a *subject* who perceives and remembers, but there is an inferential gap between claiming that a being is a subject in the *psychological* sense and saying that it is a subject in the *moral* sense, that is, subject to the moral law of rights and duties, whether only as a *passive possessor* of rights having no duties whatsoever – what Regan calls a moral *patient* – or as what he calls a moral *agent*, a being that does have duties. Regan objects to those of his opponents who claim that animals cannot have rights unless they also have duties, and that they do not have duties. He protests that a being can be a moral patient without being also a moral agent, in other words, a being with rights, to which duties are owed, but which has no duties itself. This idea will be challenged in due course, but note for the moment that such a challenge is no part of my present objection. What is being objected to here is the idea that there is no gap from 'X is a psychological subject' to 'X is a moral subject'. Here, 'subject' covers beings who have rights as well as beings who have duties, just as being a subject of the criminal law means either that one has duties under it or rights under it, and possibly both.

This general objection applies not just to memory and perception, but to a sense of the future. For if memory is a kind of sense of the past, and if it is hard to see what this contributes to the possession of rights, the same goes for a sense of the future. And the same goes for emotions, if by that term Regan means nothing more subtle than states such as feeling happy or sad, angry or affectionate, anxious, distressed or content, or perhaps tired, uncomfortable, frightened, and so on. These are all, arguably, emotions that some animals feel. Again we can ask: how does this get us to the notion that such animals have rights? It is true that a being capable of such states has a more complex mental life than a being that does not; and further, that it is in general *good* to feel happy, *bad* to feel hungry, good to be content, and bad to be frightened. In other words, as Regan says, beings capable of such states of feeling have an experiential life that 'fares ill or well for them': a dog that spends its life being beaten and starved by its master has a worse life than one that is well fed and pampered. We can even go further and say that the perceiving, remembering, feeling animal is, in virtue of such capacities, a *locus of value*, precisely because its life goes badly or well according as such capacities are or are not harmed, thwarted, suppressed, made the vehicle of unpleasant experiences, and so on. We can even agree with Regan that because of such characteristics animals' experiential life fares well or ill for them 'logically independently of their utility for others and logically independently of their being the object of anyone else's interests', *if* all Regan means by this is that in order to know whether an animal's life is going well or badly for it we do not need to know whether the animal is useful to any human being (or other animal, for that matter), or whether anyone else has an interest or is interested in the life or welfare of that animal. Indeed, we can be certain that this is the case with *all* animals, at least to some extent, *whether or not* they have complex mental lives. If a clam is dropped into water filled with toxic waste and dies, I can know that it has been damaged and its life cut short, hence that things have *gone badly* for it, without having to know whether clams are a useful source of food for human beings. What we need to know, however, is by what logic the addition of psychological characteristics such as these to the list of features of a being that is a subject-of-a-life yields the conclusion that such a being has rights, and this is not something Regan is able to tell us. Further, the addition by him of the concept of welfare-interests to the criterion of a subject-of-a-life does not bring anything new to that criterion, since welfare-interests are just the sorts of feature in virtue of which an animal's life goes well or badly, and this has already been covered.

All I have tried to show so far is that the appeal to subjective awareness on the part of some animals does not in any obvious way take us to the conclusion that such animals have rights. The same is true for the general fact that the life of an animal can go well or ill for it. There are, however, additional elements in Regan's criterion that are distinctive enough to be considered apart from consciousness, even though they probably only exist in beings that are conscious. Perhaps these further elements fill the gap in Regan's argument?

3.2.2 Beliefs and desires

As well as welfare-interests, Regan places preference-interests on his list of elements that define a subject-of-a-life. Note that he does not define a preference-interest as involving a *conscious act of preferring*:

> By [preference-interests] we shall mean those things that an individual is *interested in*, those things he likes, desires, wants or, in a word, prefers having, or, contrariwise, those things he dislikes, wants to avoid or, in a word, prefers not having. . . . However, individuals might have a preference-interest in something without it being true that they *now* are in a mental state of being for or against it . . . . Preference-interests can be *dispositions* to want, like, and so forth, not just episodes in one's mental life.[5]

One might, for instance, be interested in stamps without *right now* thinking 'I am interested in stamps' or being engaged in stamp-collecting.

The concept of a preference-interest does not add anything to Regan's criterion beyond what is added by the concepts of belief and desire, which are already on the list. The concept of a preference is in fact broader than that of mere belief and desire, but what is doing the work for Regan in his use of the notion of preference is the thought that animals have beliefs and desires, and in that sense are interested in certain things. Beliefs and desires need not be conscious mental acts, they can be dispositions to such acts (think of your belief that the earth is round, or your desire to do well in your exams). Inanimate objects such as stones have no welfare- or preference-interests, since there is nothing it is like for the existence of a stone to go well or badly, and stones do not have beliefs or desires. Plants have welfare-interests, since they do well with food, water and light, and badly without; but they have no conscious *preference* for water, or desire for it, or belief that there is water in the soil around them, or dispositions to any of these. (When we speak in such ways of plants we are speaking metaphorically.) But animals *do* desire food and water and many other things, and have beliefs about them, and have dispositions to such mental acts. Is this not the qualitative distinction that makes them sufficiently like human beings to have rights?

Before proceeding, we need to pause. For it is by no means agreed among philosophers *or* ethologists (students of animal behaviour) that animals have beliefs and desires. If they do not, then if beliefs and desires play a crucial role in the attribution of rights, animals will not have rights because they lack beliefs and desires. The present discussion is not the place to enter into an analysis of which side of this debate is correct. To do so would take us far into other areas beyond the scope of this book. Still, some brief points are worth making. One is that the debate has revolved strongly around the question of whether any animals have language, and this is a separate topic that will be broached shortly – again, without straying too far from our present concerns. Some of the claims that have been made, most notably by Donald Davidson in his important but somewhat obscure critique of the idea that animals have beliefs and desires,[6] include the claim that beliefs cannot be attributed to creatures that lack the ability to conceive of themselves as being *correct* and *mistaken* in their beliefs, and hence lack the *concept* of belief. There is also the claim that an individual cannot have a belief without the capacity to be *surprised* in the face of contrary evidence, and the claim that having a belief requires possessing the concept of *truth*, which in turn requires the concept of the *communicability* of truth, which in turn requires the capacity to *com-*

municate truth, hence language. There is the claim that an individual cannot have beliefs without being able to *represent* the world as being *this* way rather than *that*, but that it is hard to see *how* an animal can represent the world without its being able to *assent* to or *dissent* from certain propositions: you cannot ask your dog whether it believes its master is home, as opposed to whether it believes that the president of Alpha Corp. is home, even if you are the president of Alpha Corp. You might object, 'But it doesn't have the concept of *being president of Alpha Corp.*, whereas it does have the concept of *being a (its) master*, so surely we can say it has one belief and not the other.' To which we can reply,

> But *does* it have the concept *being a (its) master*? Does it know just what is involved in being master of a dog? Does it know about what it is to *own* something? Or does it just see you as a being who appears in such-and-such a way on its (the dog's) territory? If so, *what* way? How does that way differ from the way your brother presents himself? How is the fact that you are the one who disciplines it related to its supposed concept of you as master?

And so on. The questions are easier to ask than to answer. Davidson's point is that without an animal's having language, there is no way we can ever know just what concepts an animal has. Critics of Davidson naturally point out that this is an *epistemological* question, about what we can *know*, not an ontological one about just what mental states or capacities an animal possesses. Perhaps an animal does have language but cannot communicate its beliefs outside its own species, so is Davidson putting his weight on language as such, or communicability? And anyway, can't we settle most of these questions by a careful study of animal behaviour rather than worrying fruitlessly about the contents of the animal mind?

For my own part, I am at least prepared to accept that many animals have beliefs and desires, though with the reservation that *if* they do so it is probably not *in the same way* as human beings have beliefs and desires. There seems just to be an obvious sense in which Felix the cat believes that there is a mouse behind the refrigerator, or Flipper the dolphin believes it will receive a fishy reward if it jumps through the hoop. But this sense must be attenuated and hedged about with qualifications, and to speak with certainty on the matter would be rash, given the poor state of philosophical understanding of how to answer the relevant questions (and even what questions to ask in the first place!).

But the question that needs to be posed in the present context is the by now familiar one: Supposing that some animals do possess beliefs and desires, how does it follow that they have rights? What is it about possessing them that makes a being a rights-holder? Again, there can be no doubt that an animal that believes and desires has a more complex mental life than one that does not. An animal that believes and desires is more properly said to be a *subject* than one that does not. If an animal really does have beliefs and desires, it must have some kind of subjective awareness of its environment. But how, conceptually, do these facts confer *rights* on such a creature? To say that a creature with beliefs and desires can have its life promoted or frustrated in ways not possible for an animal lacking these states is an evident truth. In other words, the life of an animal that believes and desires can go well or ill for it in ways more complex than in the case of an animal that does not have these states. But what follows from that? We have already seen that there are differences both of degree and kind among species of animals in terms of the ways their lives go for them. But there is no reason for thinking that a being has rights simply in virtue of having a life that can go well or ill for it. One can *stipulate* this to be the case and go on to assert that ants, bacteria and amoebae have rights because in each case their lives can go well or ill in certain (sometimes very different) respects, in other words, because the life of each has a certain *inherent value*, that is, *goodness or badness* about it, irrespective of their utility or interest for any other animal, including ourselves. Note that when Regan speaks of the subject-of-a-life's having 'inherent value', it is not clear whether he means only this, or whether he is also claiming that 'being with inherent value' just *means* 'being with rights'. The latter is not the same as the former. No argument is needed to show the obvious conceptual connection between inherent value and the goodness or badness of a life, but an argument is certainly needed to link inherent value to rights. So one can stipulate that beings with lives that go well or ill have rights, or more narrowly that subjects-of-a-life have rights, or that to have inherent value just *is* to have rights, but a stipulation is not an argument. And if it leads to absurd conclusions, such as that ants, bacteria and amoebae have rights (which Regan himself ought to believe, if he is not able to show what is special about animals with a complex mental life), we would do well to reject it. Too many supporters of animal rights take it as obvious that rights must be conferred on a creature that believes and desires, without providing any *reason* why this is so, and the reasons that are provided do not seem to be good ones. It is difficult to see what such a reason might be.

3.2.3 Language

It would not be an exaggeration to say that most supporters of animals rights believe that some animals are linguistically competent, that they can communicate with each other using a genuine language, and that some can even communicate with human beings. This thought seems to them to provide a powerful reason for attributing rights to animals. To put it loosely, an animal with language would, it appears, be too much like us for comfort. Our sense of ourselves as a distinctive species is intimately bound up with our sense of ourselves as language users. It is no accident that many critics of the claims that animals have beliefs and desires, or emotions, or consciousness, or self-consciousness, derive their criticisms from the broadly Wittgensteinian tradition which places language at the centre of human self-understanding and understanding of the world. Davidson's critique draws importantly on ideas in Wittgenstein, as do those of R. G. Frey and Michael Leahy. The question of whether we humans are the only language users on earth has been a hot topic of debate for several decades now. It was given huge impetus by the groundbreaking research into chimpanzee behaviour by Jane Goodall, and by the numerous attempts of animal researchers to teach chimpanzees to talk. Gone (well, almost) are the days of 'talking' horses such as Clever Hans (it turned out that Hans was responding to fleeting behavioural cues on the part of the people who tried to talk to him); and it is generally accepted that 'bee dances', whereby a bee can 'tell' others where a source of honey is by an elaborate sequence of movements, do not constitute anything like a language, any more than insect communication by antenna contact or the emission of pheromones. Virtually all recent serious research into animal language has taken place with chimpanzees, and continues to do so.[7]

Once again, to explore the fascinating topic of whether animals can talk would take us too far afield. It can be stated, though, as was said in the case of belief and desire, that *if* it turns out no animals have language, animal rights supporters cannot rely on language possession to justify their case. I find the claim that animals have language far less convincing than that they have beliefs and desires. The trainers of Washoe the chimp (now living in contented retirement) are convinced that they taught her American Sign Language, and to this day when one of them visits her they begin gesticulating furiously to each other in an impressive display. Similar claims of success were made about a relative of Washoe's called Nim

Chimpsky (after the linguist Noam Chomsky), but they died away. One of the trainers published an article expressing doubts about what was achieved, and Jane Goodall herself said, after watching Nim in action, that she did not see one sign produced that she had not already seen made by chimps in the wild and who had therefore not been near a sign-language teacher. To be fair, however, Goodall *is* convinced of the linguistic ability of Washoe and other chimps and has said so publicly, both on film and in print. (For the record, it should also be said that Goodall regarded one of her greatest discoveries to be that chimpanzees were not only tool *users* but tool*makers*, thus dethroning human beings from the unique pedestal they occupied as the only toolmakers on earth. What she observed was chimpanzees stripping twigs of their leaves before using them to entice insects from their nests. Had Goodall spent some time on the Galapagos Islands, however, she would soon have found out that she had discovered nothing special; some kinds of Galapagos finch do exactly the same thing, only holding the twig in their beak and stripping it using their feet; and so do New Caledonian crows. Only armchair anthropologists and ethologists have ever thought there was something uniquely human about making tools.)

The pygmy chimp Kanzi is one of the current stars, being able, it is said, to communicate using ideograms (pictures or symbols of ideas such as *water*, *bucket* and *bring*). Film has also been shown of Booee the chimp, kept in a cage in a research laboratory, and visited after a gap of many years by the person who 'trained' him in sign language. Again, we see them gesticulating wildly to one another as though they were having a conversation. And claims continue to be made for other apes, with new stars likely to pop onto the stage on a regular basis, especially in light of the movement, known as the Great Ape Project (run by Peter Singer and Paola Cavalieri), to gain 'civil rights' for gorillas and chimpanzees.

Whatever the sincerely held hopes and the promises of success, however, the attempt to teach apes language can only be viewed objectively as a failure. No ape has ever been taught genuine American Sign Language. As the linguist Steven Pinker explains: 'This preposterous claim is based on the myth that ASL is a crude system of pantomimes and gestures rather than a full language with complex phonology, morphology and syntax. In fact the apes had not learned *any* true ASL signs.' He goes on to quote the one deaf native signer on the Washoe team, who complained that while he could not see Washoe producing even one ASL sign, the other experimenters were gleefully noting down hundreds of 'signs', and showing implicit displeasure that the deaf observer's logbook was not full enough.[8] The few sceptics who have been allowed to observe chimpanzee 'language training' at close quarters have always come away as sceptical as before, if not more so. The trainers have rarely been accused of outright fraud; rather, it seems usually to be a case of wishful thinking, where the researchers' sincere and passionate belief in the linguistic ability of their subjects leads them to interpret every gesture in the most favourable light possible, to provide unconscious behavioural *cues* to which the chimps respond (like Clever Hans), and to ignore troublesome evidence, such as a failure by the chimps to respond in the 'right' way. Pinker concludes: 'The chimp's abilities at anything one would want to call grammar were next to nil.'[9] There is simply no discernible system of grammatical rules that the chimps follow; most of the time they produce gibberish, which needs to be filtered through several layers of human interpretation before any sense can appear to be made out of it. Unlike children, who also produce gibberish in their early years of language learning, the chimps do not refine their behaviour to the point where they are regularly producing correct, grammatical sentences.

Further, chimpanzees simply do not have a *brain structure* that looks sufficiently like the human one to suggest linguistic competence (though it must be admitted that we know precious little about the relation between our own brain structure and linguistic ability). Apes do not possess vocal cords and other structures allowing them to talk, and it seems absurd that nature should have endowed them as a class with the ability to make sentences but not to speak them to each other. There is no evidence on film (at least available to the public) showing an ape 'trained' in sign language spontaneously initiating a conversation with its trainer – they both always appear on film to be 'talking' to each other simultaneously and at breakneck speed (though in fact the trainer always seems to *begin* the 'conversation', even if only by a fraction of a second). Nor has an ape been seen approaching a total stranger and initiating a conversation, or a person who does not know sign language – yet the chimp cannot know which people are able to sign and which not, and ought to expect that if one human can sign, they all can. And so on.

The evidence for the linguistic competence of animals is, therefore, disappointing. And yet maybe the sceptics are mistaken. Perhaps some animals, most likely chimpanzees, can talk. What follows from this about animal rights, at least for those that have language? Whereas my earlier criticisms were based on the lack of a conceptual link between certain features of animal life and the notion that animals with those features have rights, the criticism to be made of the language – rights connection is not that it lacks an argumentative link or makes an unjustified stipulation, but that the argument is not a good one. The claim that language users have rights *in virtue* of their being such is based on what might be called a *communitarian* view of rights, which has its most common exemplification in the contractualist theory criticised in chapter 2 of *Moral Theory*. On the communitarian view, what makes someone a rights-holder is their belonging to a community of individuals who are capable of interacting with each other in a certain way and who do so as a matter of course. Now all animals interact in some way or other, so unless one wants to elevate every social grouping of animals into a moral community (a view occasionally found on the wilder fringes of the animal rights movement), one has to specify what kind of interaction makes a grouping into a community of rights-holders who are thereby under reciprocal duties to each other. Language seems the ideal feature to single out because it is through language that community members express their beliefs, desires and preferences in a fine-grained or articulate enough way for other members to *understand* what rights a given member has, and hence what duties this imposes on the rest of the community. It is hard to see how we can tell with any reasonable precision whether an individual, say, claims this or that as his property, has this or that individual as his sexual partner, is suffering from this or that ailment (especially if the illness is psychological or otherwise invisible to the naked eye), wants to be allowed to do one thing or another, or even wants to live or die, without the individual's being able to *express* its preferences by means of the complicated conceptual resources that language makes available. (Imagine how hard it would be for us humans in such matters if we also lost the power of linguistic communication, being reduced to no more than grunts and groans.) On the communitarian view an individual is, as it were, *initiated* into a moral community by its development or possession of the means to make its outlook on the world available to other individuals. Moral beings are, to put it in the fashionable communitarian way, *beings-in-relation*. That is why, for instance, some pro-abortionists argue that the foetus does not have any rights because neither its mother nor anyone else is able to enter into 'meaningful relations' with it until after birth.

Whatever the details of the communitarian perspective on morality – and they cannot be explored here – the basic idea grounding it seems either absurd or trivial. If, as some contractualists now maintain, what matters is whether it 'makes sense' to justify a policy (whether social or individual) to an individual for that individual to have rights as a member of the moral community, we can accept the claim with equanimity. We can allow that a creature need not be able to talk to *us humans* in order for it to have rights, as long as it behaves in such a way as to suggest that it *could* understand our justification (say, of a policy of taking away its property) if only we were able to find a common language. (Whether, as Peter Carruthers maintains, it need not even be necessary for the creature to be able to talk to members of its own kind, or to anyone else for that matter, is, however, debatable. For if the creature could not even talk to members of its own kind, how would we know whether it was capable even of representing *to itself* that such-and-such a policy was one that it preferred or rejected? If justification minimally involves the provision of an *argument*, how can a creature *understand* a justification without understanding an argument; and how can it do the latter without being able to understand premises and conclusions, which require linguistic competence to grasp them? What reason would we have for thinking it 'made sense' to justify a policy to it? The fact that it engages in other complex behaviour? But what kind? And how can the contractualist spell out the nature of such behaviour while presupposing that the creature in question really is unable, structurally rather than as a matter of mere contingent fact – Carruthers is equivocal about this in this thought experiment concerning uncommunicative but intelligent Martians[10] – to communicate its thoughts to members of its very own group? I leave it to contractualists to debate the question.) We can also accept that an individual, if it *is* capable of communicating with us, need not be able to do so *right now* for it to have rights and hence for us to be under duties towards it. We can, then, allow that it 'makes sense' to justify a policy (of, say, killing) to a man in a coma or an unborn child because we know exactly what it would be like for them to be in a state of being able to communicate their beliefs, desires and other mental states and to understand the reasons for a policy of killing them: the man in a coma needs to be awake, the foetus needs to grow up and learn a language.

But if the communitarian view is supposed to mean that an individual has to be in some sort of meaningful relation of communication with members of its group *right now* for it to have rights, the view is absurd. Rights as such do not come, as a matter of their ethical origin, from communities or relationships, even though there are some rights that would not exist without, and do require, certain social facts to obtain. James has no right to Janet's fidelity if he is not married to her in the first place (or engaged to be married); Peter has no right to buy a book from his local bookshop if there *is* no local bookshop; Margaret has no right to become Prime Minister of Britain if people do not vote her into office; and so on. But to say that even *non*-social rights, in the sense of rights that do not derive proximately from social facts, are in some deep sense themselves social, or conferred by a community – whether of language users or not – is a mistake. The right to life, the right to own property, the right to bodily integrity, the right to spiritual fulfilment – these are not rights that depend for their existence on some sort of meaningful relationship with others, whatever duties they may in fact impose on others. They depend on the nature of the rights-holder *himself*, on his essential dignity as a being with a certain nature.

If the radically non-relational nature of rights is true of human beings, it should be true of animals too. If chimpanzees have rights, it cannot be because they talk to each other or to us, because their rights would depend on their individual natures every bit as much as human rights. The only relevance the search for linguistic competence can have to the debate over animal rights is in its pointing, as *evidence*, to some *other* deep-seated but essentially *non*-relational capacity. There is, then, nothing wrong with trying to find out whether chimpanzees have language, whether as a matter of ethological curiosity or as a matter of ethical significance; but to fasten upon language use *as such*, as some animal rights supporters do, as the very source of the rights an animal may have, is to make a philosophical mistake. Advocates of animal rights need to look at the *whole animal* they are concerned with, and in particular at whether there exist certain characteristics which I will propose shortly as what matter for the existence of rights.

3.2.4   Self-consciousness

Tom Regan speaks of 'a sense of the future, including their own future' as part of his criterion of a subject-of-a-life. Here he implicitly concedes that an animal may have a sense of the future (and presumably of the past and the present) without having a sense of *its own* future. And this is surely right. There is continued debate over whether, say, a dog really *expects* its master, whether it has a sense of the *future arrival* of its master, but what is beyond debate is that even if a dog has such a sense – which it is plausible to hold it does – it need not have any sense of *itself* as part of its general state of expectation. It is doubtful whether a dog does have a sense of itself, that is, is self-conscious. The fact that it licks its wounds or grooms itself is no more convincing than that it scratches itself or chases its tail. (This latter phenomenon seems hard to reconcile with self-consciousness, unless the dog is consciously amusing itself; but the phenomenon has never been adequately explained.) A dog that sees itself in the mirror will bark as though it were looking at an intruder, which does not rule out the attribution of self-consciousness, but makes it implausible. Similarly, I have seen a magpie continuously head-butting a pane of glass in which it sees its reflection. Again, the magpie *might* have a sense of itself, but such behaviour makes it unlikely. It is not clear that an animal that has a sense of *others* – as dogs and birds both do – must *ipso facto* have a sense of itself, any more than an antibody in the immune system that can distinguish between 'self' and 'non-self', that is, friendly bodies (like blood cells) and foreign bodies (like viruses), is by that fact self-conscious. (I am not implying that dogs are no more complex mentally than antibodies!) On the other hand, it is now pretty clear that chimpanzees do have some sense of self and hence some form of self-consciousness. Give a chimpanzee a mirror and a comb, and if it has seen the comb being used before, it will proceed to groom itself in the mirror with as much grace and gentleness as its less-than-fully-opposable thumbs will allow.[11]

Our question, nevertheless, is: what is the relationship between self-consciousness and rights? We need to know how the possession of the latter is supposed to follow from the possession of the former. Indeed, as will soon be argued, self-consciousness *is* an important feature of rights-holders just as much as language; but what I deny is that it is in virtue of self-consciousness *as such*, any more than in virtue of linguistic competence as such, that a creature has rights.

The first thing to note is that it is not 'psychophysical identity over time', also listed by Regan, which matters. Every animal with both a mind and a body has a psychophysical identity over time, arguably even insects. The animal need not be conscious, let alone self-conscious; all it needs is to be capable of some set of brain-based operations that regulate the rest of its life cycle for it to have an identity over time that involves, in some way and to some degree (the details are too obscure and difficult even to begin to specify), both mental and physical properties and/or operations. (Some philosophers will baulk at the very use of the term 'mental' in this context, which is understandable. If we go back to the original Aristotelian usage of the term 'psyche', however, we can see that the study of *all* life is a kind of psychology because it essentially involves a study of the *vital principle (psyche)* of living things. In that traditional sense, not even a brain is necessary for the study of psychology, which covers plants as well; though the term 'mental' is best reserved for creatures with brains.)

What, then, does *self*-consciousness contribute to the debate? As such, I do not think it contributes anything, because the important question is not whether the animal is conscious of itself, but whether the animal is conscious of itself *in a certain respect*. To put the question more precisely but also more awkwardly: As *what* is the animal conscious of itself? Merely being self-conscious does not entail that one will be conscious of oneself in all the ways in which it is *possible* to be conscious of oneself. Put more prosaically, self-knowledge need not be total. This is true as a matter of contingent fact in the case of human beings. A person may be so lacking in self-knowledge as not to understand what his real motives are, or what virtues he does and does not have, or what his weaknesses are. It is doubtful whether any person can ever have a totally false consciousness of what he is, but certainly possible that he have only a partially correct one. The point is simply that in the case of self-conscious beings the question, 'How does it see itself?' makes sense. Carried over to the animal case, the point is that if an animal is self-conscious it is legitimate to want to know how it presents itself *to* itself. We will see that for self-consciousness to matter in the attribution of rights, it must be a certain *kind* of self-consciousness, one that animals lack. In the case of the chimpanzee grooming itself in the mirror, if this does evidence a form of self-consciousness, it is hard to see how it goes much beyond an awareness on the part of the ape of itself as an individual with certain body parts, including hair, that it is able to manipulate. Perhaps there is more going on, but there is no evidence that this is the case. On the other hand, it may be that some animals have a sense of *their own future*, as is at least suggested by the behaviour of animals in abbatoirs, where cows and pigs, for instance, act as if they know what is in store for them. I cannot see that such an interpretation is forced on us by the facts, but even if it were it would not be clear how a sense of its own future in itself, any more than a sense of its own present, licensed the attribution of rights to an animal.

Nor is there evidence that chimpanzees or any other animals have self-consciousness in the sense of being able to think *about their own thoughts*, to reflect on their own reasoning processes, to make judgements about their own judgements. Apes can learn, like many other kinds of animal, but there is no credible evidence that they learn *from their mistakes*, as opposed to learning from their trainers or their environment. To learn from your mistakes you need first to know *that you have made a mistake*, that is, that your original thought about something was in some way wrong. No animal behaviour suggests this to be the case. If even this minimal kind of self-awareness is not possible for animals, still less will they be self-conscious in the way I will argue is important. In short, then, self-consciousness in itself does not legitimise the attribution of rights; it has to be a certain *kind* of self-consciousness. Second, given the minimal sort of self-conscious awareness displayed by some animals (notably chimpanzees), it is doubtful whether the morally relevant kind of self-consciousness will be a feature of any animal's mental life.

3.2.5   Action in pursuit of desires and goals

The final ingredient in Regan's criterion of a subject-of-a-life is that it should have 'the ability to initiate action in the pursuit of [its] desires and goals'. As in the case of self-consciousness, the crucial question is: in what way? Taken at its broadest, there is not a living creature on earth, plant or animal, that does not initiate action in pursuit of its desires and goals. Plants have the goal of growth and flourishing (and reproducing themselves), if by 'goal' is meant 'state whose satisfaction makes the life of an organism go well'. When they grow towards the light they initiate action, if by this all that is meant is that they operate of their own accord in such a way as to satisfy their goals. The same is true for fungi, bacteria, amoebae, worms, snails, right up to human beings.

Presumably Regan means something more. Higher animals such as primates (man, apes, monkeys) are capable of some ingenious behaviour. In 1987 the magazine *New Scientist* reported on a number of cases of intelligent deception practised by chimpanzees, gorillas and baboons. For instance:

Paul, a young juvenile baboon, approached and watched an adult female, Mel, who was digging in hard dry earth for a large rhizome to eat. Paul looked round: in the undulating grassland habitat no baboons were in sight, although they could not be far off. The he screamed loudly, which baboons do not normally do unless threatened. Within seconds Paul's mother, who was dominant to Mel, rushed to the scene and chased her, both going right out of sight.

Paul walked forward and began to eat the rhizome. Watching the incident it was difficult to suppress an intentional interpretation. ... Certainly, if you substituted 'older brother' for 'adult female', and 'favourite toy' for 'large rhizome', this scenario would be familiar to many parents, who would then have no hesitation in deciding that Paul intended to deceive his mother.[12]

In fact, it is not clear who Paul was trying to deceive, his mother, or Mel, or both. In any case, the behaviour is interesting. The authors add that Paul would not have been strong enough to dig up the rhizome himself, so he waited until it was already exposed and available to be picked up; and that he restricted his deceitful behaviour to cases where his mother was within earshot, meaning that she must have figured in his plan. (They say 'cases', implying they saw the behaviour more than once, but they do not say how often.)

Impressed as we may be by this and other such stories of animal deception, the question is how exactly we are to interpret this sort of behaviour, and again what relevance it has to the question of animal rights. As for interpretation, we must be very careful, especially when using words such as 'try', 'plan', 'intelligent', and even 'deceive', not to *presuppose* that primate deception is essentially different from other kinds of deception found in the animal kingdom. What, for example, are we to say of the trapdoor spider, which builds a trap covered in sand and dirt in such a way that it is invisible to the naked human eye (and evidently to some other animals as well!) and which then lies in wait in its lair, sometimes for hours, for an unsuspecting insect to come along, at which point the spider snaps open the door and drags the poor insect inside? Or of the incredible deceptive behaviour of the chameleon, able to change colours to blend almost imperceptibly with its environment, allowing it to catch unsuspecting prey and to evade its enemies? Or of the stick insect, which can make itself look for all the world like a twig on a branch? Or of moths and butterflies which can make themselves look exactly like leaves? The fact is that cunning and deception are rife throughout the animal kingdom, and it would have been surprising if apes were *not* capable of such behaviour. They 'initiate action in pursuit of their desires and goals' by deception just as much as by waking up in the morning and looking for food, or by making aggressive displays against intruders. They have feelings and sensations related to their goals which plants do not, such as hunger and thirst, anger, sexual desire, and so on.

The question of whether deceptive behaviour by apes is a result of 'mere conditioning', though, is not a helpful or relevant one. If by 'mere conditioning' is meant the repeated application of stimulus and response, whether to and by the ape concerned or other apes it can see, leading to a predictable response on its part to similar stimuli in the future, then it may well be that apes learn deception by mere conditioning. So also dogs learn obedience by mere conditioning, only in the case of the ape the conditioning is part of its natural environment, where for instance it sees other apes running away and leaving food behind when they hear a warning scream. Or it may be, as the authors of the article just mentioned believe, that there is more to it than that. In which case all we would be entitled to infer was that there is a certain repertoire of deceptive skills built into the brains of certain apes, though what actual shape those skills take in real life may depend to some extent on what experiences they have. Neither interpretation, however, manifests any plausible conceptual connection to the idea that animals have rights. For such a connection to be forged we need a deeper interpretation of the expression 'initiation of action in pursuit of desires and goals'.

The same goes for action of the kind that may be described as 'self-defence'. Supporters of animal rights often appeal to the way in which some animals try to escape from perceived threats to their well-being as justification for saying that they have a right to protection from such threats. Perhaps, as I suggested earlier, some animals do have an awareness of their own future, as we might conclude from the fact that pigs or cows about to be slaughtered struggle and squeal or bellow, showing definite signs of terror in their eyes. Even people who work in abattoirs say that some animals can smell the blood of their dead and dying conspecifics, and are immediately seized with panic and desperately try to escape. There is little doubt that this is the case, and we all know something about the terrible scenes in abattoirs. 'These', says the animal rights supporter, 'are animals going to their deaths and who know just what they are in for. They struggle, they try to defend themselves, just as we would in a similar situation. How can such creatures not have the right to life that we do?'

It appears that when the animal rights advocate argues in this way, he is assuming that the attribution of a right to an individual flows from the capacity of that individual – whether the capacity derives from the actual abilities of the individual or from the abilities of typical members of its species – to behave in ways defensive of the good that the right protects. Yet rights cannot flow from mere defensive behaviour. Again, every animal on earth defends what is good for it in some way or other. Killing enemies, repelling territorial invaders, adapting to hostile conditions, repairing bodily damage – we find examples of some or all such typical animal behaviour in everything from primates to single-celled organisms. The sense of the future that higher animals may display has already been rejected as licensing the conclusion that animals have rights; what is at stake here is the defensive behaviour itself. Now, an animal rights supporter once again may insist on the rights of every animal – a position absurd in itself and which I will discuss briefly later – but you may wonder whether plants will also have rights on this view. Does the behaviour of a plant when it cures itself of a disease constitute sufficient defensive behaviour to license the attribution of rights? Or when it regrows a lost branch? When a weed, say, strangles another plant to death and takes over its habitat, without which it cannot thrive? The appeal to defensive behaviour as such begins to look threadbare.

Furthermore, what is the precise conceptual connection between defensive behaviour and the attribution of rights? It hardly looks like the former is sufficient for the latter, but is it necessary? Suppose there were a species of animal that was very much like a human being except for not having the capacity to defend the goods it sought to satisfy. Not only were some members of the species unable to engage in defensive behaviour – there are plenty of young, old and sick or injured human beings who cannot do so either – but nor were typical, mature and healthy members of the species able to do so. Think of the mythical Neanderthals in William Golding's *The Inheritors* (mythical not because there were no Neanderthals but because Golding presents them as not being members of the human species, which all the evidence says they were); they are presented as innocent and lacking in guile, and are eventually killed off by the fearsome and cunning *homo sapiens*. Now think of our imaginary species as even weaker than Golding's Neanderthals. They are so passive that they do not repel invaders, do not try to adapt to extremes of climate, and do not even repair injuries to their own bodies! Naturally, they would not last long on our cruel earth, but if they had all the intelligence and self-knowledge of human beings (minus the strength and cunning, but plus an acute awareness of their own weakness and imminent demise), would we want to say they did not have at least some rights, say to enjoy their land and possessions in peace? It is hard to see why defensive behaviour is even necessary for being a rights-holder, let alone sufficient.

Finally, we should beware of circular reasoning of the form: animals have rights because they manifestly exercise their right of self-defence. Such reasoning is occasionally heard, but is obviously illegitimate. We must not describe defensive behaviour by animals in terms that *presuppose* they have rights in order to justify the claim that they have them.

3.3   The Conditions for Rights – What They Are

A right is a kind of moral protection provided to an individual in his pursuit of the good. (See chapter 2 of *Moral Theory*.) It imposes constraints, that is, duties, on other individuals. The key term here is *pursuit*. There is, as we have seen, a broad sense in which every animal and even plant pursues the goods that are proper to them. We speak of a plant's *trying* to extract water from parched soil, of a snail's *seeking out* warm, moist conditions, of a bird's *attempting* to crack a nut, of a cat's *looking for* a mate, of a chimpanzee's *knowing* that a certain fruit is poisonous. Now it is simply wrong to lump all these sorts of behaviour together by saying that just as plants have no mental life so do animals lack one; or that the mental life of each species of animal is roughly the same; or that there are no gradations of complexity in the way animals go about doing what benefits them and avoiding what harms them. It would be churlish to say that there are no striking similarities between chimpanzee and human intelligence that are not equally present as between humans and horses, or humans and insects. Nor would it be correct to deny some animals a kind of genuine *knowledge*, to deny them real cognitive abilities. Nor would it be altogether wrong to use the very word 'intelligent' in some cases. Nor would it be wrong to use terms such as 'try', 'seek', 'strive', 'act', 'understand', and others used in the description of typically human behaviour. As we saw, at least some animals are probably conscious in ways that go beyond mere sentience. Some may even have a sense of themselves.

We must not, however, apply to animals terms descriptive of paradigmatically human behaviour in anything other than an *analogous* sense. For although animals pursue the good in one way, they do not do so in the manner necessary for the attribution to them of rights. And this is because there are two conditions necessary for the ascription of rights which no animal (apart from the human animal) satisfies: (1) a rights-holder must *know that he is pursuing the good*, and hence that he is acting *for a purpose*; (2) a rights-holder must have *free will* in his pursuit of the good. Free will, and a certain kind of knowledge, are required of any being that possesses rights.

3.3.1 Knowledge of purpose

As to the kind of knowledge required, this has traditionally been called knowledge of finality (after Aristotle's *final cause*, that is, the *end* or *goal* for which an agent acts, and which exerts a certain kind of causal influence over the agent). We can also call it knowledge of *why an individual does what it does*. No one can be under a duty to respect another's right if he cannot *know* what it is he is supposed to respect. Similarly, no one can call another to account with regard to the respecting of his right if the former cannot *know* what it is the other is supposed to respect. In the paradigmatic case, calling someone to account involves the making of a conscious demand on them ('Get off my land!', 'Would you mind moving a little to the right?', and so on) and this involves communication. But as we have seen, communication is not of the essence. I do not even have to express my displeasure at your blowing smoke in my direction while I am eating for me to be able to make a conscious demand on you. My mere presence, engaging in the quiet enjoyment of my food, is enough to alert you to the fact that the pollution of my immediate environment is not something I would appreciate and may well interfere with the enjoyment of my meal. I do not need to speak to you, or make non-verbal signals, or communicate in any way. I just need to do what I do, which (one hopes) is what is good for me.

Now this conscious demand that I make on you by my presence need not involve my having at the forefront of my mind why I am doing what I am doing. After all, how many of us (Hamlet aside) spend our lives reflecting on the goodness or otherwise of our actions? We can go further and say that it is not necessary that a rights-holder even be *actually conscious* in order to make on others a demand deriving from the possession of a right, if he is, for instance, temporarily insane, unconscious, drunk or immature. All such individuals are capable of being brought to a state of reflection upon why they do what they do – all they need is mental health, or to be awake, or to sober up, or to be left alone to get on with the business of growing up. But we can go even further and say that even if an individual is senile, or irreversibly comatose, or severely brain- damaged, he makes a moral demand on others though he himself cannot be brought to a state of reflection upon his actions. It has been central to the defence of traditional morality to show that *personism* is false, and hence that mentally incapacitated human beings also have rights because of their very nature as members of a species whose paradigmatic members *are* capable of conscious reflection on why they do what they do. So the idea that a rights-holder must know why it is that he does what he does does not mean actual reflection, or even the physical possibility of reflection, on the part of the individual concerned. Human beings have rights because human beings know why it is that they do what they do. This is a *generic* truth characterising human beings *as such* and thereby justifying the application of the description conveyed by the truth to all human beings, whether or not a given individual actually exercises, or is contingently capable of exercising, the capacities in that description. And presumably the animal rights supporter would have exactly the same view of animals: *if* chimpanzees had rights because, say, they had a sense of themselves, Charlie the chimp would have rights even if he had no sense of himself at all. (Suppose he could not interpret his image in a mirror in the way other chimps could and similarly for whatever test one might propose.)

Again, the point about knowledge is not a mistaken psychoanalytical generalisation. No human being knows why he does *everything* he does. None of us is totally transparent to ourselves. We do not know the purposes of many of our actions. But even in the case of the individual most lacking in self-knowledge on the face of the earth (whoever he may be), that person knows why it is that he eats, why he drinks, why he sleeps, why he wakes, why he plays, why he works, why he has friends (let us hope he has some), why he breathes, why he sits, why he stands. Knowledge of purpose is not necessarily knowledge of anything particularly important in the grand scheme of one's life and projects. Any purpose will do.

And yet no animal, as far as any evidence whatsoever suggests, has any knowledge of why it does anything it does. What are we to say of a chimpanzee that tastes and then throws away a poisonous fruit? That it knows the fruit is dangerous? Well, we can speak in this analogous way if we like, but we really have no evidence that the chimp knows this, as opposed to sensing that the fruit smells or looks repulsive (for instance), which triggers immediate avoidance behaviour. Did Paul the baboon know that by scaring away his mother and Mel he could get the food they left behind? We can speak in this way, but we should not regard it as literally true of Paul that he had knowledge of *why* he screamed unless we are also prepared to regard it as literally true that a trapdoor spider knows why it builds an elaborately disguised trap for its prey. (There is a difference, though, in that the spider has its precise trapdoor-building mechanism built into it, whereas the rarity of Paul's exact behaviour suggests that baboons have general deception mechanisms built into them which are realized in diverse ways according to the particular sensory associations to which each individual baboon is exposed. But this difference is irrelevant to the present point.)

Does a dog know why it eats food? Or why it prefers beef to chicken? Most of us would say no to both questions – it just *does* eat, and *does* prefer one food to another, and *we* are the ones who know that food is good for it. Does a cat know why it plays happily with a mouse it has caught? If so, it would have to know that it did so *because it was a pleasurable activity*, and again most of us would baulk at attributing such knowledge to the cat, even though we speak casually as though such knowledge were present. Until, however, we are shown why chimpanzees fit into a different category from dogs and cats as far as such knowledge is concerned, we are bound to regard them in the same way. Physiology will not provide the distinction, because whatever similarities in body plan and brain function have been found between chimps and humans simply do not, as far as anyone knows, explain why there should be a mental similarity in respect of knowledge of purpose. (The objection often heard (whether it is true or not is another matter), 'But chimps and humans share 98 per cent of their genetic make-up' merely invites the reply, 'That extra 2 per cent certainly makes a difference!') Nor is it likely that we will ever know how such a thing as knowledge of purpose is correlated with brain function, either in us or in any other animal. Of course, I have been speaking very much in epistemological terms, about what evidence we have, what we know or might know. There is no metaphysical necessity here. It is at least conceivable that some crucial experiment will be carried out that conclusively demonstrates knowledge of purpose on the part of some species of animal; but there does not seem to be a great deal of research going on in that area, and whatever has been done suggests strongly that even the most 'intelligent' animal behaviour is explicable without for a minute supposing that animals act *for reasons*.

The concept of a *reason* is central to the idea now being put forward. Consider the following from Anthony Kenny:

When a human being does X in order to do Y, the achieving of Y is his reason for doing X. When an animal does X in order to do Y, he does not do X *for a reason*, even though he is aiming at a goal in doing so. Why not? Because an animal, lacking a language, cannot *give a reason*. And while a rational agent may, on a particular occasion, act for a reason without giving (to himself or to others) any account of the reason, it is only those beings who have the ability to give reasons who have the ability to act for reasons. Humans are rational, reason-giving animals; dumb animals are not and therefore cannot act for reasons. [By 'dumb' Kenny does not mean 'stupid', but 'mute', that is, lacking in language.][13]

In the first part of this extract, Kenny distinguishes between acting for a reason and aiming at a goal. We can say that plants aim at goals because they grow towards the light and extract water and nutrients from the soil. Animals also aim at goals in the sense of doing what is good for them when they can. (They may not do this all the time even when not hampered, as animals have been known to act self-destructively; note in passing that alleged mass suicide by lemmings apparently results from dangers occurring on migratory routes the following of which has been hard-wired into the lemmings' brains.) But animals do not, at least as far as anyone can see, act for reasons.

In the second part of the extract, however, Kenny explains this inability in terms of a lack of linguistic competence. Reasons – 'because I wanted a drink', 'because you made me angry', and so on – are the sorts of things that occur in pieces of *reasoning*. And pieces of reasoning consist of premises and conclusions. In the practical case, where an individual – say Fred – is thinking about what to do, the conclusion may be another proposition: 'I am hungry; there is food on the table; so I should take and eat it.' Or it may be an *action*: Fred thinks, 'I am hungry; there is food on the table', and then he *acts* by taking and eating the food. In either case, at least *some* of Fred's reasoning is propositional, in particular his reason or reasons for acting or for drawing a conclusion about how he should act. Being able to state his reasons in propositional form means that Fred can distinguish between them and other reasons that did not occur in his reasoning: did he take the food because he wanted to give it to his little brother? 'No, I took it because I was hungry.' Was it because he was very hungry? 'No, I was not very hungry, just hungry.' And so on. Without the ability to represent one's reasons in propositional form, it is hard to see how an individual can have any reasons at all.

But if Kenny is correct, does it mean that what matters in the attribution of rights is language after all, not knowledge of purpose or of finality? Kenny appears to be suggesting this, or at least to be *equating* the reason-giving capacity with the linguistic capacity; but I do not think we need to go that far. What is plausible is that, as a matter of metaphysical necessity (Kenny, Leahy and other Wittgensteinians would likely prefer to call it a conceptual or 'grammatical' truth), if an individual has knowledge of why he does what he does then he must have language, and if he has language then he must have knowledge of why he does what he does. But it does not follow that the reason-giving capacity and the linguistic capacity are the same thing. (Compare: it is a metaphysical truth that boxes have sides if and only if they have corners; but having sides and having corners are not the same thing.) Having language provides the *conditions* for being able to give reasons, but it is the capacity to give reasons that is at the heart of the ascription of rights.

Recall that when we discussed language, I claimed that the idea that rights-holders must be language-users was due to a false communitarian or contractualist view of rights, according to which rights derive from the fact that an individual is in some sort of meaningful relationship with other members of his community, and that a meaningful relationship required communication. On the other hand, it was noted that a less objectionable form of contractualism held merely that a being could only possess rights if it 'made sense' to justify to it a policy of action towards it. At its bare minimum, this would require that a being be capable of representing to itself the reasons for which another acted or proposed to act in a certain way, which in turn requires that it can represent to itself the reasons for which *it* acts or proposes to act in a certain way. Further, it was hard to see how such a representation could be made without the ability to form propositions, which itself required a capacity for symbolic or linguistic representation (and probably communication within the species, if not necessarily outside it). This, then, is the kernel that must be extracted from the 'argument from language' for the ascription of rights. No being can understand the reasons of another without being able to understand its own reasons; and no being can understand its own reasons without being able to understand the reasons of another. (Again, this is not a point about being able to grasp the true motives of oneself or others, something at which we often fail, but a point about being able to understand reasons *as such*.) It looks as though linguistic ability provides the ground for the reason-giving/reason-grasping capacity. But it is just possible that there is a sense in which reasons can be given and grasped which does not require language. If so, then this is no problem for the view being defended, since as was pointed out earlier, it is the reason-giving/reason-grasping capacity itself, the knowledge of purpose, which grounds rights, not the possession or use of language. Using alternative terminology, we can say that it is *qua* knower of purpose, not *qua* user of language, that an individual has rights.

3.3.2 Free will

The second condition of rights is the possession of free will. Now, in chapter 1 of *Moral Theory* one of the things I said would not be argued for was the proposition that there is such a thing as free will and that human beings have it. Nor is this book the place to broach the free-will/determinism debate. The questions for our purposes are (1) why free will is necessary for the possession of rights, and (2) whether animals have free will.

To take the first question first, it was said at the start of the discussion of the conditions for rights that the key word in the definition of a right is *pursuit*. A right is a moral power to do, acquire, have or hold something. It protects an individual in his *pursuit* of the good. This pursuit cannot be, to use Kenny's phrase, a mere aiming at a goal. The goal must, as has been argued, be a purpose, that is, a goal that one represents or is capable of representing to oneself as the *point* of one's action. But it is also true that the aiming must not be mere *movement towards* the goal. Plants do this, as we have noted. So does every form of animal life. By the very fact of being alive, an organism tends to do whatever it is that fulfils its nature unless thwarted in some respect (say by injury, deformation or attack). But if we are to say, as we should, that plants do not have rights, nor bacteria, nor amoebae, nor mosquitoes, and so on, we need to know what it is that separates the movement towards a goal of a rights-holder and that of a creature that does not have rights. The difference lies in the possession of free will and its accompanying characteristics of choice, decision, deliberation and intention.

But granted that plants do not have free will and human beings do, what is the ethical relevance of the distinction? Must we rest content with saying that the appeal to free will is necessary in order to prevent the *reductio ad absurdum* of attributing rights to plants? No, we can go further to explain the point of the distinction. One writer puts it thus:

Rights exist because we are obliged to guard the moral value of our being and fulfil our function by voluntary observance of the moral law. . . . To this kind of action rights are essential, because if we must guide ourselves by the use of our free will we must be guaranteed immunity from hindrance in our choice of the necessary means.[14]

As was said in chapter 2 of *Moral Theory*, the axiom of morality is 'Do good and avoid evil.' It is not a recommendation, but a *duty*. Every moral being has a duty to do what is good and avoid what is bad. It has an obligation to live well. Given that this is the fundamental obligation of morality, morality would be contradicting itself if it did not also offer *protection* in the doing of good (and avoidance of evil), if it gave no *claims* against others not to hinder an individual in his doing what is good (and avoiding what is evil). This is what the system of rights provides. But there can be no duty without the *freedom* to observe it. 'No ought without can', as the Kantian maxim has it, is another of morality's basic principles. If the moral law and the metaphysics of moral beings are not in perverse disharmony (and again, I am assuming this, not seeking to prove it), then morality imposes no obligations that a being under those obligations is not also free to discharge. Therefore, since all subjects of the moral law are obliged to do good and avoid evil, they must be free to do so. In short, the pursuit of the good must be free.

This, then, is the response to Regan's objection that an individual can be a moral patient (a bearer of rights) without being a moral agent (a bearer of free will). A being simply cannot be a subject of morality without being under the obligation to do what morality demands of it, and this requires free will. To put it in terms that might be more familiar, a being cannot be the subject of morality without being able to *choose* between right and wrong. We can also say that the individual subject of morality must be able to *decide* between right and wrong, to *deliberate* between good and bad alternative courses of action, to *intend* to do something good rather than something bad (and vice versa), to act *autonomously*.

As in the case of knowledge of purpose, however, the claim about free will must not be confused with other, highly implausible, assertions. Individuals are constrained in all sorts of ways from acting freely. They are constrained by upbringing, environment, genetic make-up, sometimes by physical compulsion, sometimes by drugs, intoxication, imprisonment, illness or immobility. All of these factors may deprive an individual of his freedom in specific circumstances, but only in the sense that the individual is not able, *at that time*, and *in that context*, to make a free decision or freely take a course of action. But that individual does not stop being a creature with free will, with the inherent freedom that is an inextricable part of its very nature, any more, as we saw, than a person ceases to be inherently rational when in a state of severe mental injury, unconsciousness, drunkenness, and so on – even if that rationality cannot be exercised in the circumstances. The idea that a person would still be a free individual in the most basic sense despite contingent circumstances preventing the exercise of that freedom is, then, the obvious complement of the truth that a person is still a rational individual despite contingent circumstances thwarting its exercise. In neither case do such circumstances (which also include the circumstance of being very young or very old) deprive the free, rational being of his rights. Hence it is humanism, not *personism*, which conveys the truth about man's moral status. Of course, whether we praise or blame a person in a given set of circumstances, whether we hold him responsible, whether we say he acted rightly or wrongly, will depend on how much, if any, freedom he had at that particular time. But the fact remains that human beings are beings with free will, and this is what makes them responsible for their actions in the typical, paradigmatic case. What would you say of a woman who was captured by some cruel dictator, tortured, brainwashed, drugged into stupefaction, conditioned to do only what the dictator commanded and to refuse what he ordered her to refuse? Would she be a free individual? In one sense, you would say, she was not. But in another, fundamental sense, you would insist that she was free and remained free, no matter how clouded her mind was by oppression, pain and conditioning. She could never lose her dignity as a free individual, she could never be turned into a robot, an automaton, something essentially different from what she was. She would still have her right to liberty even if she was incapable of exercising it, and as such she would never cease to be a subject of morality, even if she could not be blamed for anything she did under the influence of the dictator who had brainwashed her.

Granted all of this, as anyone who believes in the reality of morality and is not a determinist will do, what, to come to our second question, are we to say of animals? Do they have free will? It was conceded earlier that perhaps some animals, perhaps chimpanzees, were self-conscious; and it was objected that self-consciousness as such did not confer rights, but what mattered was the *kind* of self-consciousness an animal possessed. In particular, it was self-consciousness *as acting for reasons* that we saw to be essential. We can see now in what other respect there must be self-consciousness: are animals conscious of themselves *as free agents*? From what we know about animal behaviour, it seems even *less* plausible to say that they have free will than to say that they know why they do what they do. In fact, it may be that it is not even a question of empirical evidence as far as free will is concerned, because there is arguably a metaphysical connection between having free will and having knowledge of purpose, such that no animal can have one without the other. In other words, if it is an empirical fact that no animal has knowledge of purpose, perhaps it follows as a metaphysical necessity that no animal has free will. In his discussion of knowledge of purpose from which the above extract was taken, Anthony Kenny ties both phenomena together. After arguing that human beings act for reasons and animals do not, he goes on to say: 'We can thus justify the conclusion that the human will is the capacity for intentional action. But in the light of the discussion we can see that a better, because a less misleading, account is that the human will is the capacity to act for reasons.'[15] And he then links the possession of language with both intentional action and self-consciousness. As far as language goes, it seems more reasonable to link its possession to the possession of a capacity for giving reasons than to free will or to self-consciousness, at least self-consciousness in the minimal sense in which chimpanzees appear to have it. But whether freedom and reason-giving themselves necessarily go together is a more difficult conceptual issue.

Kenny's reasoning, which he does not make explicit, may go something like this: having a reason for doing X requires reasoning about the doing of X in a way in which that reason figures; but reasoning about the doing of X amounts to reasoning *whether* to do X; and reasoning whether to do X implies the possibility of *not* doing X (whether not doing anything, or doing Y *rather than* X); but the possibility of not doing X means that one is *free* not to do X; so one must have free will. In the other direction, it might be argued that if one is free, one must be able to act for a reason, because one is able to *choose* to do X (rather than nothing or rather than Y); and being able to choose to do X requires being able to reason for the preferability of X (over nothing or over Y); which in turn requires being able to give a reason, or the reasons, that figured in one's reasoning for the preferability of X. If both sides of this argument are sound, then freedom and knowledge of purpose go together. Still, one might at least dispute the second half, objecting that one can at least conceive of an individual who was a spontaneous, free chooser but who was unable ever to give a reason for his choices. (Do you think this is possible?)

Whatever the merits of the conceptual argument linking acting for a reason and acting freely, it seems at least from the empirical viewpoint that no animal has free will any more than the capacity to act for a reason. Animals, it appears, are governed wholly by *instinct*. The *Concise Oxford Dictionary* defines instinct as: 'innate propensity to certain seemingly rational acts performed without conscious intention; innate, usually fixed, pattern of behaviour especially in response to certain simple stimuli'. There is, I would say, a slight inaccuracy in the definition. First, the intention need not be conscious, if this means that it must be at the forefront of one's mind. When I walk to the office, although I may consciously intend to go there I do not consciously intend every step; and yet every step is surely intentional. The point about instinctive behaviour is that it is not intentional pure and simple. Second, note that it is 'especially' in response to certain stimuli that instinct can be shown to be present, but it is not essential that the stimuli be simple. The higher the animal in the developmental hierarchy, the more complex the stimuli that govern its behaviour. In any case, 'simple' and 'complex' are relative terms, and investigation shows that even what appear to be simple stimuli governing the behaviour of, say, the AIDS virus, are on closer observation very complex. (Actually, whether viruses are alive or not is hotly disputed; but the same point could be made about, say, the single-celled protozoan called *paramecium*: see the entertaining stories of the physicist Richard Feynman.[16])

Another definition of instinct is given by William James: 'Instinct is usually defined as the faculty of acting in such a way as to produce certain ends, without foresight of the ends, and without previous education in the performance.'[17] By 'foresight of ends' James means knowledge of purpose, and so he too ties free behaviour to such knowledge. The lack of need for 'previous education' should be understood correctly, however. Instinctive behaviour can be and is in many animals modified by experience and learning: for instance, although nest-building is an instinct built into birds, they often learn by experience where to build, so that the repeated destruction of a nest in a certain location will eventually cause them to build elsewhere. The point about the lack of need for previous education is that with instinctive behaviour there is some category or kind of action that the animal does not need to be taught to do, but which it knows from the beginning of its life and will tend to perform (if not thwarted) at the appropriate stage of its life cycle. The behaviour is 'hard-wired' into the animal, in its brain or other control mechanisms and/or genetic make-up.

One might concede all this and still object, 'Wait a minute. What about human beings? Scientists are discovering more and more how we humans are governed by instinct in areas where we thought we were free.' It is true that human beings are governed *partly* by instinct. Consider the instinct to eat when we are hungry: you do not get up every morning and think, 'To eat or not to eat – that is the question' – you just go and make some toast! We are also led by instinct to be attracted towards certain smells, sounds, textures, and so on. Much research of late has gone into the influence of pheromones on human sexual behaviour. These are chemical signals that have no smell but are, in humans, emitted from perspiration and other body fluids. In other animals they are emitted in diverse ways. It was found that moths, to take one example, interact to a great degree because of the impulses provided by pheromones. Perhaps humans do so as well? It was soon found that while experimentation with pheromones showed a small degree of influence over behaviour, causing subjects to report a mild dislike of or attraction to another person, it was just not possible to reduce human sexual behaviour to the emission and reception of chemical signals. Nevertheless, humans are animals (albeit rational ones), and as animals must be governed at least partly by instinct. But note that the more 'animalistic' our behaviour, the more instinctive it is. Food, drink, reproduction – these are the sorts of activity in which instinct plays the greatest role, and if it did not human life would be an intolerable round of decision-making that would doom us to extinction.

Note also that no matter how instinctive, every human activity can be brought within the sphere of choice or free will. Otherwise there would be no hunger-strikers and no celibates, to take two obvious examples. As we saw in the case of reason-giving, we may not always know the reason for this or that action of ours, but we can always at least *reflect* on the possible reasons for doing this or that. Similarly, in the case of freedom, we may sometimes behave instinctively, but we can always apply our free will to our instinctive behaviour. There can be nothing more instinctive than breathing, and yet we can – up to a point – choose not to breathe. What about, say, heartbeat or digestion? The answer is that these are best thought of as automatic bodily operations rather than activities performed by human beings (or other animals). There is no 'innate propensity' for your heart to beat or your stomach to digest food in the presence of a stimulus – they just do it. You need food before digestion takes place, so digestion might be thought of as requiring a stimulus, but food is probably better thought of as the matter upon which digestion operates rather than the stimulus that provokes the stomach or the person to behave in a certain way. (Acids and other chemicals are churning away in your stomach, full or empty, all the time, and do not do anything essentially different in the presence of food. But this is avowedly a piece of armchair physiology.) In any case, even if heartbeat, at least, is best thought of as instinctive, note that some people are able to apply their free will to it: Hindu yogis, among others, are known to be able deliberately to slow their heartbeat and/or pulse. (We can all do it to some degree by deep breathing.) Stopping or slowing digestion is perhaps more fanciful, but there is probably someone out there who can do that as well.

Even if it turned out that there was some instinctive behaviour that no human being could ever bring within the sphere of free choice, the truth would remain that human beings *have* free choice. And they can apply it to certain kinds of instinctive behaviour. There is nothing remotely parallel in the animal kingdom. Insects have been shown time and again to be programmed by instinct to behave in certain ways, even to their own detriment. I have already mentioned the plausible explanation of lemming 'mass suicide' as caused by their continuing to follow a migratory path that has long since become treacherous. Ants have been shown to behave in ways that are clearly instinctive.[18] To take another example:

Cerceris ornata is the name of a solitary wasp, which is known to kill certain bees of the genus Halyctus by means of its sting, to carry them to its nest of sand and place an egg upon the ventral side [abdomen] of the bee. One day 'while Cerceris was away hunting, some dry sand was thrown into the nest, and the entrance was then stopped with damp sand. She returned laden with prey, and seeing herself forced to resume the profession of a miner, abandoned her victim, cleared the entrance, penetrated within, came out again and flew off in search of new prey. After two successive trips she penetrated a third time into her dwelling and began to reject the dry sand which had been thrown in. In the midst of this sand was a bee (which she had dropped before). Presently the wasp flew away. The hours passed on and she returned without a bee, entered and threw out the other one which she now considered an encumbering object. Thus of two victims which were procured with great trouble, one was abandoned on the thresh-hold, and the other was dropped halfway in – neither served as food for larvae. What of that? Cerceris had given the sting

– that was enough. At another time a nest, one of the cells of which was not entirely provisioned, was destroyed at evening. On the next morning Cerceris brought a newly stung bee and placed it in the hole. One the following day she came again charged with prey and dropped her bee which rolled to the bottom of the excavation. She had not brought the full number for provisioning the nest. Instinct commanded her to bring them, and she obeyed but not knowing where to put them, let them fall.'[19]

Interesting and amusing though this story of blind instinct is, it will be objected that we cannot draw a straightforward parallel with the behaviour of higher animals. The problem is, we do not know enough empirically because this sort of research, at least on higher animals, is not fashionable. One of the pioneers of research into animal instinct, Professor N. Tinbergen, lamented the paucity of work on higher animals when he wrote his classic study in 1951.[20] There has not been a great increase in knowledge of instinct since then, though there has been an explosion of 'knowledge' of animal behaviour in the form of diffuse bodies of information obtained by observation, particularly in the field. (See the work of Jane Goodall on chimpanzees, mentioned above.) Instead, there has been an enormous amount of unscientific anthropomorphising, treating every observed behaviour of a dog, a chimp, a whale, a dolphin, and so on, as though it were 'almost human', or 'human-like', which is to beg the very question at issue.

Still, we have forceful general reasons for doubting that there is anything more to animal behaviour than instinct, whatever the obvious differences in complexity due to the fact that, say, wasps and ants are not sentient but dogs and cats are, as well as other differences in physiology. I have mentioned already the metaphysical connection between lack of free will and lack of knowledge of purpose. At a less abstract level, two reasons offered by Peter Carruthers are, first, the lack of adaptability of animals to almost any kind of circumstance or habitat, and, second, the remarkable lack of *alternative* plans among members of the same species. As to the first, he says:

> So if any animals were planners, it would be remarkable that they do not do more of it. If a dog were really capable of predicting that unless its food is hidden it may be stolen by others, and of working out that burying the food would keep it out of sight and smell until needed, then it is strange that it should not make use of these abilities in other areas of its life. Why, for example, do dogs never lay

out food as bait for an unwary cat? Another way to put the point is this. It is distinctive of human beings, and a mark of our rational agency, that we can adapt to almost any circumstance or habitat. No other single animal species even begins to approximate to this adaptability. To the extent that this is so, it suggests that no other species of animal approximates to the status of a rational agent.[21]

As to the second reason, he says:

It seems essential to the activity of planning, as we understand it, that there will always be a number of possible ways of trying to achieve a given objective, even if not all of those ways would be equally successful. It would then be strange, if squirrels were engaging in genuine planning when they gather nuts, that some individuals should not hit upon the alternative plan of observing where other squirrels have hidden their nuts, and later stealing them. And if birds were really planning for the future of their offspring in building a nest, it would be strange that members of the same species should not hit upon alternative modes of construction, or that some individuals should not avoid the labour of building altogether by laying their eggs in the nests of others, as does the cuckoo. (The cuckoo, presumably, does this innately.)[22]

True, we do see what looks like deception and/or freeloading in the case of primates, noted above. Carruthers says that of all species, the stories of chimpanzee deception are the best evidenced and least likely to suffer from being occasional anecdotes unsusceptible to regular and detailed scrutiny. He even concedes that this sort of behaviour counts in favour of rational agency, but adds that it would only be a necessary, not a sufficient condition of such a capacity, which also requires long-term planning and, on his contractualist model, 'a conception of social rules'. Still, as was implied earlier, we do not need to go that far. The only difference between chimpanzee deception and, say, the deception practised by a trapdoor spider, is that the chimp has a broad innate capacity for exploiting its conspecifics, which is realised in various ways depending on the environmental stimuli; whereas the spider's innate deceptive capacity is narrowly constrained to building a camouflaged trap. It is still the case that Carruthers's wider point, about alternative planning, holds good. We do not see in apes a variety of kinds of behaviour for the realisation of goals that even approximates to the human case. That is why, after 30 years of minute observation, behaviour such as deception and toolmaking are still emphasised by animal rights supporters as among the most notable features of chimpanzee 'intelligence'.

As I have said, it is at least *possible* that some species of animal have free will. If so, the number of such species would be very small. Nevertheless, there are no good reasons for thinking that some do in fact have free will, and very good reasons for thinking that none do. Those reasons have an *a priori* element, involving the conceptual connections between freedom and reason-giving, freedom and choice, freedom and planning, freedom and adaptability, freedom and variability, and related notions. They also have an *a posteriori* element involving the lack of evidence for the possession of any such genuine features in animal behaviour, where by not being genuine is meant that the traces of such features that are found can be accounted for it terms of instinct with or without learning, and are often described in a question-beggingly anthropomorphic way. Even the philosopher David DeGrazia, who (though he does not find the 'rights view' very helpful) believes animals do indeed have 'basic moral status' and deserve 'equal consideration', and who bends over backwards to minimise the differences between animals and humans, ends up conceding reluctantly: 'it would seem that the mental complexities involved in autonomy are so great that probably very few – if any – nonhuman animals are autonomous.'[23]

3.4   Two Dilemmas for the View that Animals Have Rights

There are two dilemmas that face the supporter of animal rights. They both follow on from the discussion of free will, but are worth considering separately. If you believe in animal rights, you will almost certainly believe that animals have the right not to be killed and eaten for food by us humans. You will be a vegetarian on ethical grounds, and your grounds will be rights-based. If you are a consequentialist, such as Peter Singer, you will perhaps still be a vegetarian on ethical grounds, but, like him, your grounds would be that animals are caused immense suffering in the food industry, especially through intensive farming, but you would, like him, concede that animals could legitimately be eaten if they were raised well and slaughtered painlessly, or at least with a level of pain that was outweighed by the pleasure we humans get from eating meat.

Leaving aside the consequentialist position, consider the rights view. If animals have the right to life, we are under a duty not to kill them for food. The problem is, though, that animals also kill each other for food. If they have rights, then they too are under duties not to kill each other for food. So every carnivorous animal should be separated from its potential prey, and fed (by whom? presumably by us) on an exclusively vegetarian diet.

You are probably thinking that this is absurd, indeed a *reductio ad absurdum* of the idea that animals have rights. Does morality really demand that we humans create an entirely new environment for all meat-eating animals, where none of them can prey on any others? Do we need a special police force to maintain vigilance 24 hours a day so as to make sure there are no violations? (After all, we do this in the case of humans murdering humans, cannibalism included.) Should there be a special nutrition squad devoted to doling out vegetarian food for each and every animal on earth? After all, the animals will not turn vegetarian of their own accord.

The consequence is every bit as ridiculous as you think. Not only does it require a change to the life cycle and behaviour of virtually every animal that exists, and to the whole of the natural environment (changes likely to be immensely damaging), but it also means a change to human activity which seems beyond the realms of our practical capacity. Furthermore, since many animals on a forced vegetarian diet will simply starve to death because they cannot tolerate it physiologically, and many species will therefore also become extinct (dogs apparently do all right on a meat-free diet, but I doubt that lions would), implementing total vegetarianism means the inevitable starvation of millions of animals and the extinction of many species. The dilemma continues as follows. As far as I can see, the only way the animal rights supporter can avoid the absurd conclusion that animals should be prevented from eating each other is the way most often heard, namely to put up his hands and say, 'But they can't help it!' In other words – although you will not hear it put this way by animal rightists – they are *only animals*. We do not need to stop them eating each other because they don't have any *duties* to each other. Why? *Because animals do not have free will.* They eat each other because of instinct; it's how they are built. But if they do not have free will, then if the arguments given above linking free will and rights are sound, they do not have rights either, and the animal rights view collapses. Further, if they do not have duties to each other, then because every right entails a correlative duty, they do not have rights either, which gives us an additional argument against the animal rights view. Hence, the first dilemma is that either the animal rightist really believes the absurdity that animals should be stopped from eating each other, or he denies that animals have free will, thereby defeating his own position.

The second dilemma is this. Morality is, as I have assumed, a coherent and consistent system. It cannot impose contradictory rights or duties. (It can entail *apparent conflicts* – collisions – as we saw in chapter 2 of *Moral Theory*, but these are in principle resolvable.) But if animals have rights, the system will indeed be inconsistent. For instance, protecting the right to life of the wildebeest means denying the right of the lion to eat it, and vice versa. Protecting the right of the swallow to nest in peace means denying the right of the cuckoo to invade its home, and vice versa. Respecting the right to life of a mouse means disrespecting the right of the cat to kill and play with it, and vice versa. It is impossible that all the rights of all the animals can be respected. Some have to be violated. By whom? By us humans, because if animals have rights, then we are bound to promote, respect and protect them just as much as have to promote, respect and protect human rights. And yet as far as animals go, we cannot do this; it is a logical impossibility. Which means that morality is itself inconsistent, which we have assumed is impossible. In other words, what is sometimes called the Golden Rule of animal rights – 'Treat the creatures below you as you would wish to be treated by a creature above you' – is not one that we could consistently follow. Again, the only ways out of this dilemma are unacceptable for the animal rights view. You could deny that respecting the right of the wildebeest means violating that of the lion because the lion has no right to eat the wildebeest in the first place. But it would still mean being *cruel* to the lion by depriving it of its natural food, and so condemning millions of animals to sickness, starvation and death. (Chimpanzees eat meat also, as Jane Goodall demonstrated – they even eat each other – but they may well be one of the lucky species capable of surviving on a meat-free diet.) Or you could deny that the lion's rights are being violated on the ground that lions are not capable of having rights since they have no free will. But then neither does the wildebeest have rights because it lacks free will just as the lion does, and so it too has no right to protection, nor does any other animal.

3.5   So How Should We Treat Animals?

The argument has been a long one, but since it is so rarely presented in detail, and is fast becoming a minority view, it has been worth giving as full a statement as possible, within the necessary limits, of the view that animals do not have rights. In itself, this statement of the position strikes many people as abhorrent. 'What do you mean, "Animals don't have rights"? Is this like saying, "Black people don't have rights"? Are you advocating we treat animals like slave-owners once treated slaves, as disposable commodities? Can we do anything we like with them? Do they exist solely for man's pleasure and utility? This doesn't sound like ethical progress to me.'

We need to understand how animals fit into the ethical system. The fundamental point is that not having rights does *not* mean that an individual can be treated in any old way. Human beings may not have duties *to* animals, but they certainly have duties *in respect of* animals. Similarly, we do not have duties *to* the natural environment, but we have duties *concerning* the natural environment. The natural environment is something we can legitimately use for our benefit, as when we adapt it for human habitation and extract resources from it. But it would be a great dereliction of duty wantonly to spoil or destroy it, both because this harms us (consider the climatic and other damage caused by the immense clearing of rainforests) and because the natural environment is a thing of beauty in its own right – it has its own inherent value – which must be preserved in a way that is consonant with the legitimate needs of human beings for housing, food, clothing, industry, and so on.

Animals, too, have their own value. The animal kingdom is full of cruelty and suffering ('red in tooth and claw'), but it is also full of beauty, charm, wonder and manifold complexity that never ceases to arouse and amaze the curiosity of the human mind. Animals provide us with a nutritious source of food, with materials that no synthetics can equal; they have served us in many ways since the beginning of mankind, and continue to do so. Without the horse it is doubtful that human civilisation could have existed (the same could be said of the elephant in Asia). Without the comfort offered by animals as pets human life would be poorer and more miserable than we might like to imagine. Animals entertain and instruct us. They provide us with important scientific knowledge, some of which is directly beneficial to mankind. With their closely knit, heavily symbiotic relationships, the diversity of species is essential to the health of the natural and human world. All of this enjoins upon us obligations of care and respect for animals, and a vigilance that we do not repay their service with cruelty and wanton suffering.

It is worth comparing for a moment this view of animals with that of consequentialists such as Peter Singer, the father of 'animal liberation'. As a consequentialist he does not believe in rights for any creature. Whereas the animal rights advocate seeks to raise the moral status of animals to that of humans, and the view I am defending seeks to preserve an essential difference between them, the consequentialist – especially the *personist* – lowers humans to the level of other animals, even though he denies that this is what he is trying to do. As a result, while generally disapproving of animal experimentation, for instance, Singer believes that it would be legitimate as long as one were prepared to experiment on a human being with the same mental capacities. Hence it would only be permissible to experiment on, say, a chimpanzee if one were prepared to experiment on a severely mentally disabled human baby. Note that Singer never says outright that experimentation on the baby would be wrong, and hence equally wrong on the ape, only that the experimenter would have to be *prepared* to do both:

> Would experimenters be prepared to perform their experiments on orphaned humans with severe and irreversible brain damage . . . ? If experimenters are not prepared to use orphaned humans with severe and irreversible brain damage, their readiness to use nonhuman animals seems to discriminate. . . . I would like our conviction that it would be wrong to treat intellectually disabled humans in this way to be transferred to nonhuman animals at similar levels of self-consciousness and with similar capacities.[24]

In other words, it would be consistent for us to condone experimentation on animals if we were prepared to do the same for disabled humans, and consistent also if we condemned both. All Singer is pleading for is consistency in our ethical policies. So if society chose the former path, if society were 'prepared' to allow human experimentation (and it is indeed practised today to an increasing degree, in prisons, hospitals, hospices, homes for the disabled and mental asylums) then it could consistently do the same for animals at a 'similar mental level'. Singer allows the possibility that his arguments against 'speciesism' might be 'misused by evil rulers for their own ends', but says that it is 'no more than a possibility'. He even acknowledges that experiments on humans 'would certainly give us a more accurate indication' of, say, the safety of a drug or foodstuff.[25] So an ethically consistent society run along consequentialist lines could legitimately allow experiments on human babies as well as animals, and obtain more useful results than if the experiments were carried out only on animals.[26]

Furthermore, the *personist* such as Singer believes that non-*persons* are 'replaceable'. As we have seen, in his view the parents of a baby with a disease as mild as haemophilia could legitimately have their child killed if they had a good chance of producing a disease-free baby next time around, and the killing 'has no adverse effect on others'. Similarly, chickens are replaceable, and so if they could be reared in decent surroundings and pain-lessly killed, they could legitimately be eaten if replaced by other chick-ens.[27] The consequentialist is not an absolutist about eating meat. Nor is he an absolutist about animal experiments, if the benefits they bring outweigh the suffering of the animals. The same goes by implication for killing ani-mals for clothing, hunting, circuses, zoos, steeplechasing, and other prac-tices that could conceivably (and often do) provide benefits to humans that outweigh animal suffering. As a preference utilitarian, Singer believes that the satisfaction of preferences should be maximised. And since he does not show why the preferences of millions of people for, say, hunting or zoos are illegitimate, or must be ranked below the desires of animals not to suffer – indeed, it is apparently central to his ethical theory that preferences count equally in the consequentialist melting pot – it is at least not obvious how he can disapprove in principle of hunting or zoos. And if he *does* in fact believe some preferences count for more than others, surely the preferences of *persons* – including the millions who visit zoos and go hunting – would count for more than those of fish, birds and other non-*persons*, and maybe even many mammals such as dogs, cats, dolphins and bears, about which Singer's views are at least equivocal.[28] Certainly it would appear to be 'speciesist' to deny us humans our pleasurable use of animals simply be-cause we were humans, and hence naturally smarter and better equipped to exploit animals than they are to exploit us.

Whatever the queries one might have about the Singerian viewpoint on animals, and whatever the criticisms that have been made throughout this book about his whole ethical system, the fact is that he has done impor-tant work in at least waking us up to the cruelties that have been and continue to be inflicted on the animal kingdom. With this aspect of his thought we can agree. Millions of animals are caused horrific suffering in experiments that, while some may and indeed do benefit humans, are for the most part pointless if not positively harmful to us.[29] Animals are taken for granted in many ways throughout the world, worked to exhaustion, maltreated and abused, denied proper food, water and medical care, and thrown away when they are no longer of any use to us. In this techno-logical age where utilitarian reasoning all but predominates, animals are treated far more viciously and with far more cruelty than at any time in the history of civilisation. We have found ways never before imagined to torture and maim animals and make their lives a misery, almost a living hell for many thousands locked in cages in the multinational food industry, in government establishments devoted to finding the newest and best weapons for humans to kill each other, and in laboratories where often the most important thing being researched is the latest in lipsticks or face creams.

We may not, as a matter of strict moral theory, be committing an injustice against these victims of human vanity and greed. We may not, as I have argued, be violating their rights. But we must stop thinking that only by violating a right can we be cruel, malicious, avaricious, conceited, vainglorious, envious and plain degrading. Every act of cruelty for cruelty's sake disgraces and degrades us. It is often said that fox-hunters, for example, glory in cruelty and bloodlust. I doubt that this is generally true, but if it were, fox-hunting would not be a justifiable use of a person's time and leisure. It is wrong to cause pain to an animal for the sake of causing pain. However, on the Principle of Double Effect, it is permissible to allow foreseen but unintended pain or suffering for the sake of a beneficial purpose if the achievement of that purpose does not have as its means the doing of an act intrinsically wrong in itself, and if there is a proportion between the benefits conferred by that purpose and the evil of the suffering. So, if fox-hunters can prove that what they aim at is the eradication of a pest that destroys farmers' livestock, and/or the benefits conferred by horse-riding in the fresh air, the 'thrill of the chase', the pleasure given to dogs who like nothing more than to pursue and kill foxes, the protection of the countryside, and the like, then their pastime is legitimate. But cruelty for the sake of it is not, and a practice such as bullfighting seems to aim precisely at the pain and suffering of the bull. The point is that each case of the use of animals must be assessed on its merits, with due attention to whether what is aimed at is cruel, degrading, or otherwise set against the virtuous life that human beings are duty-bound to live.

As I said, the scale and suffering of animals is unprecedented in our time. In previous, supposedly 'unenlightened' ages, much of what is done to animals in our day would have been unthinkable. Perhaps we can learn from a previous way of life. This was a kind of life in which modesty was the guiding principle: aversion to luxurious living, attention to necessities such as food, clothing and shelter, and respect for nature. If a return to this sort of attitude meant that 99 per cent of animal experiments were discarded, then so be it. If it meant that women did not parade around in fur coats (unless they lived in Siberia or Alaska), so be it. If it meant the end of bullfights, or of Draize eye tests for the latest kind of shampoo,[30] so be it. If it meant a return to organic farming and the end of mass production lines for inedible second-rate food, so be it. What seems to be a paradox – the denial of animal rights coupled with a significant respect for every sentient creature – is nothing of the sort.

4
Capital Punishment

4.1 A Conflict?

In chapter 4 of *Moral Theory* I outlined the case for the doctrine of the sanctity of human life, and have followed on in this volume by arguing for the immorality of both abortion and euthanasia. I have then drawn a distinction between humans and other animals, and argued that the right to life is possessed only by humans, since animals are not right-holders. Now I want to turn back. Are there cases where it *is* legitimate to take human life? In traditional moral theory, capital punishment has always been seen as just such a case.

Nevertheless, we have in the last few decades seen capital punishment coming under attack. Just as the 1960s saw abortion legalised in many parts of the world, as well as the first stirrings of the movement for legalising euthanasia, so in the 1960s some countries moved to outlaw the death penalty. In Britain, for instance, it was abolished in 1965 for all crimes except treason and piracy. (These, too, are no longer subject to the death penalty since the coming into force of the European Convention on Human Rights in 2000.) In Australia it was also abolished for most crimes in the 1960s, with full abolition in 1985. In Ireland it was abolished in 1964 for all but a handful of crimes. Other countries moved much earlier, Holland for instance banning it for most crimes in 1870 and Denmark in 1930. In the European Union (at the time of writing), only Belgium retains the death penalty for 'ordinary crimes' (not involving treason) but does not use it. Most European countries have ratified Protocol 6 of the European Convention on Human Rights declaring its illegality in peacetime, and many others have signed or ratified similar international conventions. (It is not mentioned in the Universal Declaration of Human

Rights.) Nevertheless, surprisingly many countries still retain the death penalty. According to Amnesty International, as of 1999 the death penalty was wholly illegal in 67 countries, in 14 it was illegal for all but extraordinary crimes (such as treason), and 23 have abolished it *de facto*, in other words, kept it on the statute books without ever using it. That means over 90 countries retain the death penalty.[1]

Groups calling for the abolition of capital punishment have a vocal role in the media. They, along with many other people, believe the death penalty to be a barbaric relic from a cruel, bygone age. A country with the death penalty, they claim, is holding up a sign telling the world of its lack of moral progress. Capital punishment, they say, is nothing less than state-sponsored murder. The ethical progress being made by a world that grows more enlightened every day demands that the festering sore of state execution be banned everywhere.

What is upsetting to abolitionists, however, is the continuing prevalence of the death penalty throughout Asia and the Islamic countries; and what is especially disappointing is the fact that over three-quarters of US states have the death penalty on their statute books and use it. In 1976 the Supreme Court ruled that the death penalty was not a 'cruel and unusual punishment' and hence not prohibited under the Bill of Rights. (At the time of writing there are over 3,000 Americans on death row, and there were 56 executions in 1995.) Given that the USA is supposed to stand as 'the leader of the free world', as a bastion of liberty, decency and enlightenment, how can it be that it still allows the state-sanctioned killing of its citizens?

As for opponents of abortion and euthanasia, many of whom support the death penalty, isn't their position self-contradictory and repugnant to common sense? How can they profess to defend human life in one breath while supporting its extinction in another? How can any moral theory that has the sanctity of life at its core allow support for capital punishment? Shouldn't a true humanism oppose the deliberate killing of human beings in every circumstance?

Whenever I have spoken of the doctrine of the sanctity of life, I have explicitly or implicitly restricted it to the *innocent*. I have built into the doctrine an exception as far as the lives of 'guilty' people are concerned. To leave matters at that would, of course, not answer the objections just raised. Why make such an exception? Isn't this at best an arbitrary add-on clause depriving certain people of their right to life, and isn't it at worst the very negation of what the sanctity of life is supposed to mean?

In the following discussion I will try to make good the idea that the doctrine of the sanctity of life applies only to the lives of the innocent. In recent philosophical debate, the idea of punishment as such has been given a lot of attention. Philosophers have asked such questions as: What is punishment? What is its purpose? Is it justified? On the other hand, relatively little attention has been given to the particular topic of capital punishment. Although one can only speculate, my suspicion is that most ethicists in our day believe not only that capital punishment is wrong, but that there is simply no intellectually respectable case for it. Hence the debate in philosophical circles is rarely joined. What I hope to do is to show that this belief is mistaken. There is a philosophically sound case to be made for capital punishment – it is, arguably, a scandal that philosophers have not made the case more often – and it coheres perfectly well with the defence of innocent life. Far from its being schizophrenic to espouse both positions, as many believe, I will argue that it is more than reasonable.

4.2   Punishment – General Principles

In order to make out the case for capital punishment, however, it is necessary to make some assumptions. As has been done throughout this book and its companion, I continue to assume that people have free will and are capable of choosing between right and wrong. For determinists, who do not believe in free will, the case for capital punishment cannot get started because the case for *any kind* of punishment cannot get started. If people cannot make free choices because everything they do is determined, say, by their genes, or their environment, or their upbringing, or some combination of these, then punishment as such is wrong because it implies that the 'wrongdoer' made a free choice. It would be wrong, though, to infer that determinists would not allow a kind of surrogate for punishment. Some believe every 'wrongdoer' needs medical or psychological attention, or a better standard of living, or a more supportive social network. Few people would refuse the latter two, but what if someone refused psychological counselling? Determinists would not say the person *deserved* counselling, but they may well advocate the use of *force* – that is, compelling the recalcitrant 'wrongdoer' to be counselled – in order to stop the person's being a danger to society. And while the determinist might not advocate capital *punishment*, he may well advocate the killing of a 'serious wrongdoer' in order permanently to rid society of a danger.

We can remove the inverted commas, however, and speak of wrongdoers pure and simple. People do have free will and can choose between right and wrong, whatever the influences on their behaviour. (See chapter 1 of *Moral Theory* where this was discussed.) This granted, however, does it follow that punishment is ever justified? Here I want to make another assumption, namely that there is nothing wrong, or incoherent, or absurd, or unreasonable in the concept of punishment itself.[2] True, although you are likely to be a determinist if you do not believe in punishment at all, you might still believe in liberty of the will. You might believe that punishment is cruel in itself and therefore always wrong, that wrongdoers need counselling, advice, emotional support, a higher standard of living, pretty much the same things the determinist will suggest as ways to prevent a person from harming society again. This is not a debate I will enter into; only a few observations need to be made to show the absurdity of rejecting punishment as being ever justified. The opponent of punishment, to be consistent, must think it wrong in every case. He must oppose the punishment of children by their parents, of pupils by their teachers, of employees by their employers (is dismissal a form of punishment? If so, should all employees have guaranteed lifetime tenure?), of soldiers by their commanding officers, of team members by their coaches, of congressmen by their party leaders, of presidents by the voters (should a president never be voted out of office as a punishment?), and so on. The fact is that even in the most 'democratic' society there are hierarchical structures everywhere you look; there are people in authority and people who are subordinate to authority. Without the right of lawful authority to punish disobedience, misbehaviour, insubordination, inadequate performance, and the like, authority is authority in name only. Without the discipline of punishment there would, literally, be anarchy, no matter how much counselling and emotional support wrongdoers received.

I do not propose, then, to justify punishment as such. Nevertheless, it is necessary to give a brief outline of just how punishment is conceived on a traditional ethical model, as a precursor to making the case for capital punishment in particular. On the traditional model, punishment has three main functions, all of which will be performed in the ideal case: (1) it is *retributive*, vindicating the rights of the injured party, compelling the wrongdoer to pay the debt he has incurred by his offence; (2) it is *corrective*, reforming and rehabilitating the offender so that he can take his place again as a law-abiding member of society; (3) it is *deterrent*, sending a warning to other members of the community of the penalty for breaking the law. Some remarks about each function are in order.

(1) *Retribution.* This involves the notion of 'restoring the moral balance', or 'restoring justice'. Justice is sometimes portrayed (as on the top of the Old Bailey in London) as a blindfolded woman holding a scale in one hand and a sword in the other. What this means is that the administration of justice is impartial, and involves the imposition of a penalty after the due weighing of the moral balance in order to determine the existence and degree of gravity of an offence. Retribution is sometimes thought to involve a kind of 'annulment' or cancellation of an offence against the law (that is to say, the moral law as embodied in the positive law of the land) by the imposition of a penalty on the offender. Again, the annulment might be thought of as a kind of *restitution*, or 'setting things right'. But the crucial feature common to all understandings of punishment as retribution is that it requires *guilt* or *responsibility*. Punishment *implies* guilt, in the sense that if the state penalises someone knowing or at least *believing* him to be innocent (the knowledge/belief is actually held by the judge, jury, or whomever administers justice in the name of the state), then either it has administered punishment unjustly or – perhaps a better interpretation – it has not administered *punishment* at all.

Now is not the place to go into the complex and interesting discussion of how retribution is exactly to be understood. Critics of the concept of retribution say that all these ideas of restoring the balance, cancelling the offence, setting things right, and so on, are just so many metaphors with no logical or coherent moral basis. In response, all I will say here is that we know exactly what 'setting things right' means, and 'restoring the balance' and related expressions; not everyone will be able to give a detailed philosophical exposition of the meaning, but intuitive understanding is still a form of understanding. Certainly part of the idea of retribution is the notion of *restitution*, a restoration back to good order of a world (community) in which order has been disturbed. It is not restitution *to the victim* that matters here: the victim's loss (or his family's) is made good by separate procedures for compensation, which is not itself necessarily punitive, though it may be if the compensation comes from the offender himself. (The practice of making the offender pay in dollars and cents as well as in loss of liberty is making a comeback in many jurisdictions, and should be welcomed.) The restitution brought about by punishment is made to society and to the moral law itself; and to the objection that imprisonment, or execution, or some other punishment does not really restore things to the way they were before, since no punishment can undo what has been done (Plato's objection to retribution), we can reply that *no* restitution, whether criminal or civil, can ever undo the past. Even the most severe punishment cannot bring back a murder victim, or re-create what has been destroyed.

Perhaps we can get a better handle on the idea of retribution by focusing on the concept of *forfeiture*.[3] Forfeiture helps us to understand how rights figure in moral theory (how they 'behave', as it were). For instance, George may have won a competition entitling him to attend a gala film première, but the terms may stipulate that if he does not take up the offer by a certain date the prize will go to the runner-up. If he declines the offer, he forfeits his right to go. Obviously there is no wrongdoing on his part; he forfeits by inactivity. Or again, if Fred goes insane he may forfeit his right to vote in elections or stand for office; again, there is no fault on his part. With punishment, however, there is forfeiture with fault or wrongdoing. If Maria commits a heinous crime, she may forfeit her right to liberty for the rest of her life. Punishment requires the doing of something by a person to make the infliction of some form of pain or suffering (by the lawful authority) justified.

But isn't retribution just another word for vengeance? And isn't vengeance a bad thing? To this common objection it must be replied, first, that vengeance is not of itself evil. The media in England recently reported the story of a man found guilty of the brutal, savage murder of a woman and one of her daughters and the attempted murder of a second daughter. After the verdict, the distraught husband and father of the victims was reported as saying he harboured thoughts of wanting to make the killer suffer: 'I know they [the thoughts] are cruel but I can't help it. He tortured me and Josie [the daughter who survived the ordeal]. I would like to see his head chopped off. I would do it myself.' There is nothing positively evil or bad about vindictive thoughts such as these. They come from deep in human nature, and have been felt by all of us at some time in our lives, in some context. As such, they cannot be positively evil because there *is* no positive evil in human nature. Human evil comes primarily from two sources: a *lack* or *absence* of goodness, as for instance when we say that someone lacks pity, or honesty, or integrity; and the *abuse* or *misuse* of capacities that are not in themselves bad. People say that many crimes are committed because of vengeance; the response is that just as many, if not more, are committed because of love. It is not the feeling of revenge itself that is wrong, but the abuse of that feeling by, say, taking the law into your own hands. (Even that is sometimes justified, say when an outrage has been committed and the penal system positively acts against or obstructs the administration of justice; but the details of the morality of private retribution cannot be explored here.)

(2) *Correction.* Another aim of punishment is the reform and rehabilitation of the offender. (The actual prevention of further wrongdoing by the offender is best seen as part of correction rather than of general deterrence – but only a small part, all the same.) This, of course, presupposes responsibility, as does retribution: the offender should be made to see the error of his ways, the wrong that he has done, and encouraged both to feel remorse for it and to amend his ways so that he does not break the law again. We can also speak of this aspect of punishment as chastisement, aimed at teaching the offender a lesson. Since it presupposes that the offender has free will and knows or can be made to know he has done wrong, correction can never involve treating the offender as anything but a free, rational being. Sometimes, of course, correction might involve the limited use of, say, psychological techniques that work on a person's blind impulses, uncontrollable vices, and other character traits that are not wholly under rational control. But that is not incompatible with treating the person *as* a person rather than a machine or stimulus-response unit; many of us need such techniques for eliminating tendencies to immoral behaviour, and we can even apply them by ourselves, with some training. (You might, for instance, use aversion therapy to stop overeating, or acupuncture to give up smoking.) What correction does rule out is brainwashing (think of the attempt to 'cure' Alex in *A Clockwork Orange*), psychosurgery (think of the lobotomy performed on the 1930s Hollywood actress Frances Farmer to 'cure' her nonconformity), and any other intervention that fails to respect the individual as a free, rational being who can only truly come back to the right path with the consent of his will and a genuine inner desire to make amends. Needless to say, the penal system in many countries today is barely conducive to such reform. Imprisonment can be implemented in a far better way than it usually is, with the offender reformed rather than brutalised, addicted to drugs and ready to commit another crime as soon as he is released. Penal reform groups are right to insist on the role of counselling, education, emotional support, and so on; the problem is that they sometimes seem to be saying that punishment is wrong in itself and that criminals must be 'cured' rather than corrected.

(3) *Deterrence.* The third aim of punishment is to deter other members

of the community from breaking the law, in particular from committing the same crime as that for which the offender is being punished. On the consequentialist view, this is the primary end of punishment, and the correction of the offender is seen as just another element in the general objective of deterring criminal behaviour. (On the present theory, however, correction involves more than the mere prevention of further wrongdoing by the offender.) In a famous statement, the father of utilitarianism, Jeremy Bentham, said: 'all punishment is mischief: all punishment in itself is evil'. So when is it justified? 'Upon the principle of utility, if it ought at all to be admitted in as far as it promises to exclude some greater evil.' And Bentham goes on to say: 'The immediate principal end of punishment is to control action. This action is either that of the offender, or of others.'[4]

This is the consequentialist approach to punishment in a nutshell. The notion of retribution is, for the consequentialist, either incoherent or an excuse for the infliction of suffering, something that is always at least *prima facie* wrong. Since the infliction of suffering can only be justified by the prospect of reducing a greater amount of suffering than that inflicted or promoting an amount of benefit sufficient to outweigh the suffering, punishment is only justified because of its likely deterrent effects. But what, it might be asked, if a particular instance of punishment does not have sufficient deterrent value? No doubt this is often the case: sending Fred to jail for shoplifting, say, may well have no preventive effect on him – he may well be encouraged to commit *more* crimes as a result of his stay in a 'school of crime' – and may not register as more than a blip in the thinking of other would-be shoplifters. The consequentialist response, as should be obvious by now, is typically to move up a level and justify the *institution* of punishment on consequentialist grounds. True, Fred's three-month sentence may not deter him or anyone else from shoplifting; but what if the punishment of shoplifters were abolished – wouldn't shoplifting become rampant (or more rampant than it already is)? Surely we should agree with the consequentialist on this. One can argue at length about the actual deterrent effects of punishment in modern society, but the indisputable fact remains that if punishment was abolished, crime would skyrocket. As John Cottingham points out:

In fact, between those on one side who would be determined to continue with crime come what may, and those on the other side for whom any criminal act would be inconceivable, there is likely to be a sizeable middle group who might be tempted to offend, were it not for the penalty. . . . Most of us, fortunately, do not find murder a tempting option, but in the case of crimes like smuggling and tax evasion the risk of punishment (and its associated disadvantages such as the stigma of having a criminal record) probably play an important role for many people. Even crimes people do not normally contemplate might in time become tempting if punishment were abolished. If, for example, there were no penalty for shoplifting, and every day we saw people loading up with free goods and getting away with it, then within weeks or months all but a few of the most austerely high-principled citizens would probably be tempted to join in the bonanza.[5]

Another fact the consequentialist will appeal to is that at least while Fred is in prison it is guaranteed that *he* will not offend, and this must be factored into the calculation of harms and benefits.

Although these observations about the effectiveness of deterrence (including individual prevention) are correct, they demonstrate the immorality at the heart of consequentialist thinking about punishment. For if deterrence, or 'the control of action', to use Bentham's phrase, is all that matters, justice itself goes out of the window. It will be open to the consequentialist to justify the punishment of an *innocent* man on the condition that this has sufficient deterrent value to outweigh the harm done to him, including his (and maybe other people's) psychological torment at the thought of being an innocent victim of punishment. Consider the case of the judge who is ordered by a rioting mob to condemn an innocent man lest they go on the rampage and cause far more suffering than that which will be caused to the victim. For the consequentialist, the condemnation will be positively obligatory if the calculation of harms and benefits requires it. If controlling action is the objective, the distinction between guilt and innocence is irrelevant and what matters is the 'greater benefit' to society of exerting that control. To take a real-life example, on what grounds could a consequentialist condemn Stalin's show-trials of the 1930s, which involved trumped-up charges against Party members as a means to removing the obstacles they presented to Stalin's plans for the Soviet Union? Well, the consequentialist will point to facts with which we can happily agree: that Stalin's plans were more likely to bring misery than prosperity; that communism itself is an evil doctrine (though for the non-consequentialist the evil of communism is more than a function of the suffering it causes); perhaps that the trials, once made known to the world, caused more outrage to more people than satisfaction to the much smaller group of Stalinists behind it. But what about the mere fact that people were condemned for things they had not done? Wasn't this wrong in itself, a gross injustice? It is hard to see how the consequentialist can object to *this* aspect of the trials, and if it had turned out that Stalinism did indeed bring prosperity and happiness to the people of the Soviet Union, the whole process would have been legitimate, if not *obligatory*, on consequentialist grounds.

We have seen, of course, that the consequentialist has a ready response in the form of an appeal to *rules* (see chapter 2 of *Moral Theory*). Just as punishment must be justified by its *overall* utility rather than the utility of this or that case, so the non-punishment of the innocent must be defended as an integral rule in a judicial system justified on consequentialist grounds. The abandonment of that rule might provide a net benefit in individual cases, but an almost certain negative value in the long run (however long the long run is supposed to be). Now, the act consequentialist, as was pointed out in the first volume, makes plausible criticisms of the very idea of appealing to rules rather than assessing action by reference to individual cases. But leaving that to one side, and accepting for the moment the idea of justification in terms of rules, again we may ask what the consequentialist would have to say about the conceivability of a situation in which at least the occasional punishment of the innocent maintained the very fabric and stability of a society. What about a society that practised a form of religion requiring the monthly sacrifice of an innocent girl to the Sun God? Moreover, it is certain that there *have* been such societies in recorded history. It is no use replying that *in those societies* the victims of sacrifice were considered guilty (maybe of some offence against the deity), because (1) this was not always the case and (2) what I am suggesting is the *conceivability* of a society in which, *even by that society's own standards*, the sacrificial victim is innocent, but is offered up to placate the rest. Isn't this intrinsically evil? But if it preserves the social order, and if abandoning the practice would lead to social disaster, how can the consequentialist condemn it? The very basis of rule-consequentialist thinking on the non-punishment of the innocent is, I claim, perverse: far from being concerned about the only fact that matters, namely that an innocent person is condemned, what he focuses on is the net benefit of following a rule that preserves the innocent from punishment. Not only, has it been argued, does this allow theoretically and in practice for gross injustice, but it means looking *completely in the wrong direction* for the reason why punishment of the innocent is wrong.

As for the benefit to society of keeping an offender in prison which accrues from his not being able to offend while incarcerated, this can never be the primary purpose of punishment. Otherwise, why not keep the offender in prison for years beyond what his offence merits, in order to stop him offending again? Mightn't the benefit to society of having a burglar off the streets for the rest of his life outweigh the harm to the burglar by having his liberty curtailed? And yet we would be right to regard life imprisonment for burglary as grossly unjust. Further, why not imprison people *before* they commit a crime, if they are assessed as being a risk? If someone is thought to carry a *small* risk of committing a *major* crime – say, assassinating the President of the USA – why not put him behind bars for life before he does anything remotely wrong? Again, we can see the injustice in such a proposal, but if preventing an individual from offending is what matters most, actual guilt or innocence, or proportionality between crime and punishment, are at best only secondary considerations.

Given these three primary aims of punishment, retribution, correction and deterrence, should we say that all three are always necessary for an act of punishment to be justified? First, note that these aims are ideals that are not always attainable. If perfect retribution means restoring what was lost as part of the restoration of the moral balance, then retribution can never be perfect. What is done cannot be undone – a life taken cannot be restored – but this does not mean the penal system should not try to restore moral order to the best of its ability. (Hence the relatively recent introduction of criminal injuries compensation alongside punishment is to be welcomed, even if the compensation comes from the state rather than the offender.) Similarly, some offenders are incorrigible, but this does not mean attempts should not be made to correct them, or that correction as a general aim of punishment is pointless. And some people are simply not deterred by the threat of punishment, especially those who know they are unlikely to be caught; but this does not mean deterrence is futile. We must not, therefore, think that one or other of these aims can be dispensed with because they are never completely achieved. Second, it is unlikely, I would argue, that failure to punish is always wrong when deterrence and correction are impossible in the particular case. The initial guilt of the offender is non-negotiable; responsibility is the *minimal* condition for a just punishment and penal system. But should we agree with Kant when he says that even if a society were to dissolve, the last murderer remaining in prison should be executed (assuming execution to be permissible)?[26] In other words, must every crime be punished irrespective of whether correction or deterrence will be achieved?

The reason we should not perhaps be strict about this involves the role of the state as administrator of punishment. There are several reasons why the state must punish crime rather than leaving it to private citizens. First, the state's basic function is to prevent anarchy, and leaving punishment in the hands of the citizens would create a Wild-West scenario of private vendettas, mob violence and civil unrest. (I assume the Wild West is just another Hollywood fiction.) Note that the only thing that is consequentialist about this reason for state punishment is that it is concerned with consequences! It can never be stressed enough that not being a consequentialist does not mean that as a moral theorist you shouldn't be concerned with consequences. Rather, you should not make consequences the primary or sole standard of evaluation. On the present theory, the state has the function of preventing social disorder, but it cannot do so by any means – such as punishing the innocent – because maximisation of good consequences is not the primary aim of morality, including the morality of the state. Second, the state also has the function of promoting morality, both public and private. It is never the *arbiter* of right and wrong – this is determined by the higher law of morality itself, to which all states are subject – but it is always obliged to preserve and promote the good and contain or even eliminate the bad. This means that the state has the role of punishing the *moral* infringement involved in a crime, usually indirectly, by upholding the public law. The primary concern of the victim of an offence is the *injury* to himself, his loved ones or his property. But it is for the state to deal with the crime in its moral and legal dimension. Third, private wrongs by citizens against each other, especially when they involve an offence against the criminal law, are also a breach of the public peace and social order, and hence a crime is by its nature an offence against the state as well as the individual. Hence the state has a legitimate interest in rectifying the injury to it by employing the penal system. Finally, the punishment of a crime requires *due process* (except in an emergency, such as when deserters are summarily punished in time of war), and the state is more easily capable of maintaining neutrality than if punishment is left in the hands of aggrieved individuals.

For all these reasons, which together embody the essential function of the state to promote the *common good*, it seems that the state would not be acting in an obviously wrong manner if it failed to punish where correction and deterrence really were futile (which, as noted, is hardly ever the case). Failure to punish can sometimes be seen as tacit approval of an offence – punishment works also as a kind of *denunciation* by society of a wrong done – but such a failure does not necessarily imply approval, and in the fanciful case envisaged by Kant, it is hard to see what wrong is committed if the last murderer goes unpunished. (Maybe the dissolving society should issue a proclamation denouncing the last murderer's crimes before it ceases to exist!)

To put the point in more exact terms, if only the retributive aim of punishment can be satisfied in a particular community in particular circumstances, the state is not *obliged* to punish anyway, so a failure to punish would not be wrong. But nor is the state obliged to *refrain* from punishing, so it would not be doing wrong if it *did* punish. When only retribution can be achieved, punishment is still permissible – the state is well within its rights to punish – but it is probably not obligatory. Compare this to the case where there is no guilt but punishment would have a deterrent effect. To punish in such a circumstance is *always* wrong, no matter what the other facts may be. In this way we can see why retribution is the *primary* aim of punishment: guilt is always necessary for punishment to be justified; deterrence (and correction) are not strictly necessary but usually required as part of the ideal that punishment is supposed to achieve; and all three aims are clearly *sufficient* for punishment to be justified.

4.3   Capital Punishment – The Argument

Having laid down the general principles of punishment that are a part of traditional ethical theory, I will now present the philosophical argument for capital punishment, making an appeal to those principles where necessary. In making out the case, it will be seen that there is no conflict at all between the defence of the sanctity of innocent life and the idea that the life of the guilty can sometimes be forfeited.

The first step in the argument is the proposition that punishment is sometimes justified, and we have already assumed this as self-evident. The second step is the proposition that sometimes the state has the right to punish an individual, following due judicial process. This claim has already been made out in the explanation of why it is proper for the state to punish breaches of the criminal law. Not only does the state have the right to punish, but it is *obliged* (in the usual case) to take on this job when a crime has been committed. In case the sceptic is still not convinced, consider some examples. Does the state have the right to punish unjust racial discrimination? Or child abuse? Or slavery? (In case you think slavery is an outdated subject, there continues to be a traffic in children between West and East for the purposes of cheap labour, sexual perversion and other immoralities. The traffic involves large sums of money and is arguably a form of slave trade. The same goes for young women lured from poor countries to the West for prostitution, where their conditions and the restrictions on their movement amount to a kind of slavery.) The proposition that the state has the right to punish seems as evident as the proposition that punishment is sometimes justified.

The third step in the argument is the proposition that some punishments are worse than others. Again, it is hard to see how this could be false. Ten years in prison is worse than a \$1,000 fine. A \$1,000 fine is worse than a three-month good-behaviour bond. A life sentence is worse than all of these. Naturally, which punishment is worse than which is to some extent relative to the individual: a rich person might find a \$1,000 fine much less of an inconvenience than a good-behaviour bond. But this does not negate the claim that some penalties are worse than others: we can give a rough and ready scale of penalties ordered in terms of how bad they would be for the average person (there will be plenty of vague elements in this; what do we mean by 'average', for a start?), and we can also give a scale for each individual, at least in principle, taking into account his particular circumstances. In any case, very few people indeed would ever deny that a life sentence was worse than ten years in prison, assuming the prison conditions were the same in both instancee.

The fourth step is the proposition that there is such a thing as the worst possible punishment. This is a reasonable claim; surely there must be *something* that is the worst possible thing that can be done to a person. What if the opposite were true, that there was no worst possible punishment? Then it would have to be the case that there was an infinite series of possible punishments, each one worse than the one preceding it. But since man is mortal, it is hard to see how this could possibly be the case. If he lived on this earth forever, you might say, 'Imagine someone's being in jail for a hundred years, then a hundred years and a day, a hundred years and two days', and so on to infinity, and you could plausibly say that each punishment was a bit worse than the previous one. But given our mortality, there must be a limit to how many of these punishments are genuinely possible. How else might you prove that there was no such thing as the worst possible punishment? I cannot see how, and the fact that we are mortal and in every respect finite beings means that the burden of proof is on the sceptic to make out his case. Until we see such a case, we can safely say that there must be such a thing as the worst possible punishment.

The fifth step in the argument is the principle of proportionality, which has already been touched on, namely that the punishment must fit the crime. Now as Aristotle pointed out, this does not mean that punishment must be in kind. 'An eye for an eye' does *not* mean that a rapist should be raped, or that a fraudster should be defrauded. It means simply that punishment should in some way match the gravity of the crime committed. This is a standard and essential part of judicial sentencing procedure and it is also integral to every act of punishment carried out by a parent on a child, a teacher on a pupil, and so on: if the punishment does not fit the crime then justice is compromised either in favour of the offender (undue leniency) or against him (undue severity). We should not pretend for a moment that decisions about what is a proportionate punishment for a given offence are always easy to make. Even experts such as judges get it wrong. Sometimes the answer is vague – should this burglar be given two or three years? The judge may have to make some decision, at least safe in the knowledge that neither sentence is manifestly unjust. The same thing occurs when governments decide on what the speed limit should be, or the age at which people can drink in a bar. Determining the proportionality of a punishment is often vague, always complex, and requires great sensitivity to circumstance. But the simple fact is that the principle of proportionality is about as close to a basic principle of justice as you can get. Without it, society opens itself up to the possibility of arbitrary tyranny and unimaginable cruelty. Since proportionality is bound up with the concept of retribution, and the consequentialist thinks retribution is a meaningless idea or else a relic of a less enlightened age, we can conclude that, at least in theory, consequentialism allows for just such tyranny and cruelty, whatever the hedges the consequentialist may build into his favourite system.

Granted that you accept the principle of proportionality, we can move to the sixth step in the argument, which is the proposition that there is such a thing as the worst possible crime. This is as plausible as the claim that there is such a thing as the worst possible punishment, but it needs to be understood correctly. In one sense it seems that there is no worst possible crime, particularly because of the problem of incommensurability.

How do you compare in degree of evil the crimes against humanity committed by Hitler and Stalin? What about, say, human sacrifice compared to cannibalism? What about massive drug-dealing as against blowing up a plane full of innocent people? What about raping, torturing and disembowelling a 75-year-old woman compared with the same crime committed against a ten year-old girl? It is clear that there is a certain amount of incommensurability here, where only rough and ready comparisons can sometimes be made. But this does not prevent the reasonable selection of, say, a class of heinous crimes as a rough comparison class and then claiming that no crime is worse than anything in that class. Nor is it a question of numbers. It is not plausible to say that there is an infinity of crimes ordered by degree of evil because of the conceivability of murdering ten innocent people, then eleven (worse than ten), then twelve (worse than eleven), and so on to infinity. The number of people murdered does, in a sense, make a difference to the degree of evil, but in a more basic sense it is true to say that the murder of one person is as bad as the murder of ten, and that if we select murder as the worst possible crime, this should cover *all* murders, no matter how many victims there are in each case. So it is, I maintain, plausible to say that there is such a thing as the worst possible crime, that in fact there are numerous crimes that are *all* the worst possible, even if it takes some work to state just what that class of crimes contains.

Now, with these six steps in the argument at hand, we need to make some logical deductions, before tackling one further matter and then proceeding to objections. If there is a worst possible punishment, and a worst possible crime, then, given the principle of proportionality, it follows as a matter of logic that the worst possible crime deserves the worst possible punishment. The further matter that needs to be tackled is the question of what the worst possible punishment is. Here it is plausible to claim that being put to death is the worst possible punishment, because death is the greatest possible evil, and the worst punishment is simply the infliction of the greatest evil. It will be disputed by many people that death is indeed the greatest evil. Some will say, echoing the Spanish communist fighter against Franco, La Pasionaria, 'it is better to die on your feet than live on your knees'. Others will say, following Socrates, that it is better to suffer evil than to do it, and hence better to suffer death than murder another. Millions of Christian martyrs suffered appalling deaths rather than sacrifice to pagan gods. Now whatever the correctness of attitudes such as these (and in fact they are all praiseworthy), to say that they are inconsistent with the idea that death is the greatest evil involves a confusion. These attitudes embody the idea that some acts are so wrong, so immoral, that it is better morally *to suffer the greatest evil, namely death*, than to commit those acts. It is, for instance, more noble, more fitting, more admirable, praiseworthy, honourable, courageous, and so on, to die fighting than to submit to tyranny. But such an attitude *already presupposes* that death is the greatest evil – that is precisely the reason why it is always death to which the chosen dishonourable act is compared, rather than great pain and suffering or some other evil. To say that death is the greatest evil is not in itself to make a moral claim; sometimes the point is made by saying that death is the greatest *physical* evil that can befall a person, but we can also say simply that death is the worst possible thing that can happen to a person.

Another reason that someone might deny death was the greatest evil comes from utilitarianism, that brand of consequentialism which makes pain and suffering the worst of all evils. We can see this question given a classic examination by John Stuart Mill is his 1868 speech to the British Parliament in favour of capital punishment.[7] He puts utilitarianism in a nutshell when he says: 'It is not human life only, not human life as such, that ought to be sacred to us, but human feelings. The human capacity of suffering is what we should cause to be respected, not the mere capacity of existing.'[8] And he asks:

> What comparison can there really be, in point of severity, between consigning a man to the short pang of a rapid death, and immuring him in a living tomb, there to linger out what may be a long life in the hardest and most monotonous toil [Mill is thinking of life in prison with hard labour], without any of its alleviations or rewards – debarred from all pleasant sights and sounds, and cut off from all earthly hope, except a slight mitigation of bodily restraint, or a small improvement of diet?[9]

He even goes so far as to say that to be 'so much more shocked by taking a man's life than by depriving him of all that makes life desirable or valuable' is to fall into 'an enervation, an effeminancy [sic]'.[10] But in saying this he clearly has in mind thinking, reflective souls such as himself, because he also believes that the masses are on the whole more shocked by the prospect of death than of life in prison, and that the threat of the death penalty is a genuine deterrent to serious crime; if it ever ceased to be so, he adds, then it would be time to abolish it. And since the masses are deterred, that is a good enough reason to maintain the death penalty even though, *in reality*, it is a lesser punishment than life imprisonment:

> Yet even such a lot as this [life with hard labour], because there is no one moment at which the suffering is of terrifying intensity, and, above all, because it does not contain the element, so imposing to the imagination, of the unknown, is universally reputed a milder punishment than death – [it] stands in all codes as a mitigation of the capital penalty [death], and is thankfully accepted as such. For it is characteristic of all punishments which depend on duration for their efficacy . . . that they are more rigorous than they seem; while it is, on the contrary, one of the strongest recommendations a punishment can have, that it should seem more rigorous than it is; for its practical power depends far less on what it is than on what it seems. There is not, I should think, any human infliction which makes an impression on the imagination so entirely out of proportion to its real severity as the punishment of death. The punishment must be mild indeed which does not add more to the sum of human misery than is necessarily or directly added by the execution of a criminal.[11]

Mill's implication is unmistakable. Life in prison is worse than death, but the masses fear death more than they fear life in prison, so the government should exploit this philosophical misunderstanding on the part of the populace (a misunderstanding not shared by right-thinking utilitarians) by maintaining the death penalty with all the fear of the unknown associated with it, and should indeed – one supposes – *lie* to the people about just how bad a thing death is. This sort of duplicity in utilitarian and consequentialist thinking has been observed already (see chapter 4 of *Moral Theory*, where the 'levels' thesis of Hare and Singer is discussed), and can even be traced back to Plato's belief that in his ideal society the masses should be told a 'noble lie' (a myth, that is, a useful falsehood) about why they have the lowly place they do. (Is it just a coincidence that Plato was also a deterrence theorist about punishment?)

If we are not utilitarians, however, we will see no reason for regarding life in prison, with or without hard labour, as worse than death. Death may be instantaneous, and it may even be painless, but it still means the extinction of all possibility of pursuit of any goods whatsoever. The aim of morality is to live a good life, to pursue the good, since this is what fulfils human nature. But since you cannot pursue a good life without being alive in the first place, death means the elimination of the precondition of trying to achieve the fundamental aim of morality. In other words, death frustrates the pursuit of the most important thing there is to pursue, namely goodness. So it must be the greatest evil, and therefore being put to death must, as a matter of conceptual necessity, be the greatest punishment.

As a further, *ad hominem*, point, note that opponents of capital punishment frequently base their opposition on the *finality* of death: 'But death is so final, it is irreversible, and where there's life there's always hope.' We should agree, and say that this attitude *shows* that they too regard death as the greatest evil and being put to death as the greatest punishment.

So, if death is the greatest evil, then capital punishment is the worst punishment. But since the worst crime deserves the worst punishment, on the principle of proportionality, the person who commits the worst crime deserves to be put to death. Since there is a worst crime – for present purposes we do not need to determine what it must be (but consider the examples above) – it follows that there is at least one sort of crime that merits the death penalty. This is the case for capital punishment.

4.4   Objections

4.4.1   What if an innocent person is executed?

This is by far the most common objection to capital punishment. Given the emphasis I have laid on the protection of innocent life – one of morality's guiding principles – how can it be right to condone a kind of punishment that could lead to the greatest possible evil being inflicted on an innocent man? What about the seemingly endless number of miscarriages of justice that were highlighted in the British media in the 1980s and 1990s? Some of them may even have involved the actual execution of innocent people when the death penalty was still in force, and it has been pointed out that if it had still been in force throughout the 1970s and 1980s, a substantial number of other people would have gone to their deaths without having been guilty of the crimes for which they were executed. Can we allow ourselves the luxury of thinking that the judicial process in the USA might not – has not – also led to similar miscarriages? Can we believe that any legal system is perfect? And doesn't this mean that the death penalty has no place in any society, whatever theoretical place it may have in a mythical society with a perfect legal system?

The observations about the existence of miscarriages of justice cannot be denied. Nor can it be denied for a minute that the execution of an innocent person is a terrible injustice. But the situation is more complex than the opponent allows, and qualifications need to be made. First, it should be pointed out that allowing the death penalty in a society with a flawless legal system is at least not to deny *a priori* that there is a moral case for capital punishment. Still, that does not take us very far if no legal system is in fact flawless, given that morality is not just about ideals but about the practical realities of human existence.

So what should be said about capital punishment in a world of imperfect legal systems, where miscarriages of justice are a fact of life? First, punishment without due process is wrong, no matter what the punishment. Hence we should condemn punishment without due process (except in emergencies such as wartime). Turning to the question of the *failure* of due process, this could happen in one of two ways: first, a judge (or some other person in the justice system; let us use 'judge' to cover them all) might *intentionally* condemn an innocent person to death; second, a judge might *negligently* do so. Now the possibility of an innocent person's being punished, either intentionally or negligently, should be eliminated as far as possible from the legal system. We must add 'as far as possible', because that is all we can ask of judges and the other people who work in the system. Morality does not ask of people more than they are genuinely able to do, and as we saw, a flawless system is not possible in reality. The elimination as far as possible of intentional and negligent punishment, then, is an essential part of the legal system whether it allows the death penalty or not. It is not a requirement peculiar to the administration of this penalty. So one cannot object to the death penalty as such on the ground of possible failure of due process (or of its complete absence): this is an objection to the entire penal system.

If there is failure of due process, then the system must be condemned and repaired. And this necessity should not take second place to the administration of the system as a whole. What the need for repair might mean in practice is not only that the death penalty should be suspended until adequate repairs are made, but that leniency should be shown in respect of all severe punishments, including life imprisonment and long sentences. (Again, what 'long' means will depend on particular circumstances.) So the supporter of capital punishment can and should concede that in any judicial system where there is credible evidence of intentional or negligent infliction of penalties or other subversion of due process, capital punishment and other severe sentences should be suspended until the failures in the system are eliminated as far as humanly possible. But the death penalty does not merit special treatment simply because it is the most severe punishment of all.

As for the condemnation of an innocent person after due process, where all the procedures are followed properly and there is no suggestion of intentional or careless behaviour, the system and its administrators are not at fault. The execution of the innocent person would be a tragedy, on that we can agree – but what does the opponent of capital punishment propose? That the entire administration of justice should be suspended until even the slightest possibility of a wrongful conviction is eliminated? Given that any punishment of an innocent person is regrettable, does the proposal apply to punishment as such? But since accidental miscarriages will always occur, what the opponent is advocating is the permanent cessation of the legal system. This is an absurd and dangerous conclusion to reach, and is a recipe for anarchy.

4.4.2   Capital punishment is irreversible

The opponent of the death penalty will object that the above response misses the point of distinguishing between it and all other punishments. It is the finality of death that makes a difference. At least with other punishments compensation for wrongful conviction is possible, but you cannot compensate the dead. The death penalty is irreversible. That is why it should be suspended in perpetuity in all systems where there is even the slightest risk of wrongful conviction.

In reply, I would ask: can an innocent person be adequately compensated for 30 years spent in jail? Most people would doubt that any sum of money can replace the lost years – given the choice, no one would prefer 30 years in jail with $1 million at the end of it all than not to go to jail in the first place. So should long prison sentences be abolished as well? The opponent's rejoinder will be that in the case of prison sentences at least *something* can be done to make up for time spent; money and an apology go *some* of the way, even if they do not make up entirely for the loss. In reply, I ask whether the opponent believes in life sentences without parole, i.e. where 'life' means life (which it rarely does now). Nothing can be done to compensate the innocent man who dies in jail. But to reject life without parole along with capital punishment is to say that hideous murderers like Charles Manson or Myra Hindley should not stay in jail for the rest of their lives, which does not commend itself to one's natural sense of justice. Still, if the opponent of capital punishment, in the name of consistency, also calls for the abolition of life without parole, he should be asked: why should the possibility of compensation for wrongful conviction (even if the compensation is inadequate) be an essential part of the legal system? Why is a posthumous pardon insufficient, even if we accept that it is hardly a form of compensation? (Whether a posthumous pardon amounts to compensation at all is a difficult question, which hangs on whether a person can benefit from something after his death, which I have earlier suggested is doubtful. Certainly a pardon benefits his reputation, but does it benefit *him*?) Furthermore, why is compensation of and an apology to the victim's family (if he has one) insufficient? Why is a public declaration of the miscarriage of justice insufficient? It is up to the opponent of the death penalty to show why this is so, and why the possibility of some form of personal compensation is necessary.

4.4.3   Capital punishment is not a deterrent

The objection that capital punishment is not a deterrent has implicitly been answered already, but it is worth making the answer explicit. Deterrence is not the primary aim of punishment, but retribution, as was shown above. Retribution in the absence of deterrence is not intrinsically wrong, but deterrence in the absence of retribution (that is, in the absence of the proportional punishment of the guilty) is always wrong. It follows that if capital punishment does not deter in a specific community in particular circumstances, the state does no intrinsic wrong by continuing to administer it. Nevertheless, circumstances could conceivably make it such that continued administration of the death penalty was wrong on other grounds, such as imprudence. For it to become positively imprudent to maintain the death penalty, it would have to come into such disrepute, or in some way give rise to such social disorder, that the state was bound for the sake of peace and harmony (its overriding object) to desist from implementing it. But the state would still be obliged to mete out some punishment – such as life imprisonment – that was severe enough to be at least roughly proportional to the most grave offences proscribed by the law in that society.

The case for capital punishment that I have made out *justifies* its use, but only *obliges* its use when other circumstances are met, such as due process and the absence of overriding dangers to the common good. The mere fact that it does not deter serious crime is not in itself a reason against the penalty. Indeed, it could also be argued that capital punishment is *more* necessary when there is serious social disorder, even if the disorder is caused by contempt for the existence of that punishment itself, so serious is the obligation of the state to maintain law and order using all morally justifiable means.

Consider by analogy the case of parent and child. Suppose Maria is in the habit of giving her daughter a painful slap whenever she wilfully breaks anything in the house. The daughter has at least two choices: she can stop breaking things; or she can become even *more* rebellious by continuing to break things and then kicking and screaming as hard as she can when her mother goes to slap her. If she does the latter, then Maria has two choices: she can persevere in administering the painful slaps in the hope that eventually her daughter will see that it is futile to rebel; or she can become convinced of the futility of slapping her daughter, give in, and try something else, such as sending her to her room. Now the latter choice would not necessarily be wrong in the circumstances, particularly if Maria has become exhausted by having to engage in a frightful battle of body and will with her daughter every time she tries to slap her. On the other hand, as a parent, whose primary duty is to bring up her child as a well-behaved, virtuous individual, Maria is perhaps best advised to look ahead at what her daughter may be like in five years, or ten. If her daughter sees that by protesting sufficiently vigorously she can bring about the cessation of one kind of punishment, she may well think she can do this with other punishments and may end up with the mindset that enough rebelliousness can make any authority cave in. Similarly, in the case of capital punishment (and other state-inflicted penalties, for that matter), while general contempt for the punishment might in some circumstances make it advisable for the state to desist from administering it, it is arguably also well advised to persevere in the hope of preventing further and greater unrest in the future.

I have not mentioned the empirical evidence concerning the deterrent effect of capital punishment because, given the philosophical points just made, it is largely irrelevant. Far too often, at least in the media, the debate is conducted solely with reference to whether the penalty actually deters serious crime, with no examination of the false presupposition behind this approach, namely that deterrence is the primary aim of punishment. Still, the evidence is relevant to whether the deterrent objective of capital punishment is in fact being achieved, the state being obliged to try to meet that objective wherever possible in all its penalties. The evidence appears equivocal, however.[12] For instance, since the abolition of the death penalty in Britain violent crimes against the person have increased by 200 per cent and homicides by 60 per cent. Though superficially one might posit a connection, the increase in homicides and attempted homicides is far more plausibly put down to the general decay of moral standards in society than to abolition as such. Again, the homicide rate in the USA, where over three-quarters of the states have the death penalty and are not afraid to use it, is vastly higher than in Europe, where capital punishment barely exists. One might plausibly assume (though it is disputed) that the greater availability of guns makes a difference that all but cancels out the deterrent value of the death penalty, thus showing that deterrence must be considered within the broad context of what else is going on in a community. American states without the death penalty have a lower average homicide rate than those that do, and Texas, the state that has executed more people than any other since executions resumed in 1977 (after the landmark Supreme Court decisions), has one of the highest homicide rates in the country, more than double the average in states without the death penalty. (Other factors have to be taken into account, of course, such as ethnic tension, television and Hollywood violence, family breakdown, and arguably the easy availability of firearms.)

In Zambia, to take a very different country, the introduction of the death penalty for aggravated robbery in 1974 was followed by a sharp fall in the number of reported robberies for a short time, but then they rose again to record levels. The rise was thought to be largely due to the low detection rate, which all but cancelled out the deterrent effect of the death penalty in the minds of potential robbers. And in Nigeria, where a study was carried out in the 1980s, no consistent pattern was found linking the execution rate and the rate of murder or armed robbery. In some periods an increase in executions coincided with an increase in crime, in others there was a decline. The introduction of the death penalty for armed robbery in 1970 was followed by an increase in armed robberies. It has also been found in the USA and Britain, however, that the well-publicised execution of notorious criminals (such as Gary Gilmore) leads to a definite decline in homicides over a fairly short period (usually weeks), with a resumption in the expected rate in the longer term.

What we can say with some confidence is that whatever deterrent value the death penalty has is fairly easily cancelled out by other social factors. Nevertheless, it does have a *potential* deterrent effect that would only be fully realised if the following, sometimes unpleasant, conditions were met: (1) the state made it well known to each and every citizen that the death penalty existed *and* that it was prepared to use it; (2) due process was far swifter than the years of delay and legal wrangling that nearly always occur in the USA, which has the effect of reducing in the public mind the vivid association between crime and punishment; (3) each and every execution was well publicised, instead of the current undesirable situation (in the USA) where executions are watched by a handful of people and gain little publicity, whilst occasionally some 'big name' murderer captures the public imagination and becomes the subject of the talk shows for 15 minutes; (4) the state made clear its dedication to the pursuit and punishment of crime, no matter how small, and to the rule of justice, the law, and public decency and morality.

4.4.4   Capital punishment is just state-sanctioned murder

This is another common objection, but it is easily answered: the objection begs the question. The question is whether every killing is a murder. Clearly this is not so: there is murder, manslaughter of various kinds (called in some jurisdictions second-degree murder), accidental killing, and so on. There is also capital punishment. What the objector is really saying is that capital punishment is wrongful killing, only using the epithet 'murder' to describe it. But if the case made out earlier is sound, capital punishment is not wrongful killing. In order to subvert the case, then, the opponent of capital punishment would have to undermine one of its presuppositions, in particular, the presupposition that killing is not always wrong. He would, in other words, have to make out a case against the taking of human life in any circumstances whatsoever, including war and self-defence (see the next chapter). He would also have to concede that by doing so he was implicitly denying at least one of the premises of the argument in favour, for example that the punishment should always fit the crime, that the worst possible crime deserves the worst possible punishment, or maybe that punishment is sometimes justified. Suffice it to say that attacking the presuppositions of the argument in favour of the death penalty necessarily involves denying some principles that are very plausible in themselves, and more plausible than the principles the opponent is likely to appeal to in making out the case against.

4.4.5 Capital punishment is cruel and inhuman

Again, this begs the question of whether the argument presented above is sound. If it is, how can execution in itself be cruel or inhuman? By definition it cannot be. Does that mean, then, that painful execution should also be allowed in some cases? Evidently not, since it is execution *per se* that is not cruel or inhuman. If it were painful or degrading, it might well be. Death is the greatest physical evil, but within that species of evil there are varieties: painless death is the least bad variety of death, painful death is worse, agonising death is even worse, and agonising death accompanied by degrading mockery would be just about as bad a death as you could undergo. Some varieties of the greatest evil, then, would certainly be cruel or inhuman, and hence to be condemned. But this does not make execution itself, the infliction of the greatest evil, wrong *as such*, only the way it is carried out. And the fact is that in most countries where the death penalty exists, the state builds in safeguards and conditions that render the death as swift and painless as possible. All of this might be unpleasant to have to think about, but you cannot consider this topic properly without thinking about it, and it is as much a reality in the USA as in so-called 'less developed' countries in the Middle and Far East.

4.4.6 What about mercy and compassion?

It is sometimes said that capital punishment, even if it is theoretically justified, runs counter to the better instincts of human nature. Surely, it is said, the state ought to spend its resources not on executing serious offenders but on trying to reform and rehabilitate them, on making them come to terms with the enormity of their crimes, on making them law-abiding and respectable members of society again. Anything less would be a failure of mercy and compassion.

There are a number of things to be said about this objection. For one thing, it is not wholly misplaced. Capital punishment is not a 'quick fix' solution to the problem of crime. To solve the problem of crime – which can only ever mean reduction, not elimination – a wholesale revision is needed in the way societies (at least in the 'civilised' West) are organised, of the guiding principles on which modern communities are based. Whatever the strict merits of capital punishment in the USA, for instance, it is hard not to see something bizarre in the idea that such a punishment can exist in a society governed by the principles of materialism, consumerism, egoism and the self-determination of a 'do-it-my-way' morality. (It is equally curious that these principles, while they hold sway in most of the USA, are not the whole story. The USA is still partly governed by a vestigial puritanism and semi-asceticism, long in decline, that acts as a counter to the other principles. What unites these two sets of values, however, is the principle of *individualism* – the sacrosanct nature of individual liberty and private judgement on morality and religion – on which a society can arguably not have a long-term future.) In such a society, capital punishment looks somewhat like a 'last-gasp' attempt to stem crime and disorder in the face of the failure or incapacitation of other institutions, such as family, school, church and community, to maintain public morality.

So when the opponent of capital punishment urges the supporter to look in other directions for the source of the ills that pervade society, he does so with good reason. The supporter should be as committed as the opponent to the reform of those institutions whose proper function should make severe penalties such as capital punishment all but unnecessary. (This does not mean both sides will agree on what the sources of crime are, or on what means should be adopted to reduce it.) Nevertheless, the supporter does not see mercy and compassion as the rock on which society is built. Rather, society is built first on justice, and mercy exists to soften the sometimes harsh effects of justice. To emphasise justice at the *expense* of mercy is wrong, but so is the reverse. Justice without mercy can be cruel; mercy without justice can be weak.

In fact, mercy is but one aspect of a broader feature the citizens of any well-ordered society should exhibit, namely *charity*. Charity is the virtue of loving your neighbour as yourself. Mercy flows from charity, as an inclination of the will to relieve the misery of another. People in positions of authority, whether parents, teachers, prime ministers or judges, should strive to be merciful whenever mercy is called for, but they must also not compromise justice. It would be an understatement to say that it is difficult for any person to balance these two without undermining either of them, and it is only in rare individuals that we see the balance maintained well. In the case of capital punishment, a judge ought always to look for reasons on which he can grant clemency or commutation of the sentence.

These reasons include sincere repentance by the guilty party, age or infirmity which make his reoffending a virtual impossibility, or a public act of forgiveness and call for clemency by the family of the victim. On the other hand, the judge must never forget that he is acting as the representative of the state, not as a private citizen, and whatever personal feelings he may have about the appropriateness of execution in a particular case, he must also be acutely sensitive to the state's primary function of safeguarding law and order. If mercy can be granted without subverting law and order, and if mercy is otherwise justified, then the judge should grant it, though perhaps with an additionally harsh denunciation of the particular crime, so as to make it clear to the community that justice is not being compromised.

4.4.7 Capital punishment fails to respect persons

Philosophers of a Kantian inclination sometimes argue that the death penalty fails to respect the offender as a person. A person, for the Kantian, is a free, rational agent capable of ordering his life in a certain way, devising and following certain projects, developing his character, and – crucially – legislating for himself what is right and wrong, the only constraint being that what he legislates can at least be coherently conceived as binding on all other persons. The worst thing one person can do to another, on the Kantian view, is to treat him *purely as a means* to an end (to 'use' him, in the current way of speaking). To treat a person that way is to show him radical disrespect by ignoring his autonomous personality.

Jeffrie Murphy, for instance, agrees that death is the worst thing that can happen to a person, saying that it 'represents *lost opportunity* of a morally crucial kind'.[13] He explains: 'it is by no means clear that one can show respect for the dignity of a person as a person if one is willing to interrupt and end his most uniquely human capacities and projects'. It is this radical disrespect for the person that justifies, for Murphy, 'a direct absolute ban on the penalty of death'.[14]

We can agree with Murphy's claim that taking someone's life ends his 'most uniquely human capacities and projects'; perhaps this can be seen as a variant of the central claim I have made about death, that it destroys the precondition for the pursuit of all other goods. Nevertheless, it does not follow that taking someone's life is to fail to respect him as a person. John Cottingham has pointed out the non sequitur.[15] First, he responds, if capital punishment is supposed to violate dignity and autonomy because the offender is unwilling to be executed, then *all* punishment fails to respect persons. Further, although Cottingham notes that some subjects of capital punishment want to be executed, or at least welcome the punishment in some respects – and he mentions Gary Gilmore – he could have asked: does this mean that the execution of a willing offender is permissible? If so, this seems a bizarre consequence and would mean that the death penalty was not intrinsically wrong, only that potential subjects of execution need to be taught to welcome their punishment!

Moreover, argues Cottingham, even if failure to respect a person as a person does not depend upon the state of his will, the general reply can be made that inflicting the death penalty *does* respect the person for much the same reason as any other punishment – it *recognises* the guilty party's full humanity and personhood by treating him as free and rational, and hence as *responsible* for what he did. The real failure of respect would be to treat him as nothing but a product of his upbringing or his genes, to try to 'cure' him of his 'disease', to try to fiddle with his personality so as to make him an 'acceptable' member of society. If a punishment satisfies the criterion of respect, then surely it does so whether it involves death or a two-year good-behaviour bond.

Yet there may be a lingering unease about this response. The rejoinder might go:

> Wait a minute, you're saying that by executing someone you show him such respect for his personhood that you are prepared to see it destroyed. Doesn't that sound a little bit like the father who says to his child, 'This is going to hurt me more than it hurts you', before he gives her a good wallop? And what about your condemnation, in chapter 3 of *Moral Theory*, of the idea that a doctor can take the organs from an innocent patient in order to save five others? You are against using a human being as a means to an end in that case, and now you are allowing someone to be killed in order to 'set things right', 'restore moral order', or whatever catchy phrase you want. Isn't this hypocritical?

The unease in this rejoinder can be assuaged by making some distinctions and clarifications. First, the respect for the offender's personhood is shown by the way in which he is *treated*. If he is held *responsible* and punished, rather than diagnosed as 'a product of forces beyond his control', this in itself demonstrates respect for personhood. It does not mean that such respect cannot be undermined or maybe even cancelled by other treatment, such as subjecting the offender to pointless degradation and indignity, which is why the latter is wrong. Further, it is perfectly consistent both to inflict the death penalty on someone as a responsible person and to recognise that his death cuts off the possibility of further development as a person and is therefore in itself evil. As I have implied throughout the discussion, there is a distinction between the *physical* evil of death and the *moral* evil of unjustifiable homicide. In the case of capital punishment it is not morally evil to inflict the ultimate physical evil (just as it is not always morally evil to inflict the physical evil of pain and suffering). It is not that by administering the death penalty the state is saying it respects the offender's personhood so much *that* it is prepared to destroy it; rather, it is saying that *although* it respects the offender's personhood (which it does by holding him accountable for his actions and liable to some form of penalty), it is prepared to see it cut short because of the gravity of the offence committed.

The next point is that by restoring the moral balance, setting things right, seeing justice done, punishment does not *use* the guilty person as a pure means to an ulterior end. The primary aim of punishment is retribution, and the restoration of the moral order just *is* the punishment of the offender, not some further state of affairs for whose realisation the offender is an instrument. There is nothing consequentialist about retribution; on the contrary, as is sometimes said, retribution is 'backward-looking', that is, it is concerned with what has been done, not with some state of affairs yet to be realised. Deterrence and correction, on the other hand, are 'forward-looking', because the offender is used as the instrument of preventing crime in others and, in a way, as the instrument of preventing further crime in himself. Only if punishment were inflicted without a retributive element would its recipient really be used as a pure means to an ulterior end, and thereby treated as something less than a person.

Compare this to the situation of the doctor who uses a patient as an organ bank from which he can withdraw the spare parts to save five other people. Here there is no sense whatsoever in which the patient is anything more than a means to a further end, the saving of other people's lives. If the patient volunteered a kidney, for instance, the doctor could accept it without disrespecting the donor's personhood because the donor acted freely. (As we saw in the discussion of euthanasia, however, a person is not entitled intentionally to give away his life. It is one thing to say that acting freely is a necessary condition of acting as a person, and another to say either that acting freely is sufficient for acting as a person – doctrine of the paramountcy of the will – or – which is the same thing, for the Kantian – that acting freely is sufficient for an action to be morally legitimate.) But for the doctor to ignore or override the patient's wishes and help himself to his organs is fundamentally to disrespect his personhood because it involves seeing the patient as a mere receptacle, and these are incompatible viewpoints.

There is still a small problem. The transplant doctor who helps himself to a patient's organs might have recourse to some remarks of John Stuart Mill on capital punishment. In the speech quoted earlier, Mill says the following:

> Does fining a criminal show want of respect for property, or imprisoning him, for personal freedom? Just as unreasonable is it to think that to take the life of a man who has taken that of another is to show want of regard for human life. We show, on the contrary, most emphatically our regard for it, by the adoption of a rule that he who violates that right in another forfeits it for himself, and that while no other crime that he can commit deprives him of his right to live, this shall.[16]

Now the transplant doctor might read this and think: 'Just as Mill says that we show respect for life by inflicting the death penalty only on someone who has taken life himself, so what I am doing is respectful of life because I am only prepared to take the life of Fred because I can use his organs to save the lives of George, Harry, Ian, Julie and Kate. Otherwise I would never consider such a thing.'

There can be no doubt about the seductiveness of the analogy, nor about the fact that consequentialists often try to justify actions such as the transplant doctor's by reasoning similar to that just mentioned, even if they do not do so by reference to capital punishment in particular. The fact that it finds a place in the moral thinking of an arch-utilitarian such as Mill ought to make opponents of consequentialism think carefully about whether such reasoning is acceptable. Nevertheless, I would suggest that there are two aspects of the reasoning, one unacceptable and one *probably* legitimate. The unacceptable part involves the thought that one can show respect for life by setting the conditions for taking it sufficiently high. If this is the guiding thought of the transplant doctor or of the state when it inflicts the death penalty, it is clearly consequentialist: for it is irrelevant whether the conditions for taking life include the taking of another person's life (Mill's reference to capital punishment for murder), or the prospect of saving many other lives (the transplant case or the execution of an innocent man) or, for that matter, the prospect of achieving a sufficient amount of benefit, such as the cure of many other people's serious illnesses. I am not saying that Mill was necessarily thinking in a consequentialist way when he said that life is respected by taking it only when the life of another has already been taken. The most natural reading of this statement is retributivist, as an enunciation of the principle of proportionality in punishment. Nevertheless, as a utilitarian Mill's justification for all punishment is ultimately deterrence (see the discussion of his views above), and whatever his official abhorrence of the thought of condemning an innocent man, it is just possible that in the passage quoted earlier there is a confused mix of consequentialist and non-consequentialist thinking. If there is a consequentialist element, and if this is what the transplant doctor is relying on, that reasoning should be rejected: treating any human being, guilty or innocent, as a pure means to a further end is fundamentally disrespectful of human life.

The non-consequentialist aspect of Mill's thinking, however, is not something on which the transplant doctor can rely. The doctor says that he respects life because his ultimate aim is to save life, even if it means taking a life in the process. Mill says that we do not disrespect life by taking the life of someone who has *forfeited* his right to it any more than we disrespect a criminal's liberty by depriving him of it. The point here is that it is the offender who forfeits his rights, not the punisher who violates them. It is *guilt* that makes the crucial difference. The state can consistently respect life while taking the life of someone who has forfeited his right to it because it recognises that *nothing less than forfeiture* makes its penal act justifiable. It does not use the offender as a pure means to a further end because the offender has *already* so changed his moral status by his crime that *he brings himself* within the sphere of the state's moral competence to punish. By contrast, the innocent victim of an organ-harvesting operation has done *nothing* to bring himself within the sphere of the doctor's moral competence to carry out a transplant operation: he has not waived his right to his organs (which he could lawfully do if it didn't result in his death, to which he could never lawfully consent); he has not forfeited his right to his organs; he will not benefit from the removal of his organs (if he will, then the principle that a part may be sacrificed to benefit the whole, the Principle of Totality, comes into play); in short, his moral status has not changed in any relevant way when the doctor goes to remove his organs. Hence the disanalogy with the case of capital punishment.

Consideration of the passage from Mill makes another clarification necessary. He says that respect for life is shown by taking it in the case of someone who has violated the right to life in another. Taking this in its natural non-consequentialist sense as reflecting the principle of proportionality, does it mean, if Mill is right, that capital punishment is only justified in the case of murder, because otherwise respect is not shown for life? In the abstract case for the death penalty that was made out earlier, I said that the worst possible crime deserves the worst possible punishment; most of the examples I gave of potential candidates for the title 'worst possible crime' involved murder, though massive drug-dealing, whatever deaths it leads to, typically does not. Is the state ever justified in inflicting the death penalty for a crime other than murder?

The first point to be made in answering this question is that whatever Mill may have had in mind, his words, on the face of it, allow for capital punishment for crimes other than murder; more importantly, if you want to interpret him as saying something *plausible*, this is how you should read him. He does not say that the state should only fine a criminal if he has stolen the money of another, or that he should be imprisoned only if he has taken the liberty of another. His point is (or ought to be) that we do not show disrespect for property or liberty as long as we take them away from a person who has *forfeited* his right to them by his own deeds, in the way I explained earlier. As long as the subject of punishment is guilty, and as long as the penalty is proportionate to the gravity of the offence, no disrespect is shown to those rights of the offender that are forfeited. By parity of reasoning, then, we should not say that respect for life is shown *only* by taking it from someone who has himself taken life. Certainly, if he has done so this is a *sufficient* condition for its being true that the state has shown respect for life when it executes him. But why should we think it is *necessary* that the executed person be himself a killer in order for respect for life to be shown? All that is necessary is that the crime be the worst possible and that the punishment be proportionate. What is the worst possible crime, however, must depend in part on the circumstances of the community in which the crime is committed, including the *potential effects* of that crime on the community. Can we dispute that it is at least possible for massive drug-dealing to be the worst possible crime in a community even when the drug-dealer – as is nearly always the case – does not *intend* to kill anyone by supplying his wares? Speaking in a strict legal sense, the drug-dealer is hardly ever guilty of more than manslaughter, or homicide in the second or less degree, because he causes death through the reckless or negligent supply of dangerous objects. He is not a murderer. And yet many people reasonably think that because of the damage he can do to a community, in terms of young lives lost, families devastated, poverty created, diseases spread (such as hepatitis), and further crimes provoked by people desperate for money to finance their habit, he deserves nothing less than death. That is certainly how many Asian and Islamic countries see drug-dealing, and we would do well not to make hasty and prejudiced judgements about how they handle their affairs.

The point is that a crime may be the worst possible in a community because of its effects on that community and the peculiar circumstances of that community. The state, as I have said several times, has as its primary function the promotion of the common good, and central to this function is the promotion of public peace, law and order, and the harmonious relations of its citizens. As such, its remit is wide in the way in which it handles crime. To take another aspect of the issue, it is also open to the state to inflict exemplary punishments on certain offenders. At first this might seem to involve consequentialist thinking, but that is not the case. In punishing an offender, the state's first duty is to observe proportionality. Typically, a judge has a range of sentences he is allowed to inflict on a criminal. That range, normally set by the legislature, must not exceed what a criminal falling into the relevant category can legitimately be subject to according to natural justice. For instance, penalties for burglary might range from two to ten years. There is nothing disproportionate in handing out any penalty within that range to a burglar as such. (We cannot use mathematical precision here; remember Aristotle's dictum that ethics is only as precise as the subject matter allows.) However, the circumstances of a particular case – the amount stolen, whether there was any violence, whether the offender shows remorse, and so on – will affect how severe a punishment in that range he can legitimately be given. In addition, though, there might be factors *extrinsic* to the particular case that justify a severe sentence for a relatively minor offence. For example, if a person is convicted of hacking into a military computer and stealing information that turns out to be relatively unimportant, so that there is no significant threat to national security, a judge might think that although the hacker has not in material terms done anything worse than stealing someone's purse, he should be given a sentence at the higher end of the scale so as to deter others who may, as potential copycats, be tempted to do really serious damage to national security. The judge might, in other words, make an example of the hacker. Even though deterrence plays a large part in influencing his decision as to the gravity of the sentence, he has not been unjust to the hacker as long as the penalty actually inflicted is within a range that is already proportionate to the category of offence – burglary, say, or theft – and as long as that scale of penalties is publicly promulgated for all citizens to know.

What the state must always do, however, is respect the basic principles of justice and fairness; if, having done so, it is bound by its essential function to act more severely than normal so as to protect public welfare, so be it. But if it is in a position to show mercy and clemency without endangering public welfare, and if the particular case merits it, it should also do so.

4.5   Concluding Remarks on Hypocrisy

It is unusual, in the current moral climate, both to argue against abortion and euthanasia and for the permissibility of capital punishment, even if this was by far the prevailing view in society until comparatively recently. If one does so, he is likely to be accused of inconsistency at best, of hypocrisy at worst. There are two points I want to make in response to this charge.

The first takes us back to the concept of mercy, discussed earlier. Mercy, as I said, is a virtue involving the inclination to relieve others of their misery. It springs from charity, that is, love of one's neighbour. Now the opponent of capital punishment believes that the merciful thing to do in the case of serious criminals is to help them come to terms with their wrongdoing, to help them understand their position, reform themselves and prepare to re-enter society as law-abiding citizens. At the institutional level, the way to deter serious crime is to look to its alleged causes in poverty, family breakdown, poor education and the like, not to execute serious criminals.

Just as it is rare for moral philosophers to be against euthanasia and in favour of capital punishment, so it is common for them to be against capital punishment but in favour of euthanasia. When it comes to the latter, however, there seems to be a different understanding of the concept of mercy. Whereas the attitude towards serious criminals is that they should be helped to come to terms with their wrongdoing, the attitude to the terminally ill, or the elderly, or the handicapped, is not that they should be helped to come to terms with (and manage) their illness, or their age and infirmity, or their disability, but that the merciful thing is often for them to be killed; hence the term 'mercy-killing'. In the case of euthanasia, it appears, 'relief from misery' means 'release from misery'; hence the term 'merciful release'. It may not be possible to give someone back their youth, or their health, or their able-bodiedness, but much can be done to relieve a large part of their misery by the appropriate care, concern and material assistance. (Witness, for example, the excellent hospice system in Britain, which is continuously under threat and whose very existence is a stumbling block to advocates of euthanasia.) This would be true mercy, on a par with the mercy that opponents of capital punishment want the state to show to the community's worst criminals. If one were to say to an opponent of capital punishment that the truly merciful thing to do to a murderer is to release him from his wretched and depraved existence, he would shrink back in horror. When it comes to the sick, the old and the disabled, however, these same opponents of the death penalty who also advocate euthanasia believe that the truly merciful thing to do is to release them from their miserable existence.

On the contrary, to seek to relieve someone's misery by killing him is a perversion of the concept of mercy. It is to treat people as mere receptacles of pain and pleasure – destroy the receptacle and you eliminate the pain that is in it. As we saw in chapter 2, it is this sort of thinking that R. M. Hare displays when, in response to the charge that Peter Singer's advocacy of euthanasia for the severely disabled is a form of discrimination (a charge common in Germany, where protesters have tried to stop Singer from speaking publicly), he replies: 'Singer's position no more involves discrimination against cripples than does the setting of broken legs. One sets fractures because one thinks that it is better to have whole legs than broken ones; but this does not imply any contempt for cripples who for some reason did not get their legs restored to normal.'[17] Surely, however, it is a perversion of the concepts both of mercy and of non-discrimination to say that just as you can cure someone of a broken leg by setting it, so you can sure someone of a painful life by killing him! To say that someone who is, say, severely handicapped, is 'better off dead' is not to show him mercy, but contempt. It is to fail to see how genuine mercy could be exercised in such a case, the sort of mercy that opponents of the death penalty want to be shown to society's gravest offenders. Perhaps, then, the charge of hypocrisy or inconsistency has been launched in the wrong direction.

The second point is not just about hypocrisy and inconsistency but about the relative peculiarity of moral viewpoints. According to many ethical thinkers, support for capital punishment and opposition to abortion and euthanasia is a bizarre combination, because it seems to display an inconsistent attitude towards the taking of human life. What the advocate of such a position should say, however, is that the viewpoint that is truly bizarre is support for abortion and euthanasia and opposition to capital punishment. Why might someone support abortion and euthanasia? Two principal reasons are (1) the consequentialist belief that they are sometimes justified by the greatest balance of benefit over harm, or (2) the rights-based belief that a woman has the right to control her body, that a person has the right to determine whether he lives or dies, and that the state has the right to minimise the social burden of people the resources for whose maintenance could best be distributed elsewhere. (There may or may not be an element of consequentialist thinking in this last position.) Both (1) and (2), however, depend on reasoning that, if one is consistent, carries over to capital punishment. If you believe (1), why should you not also believe (3), that capital punishment can, at least in theory, bring about the greatest balance of benefit over harm for the community? Even if it never does so in practice, it could never be opposed *in principle*. If you believe (2), why should you not also believe (4), that the state has the right to distribute harms and benefits fairly, say by penalising someone who shows ultimate disrespect for the rules of society in a way that makes him pay the ultimate price? (Such reasoning is deeply dubious, but then so is the reasoning in (2).) Or that the state has the right to minimise burdens on society by choosing not to house someone for decades, at the cost of hundreds of thousands of dollars to the taxpayer, but instead to dispatch him at a much smaller cost to the law-abiding members of society?

Contrast the inconsistency in support for abortion and euthanasia, and opposition to capital punishment, with the reverse position. The charge is that the reverse position involves an inconsistent attitude to the taking of human life. The reply is that there is no more inconsistency in saying that killing is permissible in some cases and not others than in holding that taking purses is permissible in some cases – when the purse is your own –

but not others – when the purse belongs to someone else! It all depends on what exactly is involved in each case. If you make a distinction without a difference, that is, you do not make a distinction of *principle*, you are liable to the charge of inconsistency. But if you do, the inconsistency is an illusion. And the fundamental, pivotal distinction of principle between abortion and euthanasia on the one hand, and capital punishment on the other, is the distinction between innocence and guilt. Guilty actions put a person in a different category, for ethical purposes, from that of innocent people. Guilty actions place a person squarely within the fields of retributive justice and of the competence of the state to administer it. As we are social creatures, we naturally form communities and we naturally look for forms of government to maintain order in those communities. The state, which has the guardianship of the community as a whole rather than of this or that part of it (which is left, in the first instance, to other institutions such as the family, the school and the church) has a fundamental right and duty to exercise that guardianship.

But it is also a basic rule of social organisation that the authority of the state has limits. For one thing, it has no legitimate business interfering with citizens who obey the law and do not threaten the common good. An innocent person is by definition just such an individual. He has, therefore, the full backing of morality against incursions into his life by the state, including the most severe incursion of all, namely the taking of his life. The innocent person, by his very innocence, also does not threaten the legitimate interests of other people. By his very innocence he does not interfere with their legitimate pursuit of the good and so does not come within their proper sphere of self-protection. Morality, therefore, gives the innocent person absolute and unconditional protection both from the state and from other people. His moral status is qualitatively different from that of the guilty person. And it is this basic difference that ensures, not only that there is no inconsistency or peculiarity in support for capital punishment and opposition to abortion and euthanasia, but that an ethical viewpoint encompassing these positions is eminently reasonable and commendable to common sense.[18]

5

War

5.1 Some Questions

There is something deeply mysterious about war. Humanity has been plagued by it throughout history, with recent times (the last couple of hundred years) worse in this respect than any other time; and yet the truth is that, *taken as a whole*, the people of one country never have the genuine desire to make war on the people of another country. Unless, that is, they are deceived by fraudulent propaganda, or are impelled by a motive that has not been applicable for a very long time.

If you are sceptical of this generalisation, consider the possible motives that might drive a nation to make war. Hatred of another people is one possible motive. Suppose you met someone from another nation, say Ruritania. You might be indifferent to him. You might like him. Or you might dislike him, perhaps intensely. Suppose you disliked him. It is hardly likely that you would want to kill him, and inconceivable that you would consider destroying his family, his neighbours, his home town and his country. What about the possibility of disliking individually *all* the citizens of Ruritania with sufficient intensity that you were prepared to interrupt your career, abandon your family, suffer deprivation and risk your very life in order to relieve your feeling of hatred by attacking Ruritanians? It is inconceivable. How would you meet them all, anyway? But imagine you could find every last Ruritanian and set about assaulting them; now try to visualise all your fellow citizens, without any help from yourself, experiencing the same feelings of intense hate to the point of suffering the same deprivation and incurring the same risk to life and limb in order to embark on the slaughter of Ruritanians with you at exactly the same time. Now this sort of united mass action might have been possible in the days when religion was considered to be the only cause worth fighting and dying for, and when all the inhabitants of a country adhered to the same religion. In the present day, such unanimity is unlikely to occur even in your own family.

So what motives other than blind hatred might conceivably have the power to unite a whole nation in the desire to fight a war, the most physically damaging, disruptive and sorrow-generating activity known to mankind? Maybe greed, perhaps the desire for territory, perhaps the lust for adventure and the extremes of agony and ecstasy that no doubt exist in war; or maybe religion?

Greed is certainly a powerful motive behind war, but history shows that it is the greed of a few rather than the greed of many; and the greediest will seldom be doing the fighting. There may well be those who see great financial advantage in fighting a war, so much so that they will abandon kin and comforts and risk being maimed or killed. But they do not comprise the whole nation, only a tiny minority; for the rest, war involves nothing but sacrifice.

The same goes for the desire for territory. Again, it has been a strong motive in many wars, but the vast majority of a population at war neither see nor receive any obvious material benefit from the acquisition by a nation of extra land. Moreover, there are far less painful ways of benefiting from additional or better quality land, such as emigration. How then could the desire for land figure dominantly in the thinking of the average citizen, it being remembered that wars are fought primarily by average citizens?

The same can be said about the lust for excitement and adventure. Everyone likes adventure up to a point, and some people relish it so much that they are not happy unless they are fighting a war. But it is hardly realistic to think that most inhabitants of a nation are so anxious to satisfy their desire for adventure that they would take the extreme step of going off to fight a war.

It seems that religion is just about the only motive capable of uniting a whole nation in the desire for war, for invasion and conquest, even at considerable sacrifice to the invaders. It is conceivable that secular ideologies, in particular, political ones like communism and fascism, could drive a people to desire war; but to the extent that this is so the ideology simply approximates in a perverted way to the essence of religion, otherwise what looks like spontaneous militaristic fervour is nothing but a display of manipulation by state propaganda. For religion to unite a nation in the desire to make war, however, it is necessary that almost every inhabitant of that nation have the same religious beliefs, and the majority must hold them with great fervour. With the exception of the Islamic countries, unity and intensity of faith has not been a characteristic of any of the major nations of the twentieth century, nor has it been so for at least 200 years.[1]

And yet we have been and continue to be plagued by war. What really drives it in the modern era requires extensive investigation, and it may well be that the true causes of most recent conflicts have involved far more political manipulation, far more in the way of self-aggrandisement by a few at the expense of the many, than we would like to admit. Even we, however – the people who are not remotely involved in the decision-making about whether and when to go to war – tend to have a certain uneasiness about most recent wars. When we think about it, we tend towards the idea that the First World War was a hideous waste of millions of lives for no obvious purpose, the destruction of the flower of European youth from which Europe will probably never recover culturally and psychologically. We tend towards the idea that the Second World War began with the noble motive of defeating Hitler's Germany, and ended up enslaving half of Europe in the tyrannical grip of Stalin's Soviet Union, an enslavement that continued for decades. Many people think Vietnam was a costly tragedy, whatever the ostensible motive of stemming the tide of communism. And wasn't the Gulf War all about oil? It may have been provoked by the wrongful invasion of Kuwait, but couldn't oil supplies have been secured without the loss of tens of thousands of lives and the devastation of Iraq?

The purpose of this chapter is not to examine in detail the rights and wrongs of particular wars, although reference will be made to factual situations and the morality of particular actions, and examples will be used to illustrate general points. Rather, the purpose is to look at the general principles governing war, both conduct leading to and conduct during it. For whatever the extent to which one may find war mystifying for the reasons I have just presented, and whatever the scepticism one may have about the way many recent episodes in our history have been standardly interpreted, the fact is that morality does recognise the legitimacy of war in certain situations. It is of crucial importance to distinguish negative judgements about particular cases from general principles that are justifiable by moral reasoning. In the case of capital punishment, it was noted that miscarriages of justice might well call for the suspension of the penalty until adequate reforms can be made, but that this did not invalidate the general case for the death penalty. Similarly, one might even think that no war has been fought for a legitimate cause since, say, the thirteenth century, and yet still be compelled by general reasons to accept that war as such can be legitimately fought. The purpose of the following discussion is to outline those reasons and the principles to which they give rise.

5.2   War, Pacifism and Self-Defence

There are two principal sources for the claim that war does *not* come within the province of moral thinking and hence that there can be no ethical principles governing it. On the one hand there is what we might call the *cynical* view, which is sometimes – and misleadingly – called 'realist'. It is encapsulated in the famous slogan 'War is hell', and in these comments by General Sherman in the American Civil War: 'If the people raise a howl against my barbarity and cruelty, I will answer war is war. . . . War is cruelty, and you cannot refine it.'[2] In fact these remarks only concern conduct *within* war, but since there are two ethical aspects to war – the morality of *going* to war and the morality of conduct *during* a war – the complete cynic not only echoes General Sherman, but says that the reasons for going to war in the first place are so bound up with circumstance and national self-interest that it is a sham to pretend that one can distil ethical principles governing reasons for warfare from the complex morass of history as it is actually played out.

Cynicism is not a view we need to pursue in any detail, because it is absurd. Why should the cynic believe that there is anything special about war as a form of human activity that takes it beyond morality? Human life is in fact a continuum, from the actions you perform in private, or in your family, to those you perform within a small community, or a larger community, or as part of a socially organised political unit such as a state or nation. If morality governs what you do as a member of a family or as a neighbour, why doesn't it govern what you do as a citizen, whether a private citizen listening to your government or as a public citizen – maybe a president or prime minister – deciding what your country should do, such as go to war? If the cynic believes that war is hell, it can only be because he believes *life* is hell and hence beyond morality, which is nonsense. Or the cynic may be subject to confusion about what 'war is hell' means: he may recognise that terrible things are done within war and to 'justify' it, but draw the invalid conclusion that morality is therefore irrelevant. We can agree with the cynic's *factual* observation and reply: 'All the more reason for proper moral guidelines!'

The other, philosophically more important, source for rejecting the idea that the conduct of war can be governed by moral principles is the doctrine of *pacifism*.[3] Pacifism has a long history, finding exponents throughout the ages, in every religion and system of thought. It has a strong appeal to the imagination and is perhaps more influential than ever. 'Pacifism' is in fact a name for a number of different theories and ideas, but as a general doctrine it advocates the *renunciation* of war on moral grounds. In other words, while the pacifist believes morality has something to say about war, it is in the limited sense that it says one thing only: war is wrong. As such, pacifism is opposed to any theory, such as the one I will defend, that war is sometimes right and sometimes wrong, and that some things can legitimately be done in war and some things cannot. This theory is also called 'just-war theory', though what I will defend is the traditional version, that is, pure just-war theory, while recognising that other writers also hold that some wars are right and some wrong without subscribing to the full traditional theory as I will present it.

The statement 'War is wrong' can be taken in more than one way, however. It could mean, on the one hand, 'Every war is wrong' – absolute pacifism, or pacifism pure and simple – or it could mean 'This war is wrong', or 'These wars are wrong', or 'Most wars are wrong.' These latter assertions are versions of what is sometimes called 'contingent' pacifism, because its advocate does not disapprove of war in principle, claiming only that in the contingent circumstances of a particular case a given war is wrong, or a class of war is wrong in certain general circumstances. One might, say, have been a pacifist *about* the Vietnam War, or about colonial wars, without being a pacifist pure and simple. Contingent pacifism, whatever the merits of the name (it is perhaps misleading) is not a view I wish to discuss in its own right, because it falls squarely within just-war theory: if the contingent pacifist believes, say, that Vietnam was wrong, his only disagreement – *if any* – with the just-war theorist will be over this particular case, not the rightness or wrongness of war in general. The just-war theorist also objects to certain kinds of war, and if he disagrees with the contingent pacifist who says 'Some wars are wrong', it will be over the particular class in question.

Absolute pacifism, on the other hand, or just plain pacifism, rejects war in its totality. The pacifist almost always believes that war as such is not so much hell but rather a moral obscenity, like capital punishment (to which he is almost certain to be opposed as well), a relic of a more primitive, barbaric age. Just as we regard it as brutish and petty for individuals to settle their arguments by a physical fight, so we should say the same about war. In particular, the pacifist will point to the fact that we live in an age of increasing interdependence between nations, and are seeing the rapid growth of international and supranational structures that are the instruments by which conflicts between nations must now be settled – international courts and tribunals, the UN, the various international treaties and conventions. War, says the pacifist, should go the way of tribal fighting before the development of the modern political state.

As I have just presented pacifism, however, there are still subtle distinctions to be made. One kind of pacifism is the pure ethic of non-violence associated with certain versions of Buddhism, with the thought of Mahatma Gandhi, or with that of the novelist Leo Tolstoy in his later years. This form of pacifism does not even begin to inquire into the circumstances of war, since it argues from *a priori* views about the wrongness of violence in general. On the other hand, just-war theory has faced a challenge, sometimes from within its own quarter, involving a pacifism that says something like: 'It is true that war may have been *justified* in the distant past, perhaps in the Middle Ages or earlier, when the conditions of war were so different from today. But times have changed radically, and modern warfare in *all* its forms excludes any possible justification for its practice.' This kind of pacifism is still absolute in the sense that it recognises no case in which war is justified now, even though it admits the bare theoretical legitimacy of war in radically different social conditions belonging to the distant past. It is particularly challenging to just-war theory because it is presented as the *logical extension* of that theory: if you interpret it with strict accuracy, *no* war ever comes out justified in the modern age. The pacifist of non-violence and the modern-age pacifist, as we might call them, coincide in what they recommend when it comes to decisions about warfare today: don't engage in it.

It still has to be said that I have only scratched the surface of pacifism, ignoring all sorts of variations. I have also not mentioned the *positive* aspect of pacifism: the pacifist does not merely say 'no' to war, but urges the exploration of ways of *promoting peace*, and this has led to fruitful theoretical developments and practical work such as we have seen coming from the religious sect known as the Society of Friends (Quakers). The just-war theorist, who is also committed to the promotion of peace, can welcome the positive contribution of the pacifist movement to international politics, but disapproves both of the theoretical position behind it – that all war is wrong – and of any pacifist activity that seeks to thwart the conduct of a war that has a legitimate reason for being conducted.

I will consider modern-age pacifism in the course of sketching the principles and applications of just-war theory. Again, there will be no room for detailed exploration, but it will be argued that war can sometimes be justified even in the modern age, though the conditions for its exercise are very limited. But what about non-violent pacifism, which argues from the wrongness of force in general? It may seem noble and peace-loving to oppose violence in all its forms – and which of us does not desire peace? On the other hand, one can soon see how such a position leads to absurdity. One issue that should be raised immediately involves the question of whether the pacifist (and from now on I mean the non-violent pacifist unless I state otherwise) believes non-violence in a society needs to be enforced by the government. After all, most people will not go along with the idea that violence is never justified, say to defend themselves against attack; others of a criminal inclination will still use violence against innocent people. So should the government enforce non-violence? If so, then the pacifist contradicts himself by approving of force in some circumstances, and we can ask: if the government is allowed or even obliged to use force to keep the peace, why shouldn't individual citizens also be in the same position, say when the government (via the police or the legal system) is not able or prepared to help them? And if this is the case, the whole ethic of non-violence collapses and we can inquire further into parallels between violent action by the state against its citizens, violent action by citizens against other citizens, and violent action (that is, wars) by states against other states. Furthermore, if the pacifist really believes it is obligatory and *feasible* for the state to maintain total non-violence in a society, what he is advocating is nothing less than tyranny, because that is what it would take to maintain a condition of non-violence in society.

But suppose the pacifist says (for the sake of consistency) that not even the state is allowed to use violence, even in order to prevent violence by its citizens. Then we would not have tyranny but anarchy, because the total cessation of the use of force by the state would lead to an equally total breakdown in law and order: a state that is not prepared and able to use force on at least *some* occasions is not a state but at best a kind of counsellor to the citizenry, exhorting the people to pacific behaviour while watching the opposite occurring all around it, powerless to act by the very dictates of the pacifist's 'moral' vision. So pacifism leads to inconsistency, tyranny or anarchy. If the pacifist does not even have plausible basic principles, then we have no reason to listen to him about the way states themselves ought to conduct their relations with each other.

At a more fundamental level, pacifists are wrong to insist that human beings are never right to use force against each other. They frequently invoke biblical injunctions to 'turn the other cheek' and not to 'resist evil', and say that 'those who take the sword shall perish by the sword'; but they will find no comfort for their ethic of non-violence in biblical ethics. (I leave it to the reader to explore this issue.) Speaking in terms of natural morality, that is, what is proper to the human being as seeker of the good, it is true to say that one should strive to be peaceful in one's dealings with others – this is what is sometimes called a 'counsel of perfection', not a strict obligation applicable in all cases. Again, pursuit of private vendettas, the resort to force when there are instrumentalities – namely the state and its organs – whose *job* it is to enforce the rights of the citizen, are something a person *is* obliged not to undertake, no matter how legitimate that person's feelings of outrage and how just his complaint against his neighbour. These are principles that traditional morality has always recognised, and the pacifist should be applauded for emphasising them in an age when people are only too ready to take up arms against each other whenever they are aggrieved.

Nevertheless, morality also recognises the *right of self-defence*. By self-defence I do not mean simply the kind of 'militant clash of wills' advocated by Gandhi, the 'dynamic non-violence of the strong' (which he called *satyagraha* and opposed to 'passive resistance' or the 'non-violence of the weak'),[4] but the actual use of physical force to defend oneself against physical attack. Morality, as I have said, gives the individual certain powers over his pursuit of the good: those moral powers are what is meant by rights, that is, claims or strict titles against other people binding them not to interfere in certain ways with the individual's pursuit of the good. It was argued in chapter 2 of *Moral Theory* that morality would be inconsistent in its very nature if such rights did not exist. Equally, morality would be inconsistent if, among those rights with which it equips the individual, there did not exist the right to use force against an aggressor, that is, against another person who threatens the individual's life, bodily integrity or even property. Not to have that right of self-defence would mean that an aggressor had the right to attack without interference or repulsion, and this would contradict – even render meaningless – the individual's right to life *itself*, his right to bodily integrity, his right to enjoy what he owns undisturbed. What would it *mean* to say he possessed such rights if other people also had the right to interfere with his life, bodily integrity or possessions without his physical resistance? The only response would be to say that it was always the job of the state to enforce the individual's rights: the aggressor may have the right to attack without physical resistance by the right-holder, but not without resistance by the state. But apart from the tyrannical political organisation that would be needed to maintain such a state of affairs, making the moral system that dictated it absurd, the fact is that the state is not always in a position to enforce a person's rights. In many cases a person has only himself to rely on for protection, and to say that morality allows the state to protect a person but does not allow a person to protect himself is to condemn the individual to harm or even death in many situations where the state just cannot or will not help. The state has as its proper task, as we have seen, the promotion of the common good: hence such actions as private vendettas, which directly threaten law and order, are wrong, and it is for the state to administer punishment as a public act in defence of the peace. But there is no threat whatsoever to law and order or the public peace by an individual's use of self-defence. The whole *point* of defensive as opposed to offensive action is that is directed at *maintaining* peace, not upsetting it. A person engaged in a private vendetta might think that he is contributing to public peace, but the real effect of his actions is to encourage others to make private judgements about who should and shouldn't be punished, without due process and impartiality. This is a direct threat to law and order. Defensive action, on the other hand, does not encourage any behaviour that usurps the proper role of the state; it does not threaten law and order, and as such is exercisable by the individual without the need for any sanction from the public authority. Furthermore, whatever our nature as social creatures who incline towards forms of political organisation, history sometimes finds people in situations of social breakdown, absence of government, failure of law and order, and the like. To say that morality gives them no assistance with physical self-protection in such cases, when self-protection is more necessary than ever, but *does* give assistance when the state exists and is competent – when self-protection is less likely to be necessary because of the threat of punishment – is again to make of morality an absurdity, or at least to reduce human rights to a gift of the state rather than a gift of nature and of the objective order of things.

5.2.1 Self-defence – basic principles

Self-defence is, then, the proper right of every human being. By considering in outline the principles that govern its use, we will gain a better idea of the principles governing war, because the paradigmatically just war is the war of self-defence against wrongful attack. In particular, because the ethics of war centres on the ethics of killing rather than that of causing harm *per se*, we need to concentrate on the morality of killing in self-defence.

First, the intention when you use lethal self-defence must be *to protect yourself*, not *to kill*. Your motive must not be revenge, or greed, or to 'teach the attacker a lesson' – it must be genuine self-protection. Now there is a well-known difficulty here when self-defence is compared to capital punishment, and it needs briefly to be considered. Killing a human being is, *considered in itself*, an evil, because death itself is an evil, a bad thing. Killing the innocent is, as I have argued throughout this book, always wrong. The state, on the other hand, is allowed to kill one of its members when that member has committed a serious enough offence, that is, when the offender is guilty to a high enough degree. But then if you are attacked by a violent mugger, why should you not also be allowed *intentionally* to kill the mugger? Why does the traditional ethic say that your intention must be, *not to kill*, but to *defend* yourself? After all, the mugger is guilty of an offence against morality. If he murdered you in the course of his attack, he too might be liable to having his life taken by the state. And yet I am claiming that the state could, all things being equal, inflict death on him deliberately, but you would not be allowed to do so in the course of defending yourself.

The reason for the difference lies, I would argue, in the very nature of the two acts, self-defence and capital punishment.[5] The death penalty is, as an act of punishment, first and foremost *an act of justice*. Punishment is, as I argued in chapter 4, a social good – it is right and proper. By inflicting it on an individual, even if it means deliberately killing that person, the state does something that is good *by its very nature* – it administers justice. Hence what would otherwise be a wrongful killing becomes a qualitatively *different* kind of act. Self-defence, on the other hand, while it does involve the securing of justice (as between the attacker and the victim), can be described as doing so *only insofar as it is an act of self-protection*. What is just about an act of self-defence is that it is an act of self-protection; to the extent that it involves *taking a life*, it is not to be described as an act of justice but quite simply as the taking of a life, and this is the infliction of a great evil. Since you are never allowed intentionally to do evil, you are not allowed intentionally to kill someone even in the defence of your own life. As an act of self-protection, however, which is not an act of evil but an act of justice, you are entitled to do whatever is necessary to defend yourself, even if it means bringing about the death of the attacker as a *foreseen* but *unintended* side effect of your permissible act of self-protection, following the Principle of Double Effect. (The proportionality requirement is satisfied, because the good effect is the preservation of your life and the bad effect is the loss of the attacker's life.) Compare this with capital punishment, where the infliction of death is *an essential part of the act of administering justice*, because of the principle of proportionality that is itself essential to every act of punishment. The killing of the offender becomes, then, part of the very act of justice that punishment is, and so may without wrongfulness be inflicted deliberately. This, I would argue, is what puts self-defence and capital punishment in morally different categories, and why killing in self-defence must not be intentional and in capital punishment may legitimately be intentional. This part of the argument is rather abstract, I admit, but it will help you to understand why killing in war is permissible, when we come to consider it.

(For the sake of completeness, we should note another argument for the distinction between self-defence and capital punishment, based on the Principle of Totality mentioned in chapter 2 of *Moral Theory*. That principle says that it is permissible, sometimes even obligatory, to sacrifice a part of something for the sake of the whole: for instance, if Brenda cut off Charles's leg she would, all things being equal, have inflicted a great evil on him, and so have acted wrongly. But what if Charles's leg had been mangled in an accident and he was bleeding to death, and Brenda was a surgeon? Then she would be *entitled* to cut off his leg in order to save his life – all things would not, in such a case, be equal; the very nature of the case would be different from your run-of-the-mill Texas Chainsaw Massacre leg-cutting. It is said by some writers that capital punishment involves the Principle of Totality:[6] citizens of a state are its members (the very term 'member' is suggestive, isn't it?), and the state has the right to 'cut off' one of them, the guilty offender, in order to save the whole. Some people even speak of the heinous criminal as a 'cancer' on society, who should be 'excised' by being executed. I am not sure about the persuasiveness of such reasoning. Certainly the Principle of Totality is the justification for saying that cutting off a part to save the whole does not violate PDE – which prohibits doing evil for the sake of good – and this is generally thought to make such reasoning, when applied to the death penalty, not consequentialist; but it is not clear that the 'saving of society' that execution justifies on this way of thinking is any more than the deterrent effect of punishment. It is hard to see how society is *saved* by retribution as such, even if retribution is justified. The implication would seem to be that such reasoning would *not* apply if deterrence could not be achieved in a given case, and we saw that the state *is* within its rights to use the death penalty even if deterrence will not be achieved on a particular occasion. Furthermore, it is a thorny question just how far to take the idea of the state as a whole of which the citizen is a part; one can see the evil directions in which such reasoning could lead (and has notoriously led), so we must be very careful about how to interpret the Principle of Totality in the political sphere.)

The second requirement of self-defence is that there be a true aggression. In other words, there must be an actual act of violence, as opposed to the mere threat of future violence. If Michael says to Neil, 'One of these days I'm going to get you!', Neil is not allowed to carry out a pre-emptive strike by shooting Michael, or poisoning his beer even if the poisoning involved a purely defensive and non-lethal intention to ensure that Michael would never be in a position to 'get' Neil. On the other hand, self-defence would often be futile if you had to wait until the attacker was coming right at you: what this means is that the true aggression need not yet involve physical attack, but may involve no more than an *advance* that has barely commenced, the *beginnings* of an attack, a clear *attempt* to set an attack in motion. The mere *planning* of an attack, on the other hand, is not enough. (Some writers use the term 'moral' aggression to specify when defensive action is allowed, meaning that the aggressor has to be 'on his way', or embarked on his attack.) We will see that similar reasoning applies to war, but with important qualifications.

Third, the aggression must be unjust. So, it would be wrong for someone to defend himself against a police officer making a lawful arrest, and for a prisoner to defend himself against lawful restraint by a guard or against lawfully imposed punishment, including capital punishment. But the injustice of the aggression need not involve full knowledge and advertence, what is called *formal* injustice (see chapter 1). So, while it is permissible to defend yourself against a mugger who has the express intent of causing you harm, it would also be permissible to defend yourself against a *materially* unjust attack where the aggressor was not in his right frame of mind, say drunk, drugged, or insane (what is called 'innocent' aggression – innocent because of the lack of a right frame of mind proper to guilt, but materially unjust because the harm threatened is just as bad as if the attacker knew what he was doing). Even if you were responsible in the first place for another person's getting angry and wanting to attack you, you would still be permitted to defend yourself, because of the wrongness of private vendettas.

The fourth requirement of legitimate self-defence is that the force used to repel the attack must be *moderate*, meaning *proportional* both to the type of attack and the difficulty of repelling it. As far as the type of attack goes, you cannot, for instance, use deadly force against someone just because he is trying to steal your car, or beat him unconscious just because he pushes you out of the way. If, however, he comes at you with lethal intent, carrying, say, a knife or a gun, or saying 'I'm going to kill you!' and looking as though he means it, you are entitled to use maximum force in the knowledge that you may end up killing the attacker, without yourself intending to do so. But the other dimension of proportionality involves the difficulty of repelling the attack, and this may affect the degree of force you can use. So, if someone comes at you with a gun, and you also have a gun but have never used it before and are simply not skilful enough to shoot the attacker in the legs, or else the attacker is so close to pulling the trigger that shooting him in the legs is unlikely to stop him shooting you, you may shoot at his upper body in the full knowledge that he may well be killed. In other words, your task is to *repel the attack* (or avoid it), and wherever possible you should use only the means necessary to do this. If you can call the police, you should do so. If you can escape, you should do so. (These options are not mutually exclusive! Some people think that if your escape will make you look a coward in the eyes of reasonable members of the community you can stay and fight, but the question is controversial. In the case of war, dishonour is far more potent a motive and may well legitimate military action.) If you can't escape, you should aim for the minimum force necessary. If you can repel the attack by pushing rather than hitting, you should do so; you should hit rather than stab; stab rather than shoot; shoot at the legs rather than at the chest; and so on. (The extent to which, in gun-owning societies such as the USA, people seem to think 'shoot' means 'shoot to kill', is disquieting and contrary to ethical norms.) In all cases, you should try *words* before *deeds* – it is amazing (but should not really be) how effective well chosen words can be in repelling an attack.

Still, it might be objected, 'You are laying down dry, abstract principles with no application to the heat and mayhem of a real-life case – typical ivory-tower talk from someone who has never been mugged.' The reply to this should be, first, that without principles to govern physical conflicts between people we have nothing but chaos and barbarism, and second, that it is of course true that in real-life situations it is often hard to think rationally about what should be done. Someone may attack your beautiful new gleaming red sports car, and you naturally go berserk and want to kill him. Things get out of hand, the conflict escalates, and someone gets seriously hurt – all over a car that is probably insured anyway. The point is that morality carries degrees of praise and blame, something consequentialists for one have a hard time describing, given the skimmed-down, denuded ethic they usually work with. It may be wrong to knock someone unconscious because he called you an idiot in front of your friends, but if your embarrassment was acute and understandable you will not be guilty of the sort of malicious intent that goes with a wanton attack on a total stranger. The courts know this, and usually apply moral rules with great skill and prudence when assessing degrees of guilt incurred during heated conflicts that get out of control. Gross negligence, recklessness, mild carelessness, thoughtlessness, oversensitivity, overreaction, and so on: these are the sorts of moral category that are indispensable to the ethical evaluation of conflict, whether between individuals or between nations.

Is self-defence obligatory or merely permissible? In most cases, it would seem to be obligatory. As pointed out in chapter 2 of *Moral Theory*, the first duty of charity is to yourself, and it is quite wrong to take this to be a recommendation of selfishness. 'Self-love' does not mean 'self-benefit all the time or at all costs', it just means that our first job is to do what fulfils our nature, and that must include the preservation of *our* lives before that of others. What about martyrs and people who work themselves to death for the benefit of others? Such behaviour is commendable and does not contradict the principle that charity begins at home. You should never *intend* to find martyrdom, or *intend* to kill yourself in the service of others – this would be suicide, and the taking of an innocent life is wrong, even if that life is your own. This does not, however, stop you from ordering your priorities in such a way that you do not strive to preserve your life or health at all costs, but place it below the service of others or of the common good. Even the greatest martyrs in history do their best to *avoid* martyrdom, and only welcome it when it becomes an inevitable consequence of doing what is right, having always been *prepared* to accept it as a gift from God. (Think of the life of St Thomas More, for instance.) In addition, it may be that your duties to *others* make it obligatory for you to defend yourself, so you can continue to look after your family, for example, or your community, if you are in a position of responsibility. It is especially necessary for a good ruler or governor of a society to resist an assassination attempt, since the world needs the good leaders it has, there being enough bad ones already. Again, in the case of war the government must have the good of its people firmly in mind before embarking on such a dangerous enterprise, and must look to secure a really necessary good as the reason for exposing the citizenry to the immense hardship that war brings.

What about the defence of a third party? According to traditional morality it is sometimes permissible, sometimes obligatory. It is certain that a person is obliged by natural duty to defend his family against attack and also anyone else for whom he has a natural responsibility of care and concern, such as friends and loved ones. It is equally certain that a person under a lawful contract containing the defence of another as a requirement (policemen, bodyguards) is under a duty to defend the people for whom he is responsible. What about the defence of total strangers? If I see an old man being beaten up in the street, I am certainly allowed to come to his aid by repelling his attacker, and if I can do so at little cost to myself in terms of life and limb I may be obliged. Whereas the defence of family and those for whom you are responsible is primarily a matter of justice, something to which they are entitled, the defence of strangers is more a matter of charity, and while charity is something we are all advised to practise, it is not always a strict duty. (To take an extreme example, it is commendable to travel to a foreign country and help the starving, but hardly a duty.) The risk or cost to ourselves partially governs charity towards strangers, and it is doubtful that there is a strict duty to risk your own life in their defence. On the other hand, public safety may require you to come to the aid of a stranger, say in order to prevent a riot.

In any case, the rules of self-defence carry over directly to the defence of a third party. The life of the innocent person whom you have undertaken to save must be under genuine threat, and there must be more than the mere planning of an attack. Also, the degree of force must be proportional to the kind of attack and the means necessary for repelling it. What about the case, for instance, of a hit man or serial murderer who periodically kills innocent people? Suppose you find out that he is almost certainly going to kill someone tomorrow, or in a week, but you don't know whom, and he is not engaged in any physical attack in between killings. What are you to do? For a start, there are few cases in which you have any business doing anything as long as the police are prepared to take action. But suppose they are not? You do not have any strict duty to take action, only a duty of charity, unless it can plausibly be argued that, *qua* citizen, you have a duty to uphold the common good if the law will not do so and if your actions will not harm public welfare even more than the periodic killings harm it already. In any case, it is at least arguable that where a person is engaged in periodic murders as a pattern of behaviour, even though at a given time he is not attacking anyone, it is open to another to come to the defence of innocent third parties even if he does not know who they are. To take a concrete example, suppose you were a German citizen during the Second World War, and you knew that a certain German officer was responsible for periodically ordering the execution of innocent Jews. Would you have been entitled to come to their aid by killing the officer on a day when he was not ordering anyone's execution, but was, say, sitting in his barracks having a cup of tea? I would say you were entitled, even though there was no actual aggression under way and you did not know who the next victims would be. In other words, a *pattern* of homicidal behaviour can constitute sufficient 'actual violence' to justify defence of a third party, where it is morally certain (that is, reasonable and rational, given the objective evidence, to believe) that further killings would be committed.

In the case of defence of a third party's property, it is nearly always permissible and not obligatory: there is far more call on your charity to prevent muggings than purse-snatchings. The most obvious case where it would be obligatory as a duty of charity (and justice if it involved family or others for whom you were responsible) is where the attack on property is tantamount to an attack of life itself: you should, for instance, prevent someone from taking the last piece of food from a starving man when there is no threat to your own life in doing so. Property is generally less important than life and bodily integrity; the problem is, defending an attack on someone's property is likely to involve less risk to yourself than defending his life and limb, since the more violent an attack, the more likely it is that the attacker will be violent towards anyone who comes to the victim's defence! It is the nature of the attack that should come first in your deliberations, however, not the risk to yourself. Since an attack on property is far less severe than an attack on life, it is less likely to be the kind of thing charity *calls* you to defend, however commendable your defence might be, unless, as was implied earlier, your tie to the property is especially close by virtue of your personal relationships of family and friendship (or by virtue of prior obligation, such as that incurred by a security guard employed to prevent theft).

5.3   Going to War

All of the principles of self-defence and defence of a third party that have been outlined carry over, with modifications, to the case of war. And many of the same problems arise, both those of a conceptual nature and those involving the application of principle.

One of the prime conceptual problems, paralleling the problem of distinguishing killing in self-defence from killing in capital punishment (which I discussed at some length earlier), concerns the fact that war seems to involve the killing of innocent people. I am not talking about the killing of people who are not fighting the war (innocent civilians, non-combatants), but the killing of soldiers themselves. After all, very few soldiers *prefer* to be in a war; *they* didn't declare it; many will be unwilling conscripts; most would rather be anywhere, doing anything, than killing other people; so isn't it a fiction to think of many soldiers as anything other than innocent men? I said earlier that one may not intend to kill in self-defence, only to protect oneself, because killing involves the infliction of a great evil that can only be permitted as the side effect of a proportionate good. Only the state can perform the deliberate infliction of death as a punishment, which it is not up to private individuals to carry out. Isn't killing in war more like killing in self-defence than killing as punishment? The novelist George Orwell found war puzzling and deeply disquieting for this very reason. Human beings, he wrote, who are in private life peaceful, law-abiding citizens, in wartime become cold-blooded killers and lose not a minute's sleep after having bombed 'the enemy' to smithereens. (In fact, soldiers lose plenty of sleep over this, but leave that to one side.) The soldier, says Orwell, 'is serving his country, which has the power to absolve him from evil'.[7] Tolstoy did not deny that soldiers have a conscience, but said that it is somehow 'kept dormant' within them once they have donned their uniform. Pacifists object to war as a 'desensitising' experience involving a kind of 'moral anaesthesia'. Modern-age pacifists, in particular, point to war as it is now fought, often anonymously, at great distances, with human beings hiding behind faceless technology, and call the whole thing an obscene, conscience-numbing experience that masks the truth that innocent men are slaughtering one another.

On the other hand, just-war theorists insist that it is *precisely* the public, state-authorised nature of war that *permits* acts that in private life would be immoral, such as killing, maiming and destroying property. Although soldiers may well feel hatred and animosity towards the enemy, the very structure of warfare allows them to do their duty to their country *without* having such unworthy feelings. War may not usually be an ennobling experience – though many men, both commanders and front-line soldiers, have testified throughout the ages to its more noble aspects, such as the extremes of heroism and virtue to which it gives rise – but at least the soldier does not have to feel personal hatred in fighting for his country.

The just-war theorist is, I would argue, right to point to the structure and nature of war as the ground for saying that warfare does not essentially involve the killing of the innocent. It may be true that individuals fight wars, but it is states that conduct them. When a person fights in an army, he is acting as the *agent* of the state unless he exceeds the authority given to him. That authority involves the duty to obey his commanding officers in carrying out whatever he is ordered to do as part of the prosecution of the war, subject to the limiting principles that just-war theory provides and which will be outlined shortly. Now, according to just-war theory, when a state fights a war it will do so either legitimately or illegitimately. Either way, it will have *reasons* for waging war. The individual soldier, however, is in a special condition relative to the state's reasons for action. On the one hand, he is not a microcosm of the state: he does not take on, in an objective sense (whatever his personal motivations), the state's reasons for waging war. So it is not as though he is innocent when the state fights for a good reason, so that killing him is murder, but guilty when the state fights for a bad reason, so that killing him is permissible.

To take an analogy, suppose Alpha Corp. and Beta Corp., who were once on friendly terms, engage in commercial hostilities because Alpha suspects Beta of illegal practices. Alpha takes Beta to court; meanwhile, the CEOs of each company order their employees to cease all further commercial assistance to employees of the other company, such as the swapping of ideas and technical information. Alan works for Alpha Corp. and Brian for Beta Corp. How should they deal with each other on a *commercial* basis, if they happen to meet? (Whether they know each other personally is irrelevant.) Surely it will not depend upon whether Alan knows that the law is or is not on Alpha's side, and the same for Brian. Once they have decided to continue serving their companies throughout the commercial 'war' (and we will see that, in just-war theory, a person is bound to decide *whether*, in the first place, he should fight his country's war), they are bound, as faithful employees – that is, as *agents* of their respective companies – to do what their CEOs have ordered, namely not to swap ideas or technical information. If Brian, for example, knows that the law is in fact on Alpha's side, he should not say to himself, 'Well, the truth of the matter is that Alpha is innocent and my company is in the wrong, so Alan is innocent himself and I can give him some useful commercial information.' Nor should Alan say, if he knows that Beta is in the wrong, 'Ah, I know that Beta is guilty, so Brian is guilty, and *that* is why I won't tell him about that new product Gamma Corp. is releasing onto the market.' No, Alan should obey his CEO and not hand over information.

The same goes for war. The individual soldier does not embody the guilt or innocence of his country, and so is not innocent because his country's cause is just. On the other hand, however, it is not as though the soldier has *no* relationship to his country and its actions: he is its agent and representative. As a soldier, he does what his country, in its lawfully constituted authority, has every right to tell him to do. So whatever his personal preferences – he may want to do anything rather than kill another – he is not innocent by virtue of a lack of homicidal intent. He 'takes on' the homicidal intent of his country, that is the decision of his country to kill the citizens of another country, and as such is a killer, just as Alan, when he carries out a decision made by his CEO against the interests of Beta Corp., 'takes on' that decision, and is responsible for its execution, whether or not he personally wants to do what he is told to, and even if he thinks it is the worst decision ever made. If Brian, knowing Alan was about to carry out some decision that had 'come from the top', were to ask his own CEO what to do in response, he would be obliged to respond as ordered (assuming, as always, that he was not ordered to do something intrinsically immoral, such as murder Alan). He could not legitimately say to himself, 'Poor Alan is innocent, he is only doing what he was ordered to do.'

The pacifist is wrong, therefore, to think that war essentially entails the killing of innocent conscripts and soldiers who do not want to fight. Once a soldier puts on his uniform, he is an agent of his country; and it is this very public characteristic of warfare that enables it to be conducted in the first place, that is, enables states to resort to force in the defence of their interests. Soldiers have a difficult enough time coming to terms with the killing of the enemy in war; they would go positively insane if they did not have principles of subordination and authority to justify their actions. The pacifist might insist that this points merely to the hypocrisy and obscenity of war, but if what I have argued against pacifism is correct, such protestations are without rational foundation.

5.3.1   Basic principles of the just war

The fundamental principle of just-war theory is that some causes for fighting a war are just and others are not. A paradigmatically just cause would be a war of independence by a state against an oppressive state that had enslaved it. Conversely, a paradigmatically unjust war would be one aimed at enslaving another people. Once a war is commenced, the enemy is not limited to those in uniform carrying a weapon: the enemy includes active combatants on land, in the air or the sea, all commanding officers whether actively engaged in combat or not, all administrative personnel, operators of communications and computer equipment, suppliers of food, weapons and other material, manufacturers of the same if they are for use by combatants active or not, advisers, counsellors, intelligence agents and anyone at home or abroad who participates in or co-operates with the prosecution of the war. What constitutes the requisite degree of participation is, however, sometimes difficult to answer, and we will return to this question when discussing the distinction between combatants and noncombatants. The long list of members of the enemy I have just given might remind you of the expression 'total war' and of the consequent thought that, since war in the modern age involves just about every citizen in one way or another, it is a barbarous and unredeeming exercise in mass destruction. This question will also be discussed later, but for now it should be noted that whatever the difficulties of drawing the line (as is often the case in ethics), principles can be given that enable fair distinctions to be made.

The just war can be offensive or defensive, and it is at this point that the parallel with self-defence by an individual, which I have been so concerned to draw, shows its limitations. A typically just war would be one involving resistance to an unjust attack, such as an invasion for which there was no justifying cause. Polish resistance to the German invasion of their country in 1939 looks like such a case. On the other hand, to reach further back into history, Turkish resistance to the Hungarian attacks on Serbia and Bosnia in 1463 was not justified on the reasonable assumption that the Turkish presence was already that of an invading army of expansion. But then this seems to imply that the Hungarian *offensive* was justified; and yet we have seen that any attack on an individual is unjust (whether formally or materially) unless it is part of the exercise of lawful authority, such as a policeman arresting a suspected criminal. How was Hungary acting lawfully by seeking to oust Turkey from the Balkans, given that there was no higher political authority to obey?

It is here that we see the justification for war going beyond that of self-defence. Within a state, the individual citizen has no authority to go around using force to secure his rights. He has a higher authority, namely the state and its legal system, to appeal to. All he is justified in doing, in the absence of total political breakdown, is protecting himself, his family and his property (and maybe strangers, as suggested above) from physical attack. As far as enforcing his rights that go beyond mere protection, however, he must in the interests of law and order rely on political and legal authority for their enforcement. So, for instance, suppose Harry has some next-door neighbours who play loud music and make his life a misery. He is entitled to do what he can to his own property to soundproof it, but he is not entitled to enforce his rights further by breaking into his neighbour's house and taking away his stereo equipment. In the interests of public peace he should go to the local authorities for redress (something, at least in Britain, that local authorities are only beginning to provide in a meaningful way; but any laxity on their part still does not justify trespass). On the other hand, states never had such authorities to appeal to – certainly not in the fifteenth century – and even now this avenue is fairly limited. 'What about the UN, international conventions and all the international legal mechanisms for enforcing states' rights?', you may object. I will consider this difficult issue later in the chapter, because of its separate and important implications. For the moment, leaving aside current international structures, the point is that states (and the same would apply to tribes or other forms of government) generally do not have higher authorities to appeal to, and so must fall back on their own resources to enforce their legitimate claims. This puts them in a different position from individuals within a state when it comes to the enforcement of rights.

So, wars can be defensive or offensive. As far as the former go, a war can be defensive in the strict sense when the defending state repels an attack or invasion, having not itself begun hostilities: we see this in the case of the German attack on the Soviet Union in 1941, the Japanese attack on the United States at Pearl Harbor, and the Argentinian invasion of the Falkland Islands which prompted a British response to what it saw, with some good reason, as an attack on territory within its possession. (Let us leave aside the many questions about the rights and wrongs of these conflicts and confine ourselves to plausible, if perhaps superficial, assessments.) A war can be defensive in a broader sense, however, when an innocent nation launches an attack, even perhaps declares war, as a pre-emptive strike against another nation's plans and preparations for war. Now in the case of individual self-defence, we saw that pre-emptive strikes are illegitimate: I simply may not clobber you over the head today if you are planning to assault me in a week's time. I can warn you of my intent to defend myself vigorously, I can try to scare you off, but I may not act first. So why should states be allowed pre-emptive strikes? Again, the difference comes down to the respective roles of citizen and state. As has been argued, it is not the place of the citizen to use force in order to administer justice, to 'teach a lesson' to an aggressor, to 'send a warning' to the community that force will be met with force. These are the proper functions of the state as protector and promoter of the common good, and as we have seen, deterrence and correction are central aims of punishment and the administration of justice. When it comes to relations between states, however, there is no way deterrent functions can be performed without this being done by the states themselves. So, to take an example, when Israel attacked the Iraqi nuclear reactor in 1981, it was at least arguable that it was permissible for the Israelis to 'send a message' to Iraq that any attempt to build a nuclear arsenal, with the ultimate aim of destroying Israel, would be thwarted as early as feasible. Whatever the facts of this particular case, the general principle holds that a state may launch a pre-emptive strike if it has very good reason for thinking that another state is preparing for war, in order to deter the execution of such plans. If the preparations are long-range, as Iraq's would have been on the assumption that there were any military plans at all, the application of PDE means that the evil of the attack – risk of death, injury and property destruction – would have to be proportionate to the good the state aims to achieve, namely the lessening of the risk of future aggression. If that risk is relatively small, as it would have to have been in Iraq's case, as not a single nuclear weapon had even been built to the best of anyone's knowledge, the severity of the possible damage – in this case by the most horrendous weapons in existence – would have to be great. In short, a small risk of massive destruction would be proportionate to a certain risk of minor destruction (for example, the loss of a reactor and several deaths), and so the prevention of the former would justify the bringing about of the latter.

The case of the Iraqi nuclear reactor is at the borders of a legitimate pre-emptive strike. What about, say, the Six Day War of 1967, when Israel launched a first strike against Egypt?[8] Here, it seems, a pre-emptive strike had greater legitimacy. Egyptian war plans were not merely being drawn up: there had been a blockade of Israeli shipping, incursions into the Sinai (which then belonged to Israel) and increasingly bellicose speeches by Nasser and other Egyptian political leaders. On the other hand, the Egyptians had some cause for thinking Israel was preparing for war before it took some of its own threatening action. In other words, the situation was volatile, there was much disinformation, propaganda, posturing and interference by outside powers such as the USA and the Soviet Union. On balance, however, it seems that Israel reacted to what it at least believed on substantial grounds to be the threat of imminent attack. Whether there was any deterrent effect of Israel's massive strike against Egypt, however, is doubtful, as the latter invaded Israel only six years later. This shows the perilousness of attempts to 'teach a lesson' to another nation, as the result may simply be a desire for vengeance rather than peaceful amendment.

Wars may also be *offensive*, when a state attacks another to avenge an injury or enforce a right, such as to obtain compensation for unjustly inflicted damage. Again, the parallel with action by the individual breaks down, because the state has no higher authority to which it can appeal to administer punishment and enforce rights. For example, in the early years of the twentieth century the USA used force against Caribbean nations such as Haiti, Nicaragua and the Dominican Republic to secure the repayment of debts owed both to the USA and European nations.[9] On the one hand, this caused long-standing resentment in Latin America against the USA; on the other, it arguably prevented European military intervention of a more substantial kind than the USA undertook. Trade embargoes, boycotts, economic sanctions and other commercial injuries have all been reasons why states have gone to war, and just-war theory sometimes allows offensive action in such cases.

As we saw in chapter 3 of *Moral Theory*, however, there are three determinants of the morality of an act: its object, its circumstances and its motive. No act can be good if these three elements are not all good, and this applies as much to the actions of states as to the actions of individuals. Hence state acts, including military ones, will only be justified if they too abide by the determinants of morality. No state, then, will be justified in its use of force against another state unless several conditions are satisfied. I will begin with the three core principles and bring in other subsidiary ones as we go along.

First, the use of force must be sanctioned by the lawful authority of the state, the agency of government responsible for decisions as to military action (whether Congress, the cabinet, the Prime Minister, the king or queen, and so on). War is an act of state, not of private individuals, and as such must be authorised by the state, that is, by individuals acting as representatives of the state.

Second, there must be *just cause*, in other words *fault* on the other side which justifies military action. After all, if a state may not use force against its own citizens without sufficient reason (such as the administration of justice), still less can it use force against citizens *not* within its jurisdiction without good reason. In no case can a state violate the legitimate rights of another, but whereas in the case of its own citizens it can use force for a range of reasons, say to compel the payment of just taxes or promote this or that arrangement, when it comes to another state it does not stand to that state's citizens as lawmaker to subjects, but *only* as protector of its own rights or of the rights of other states to whom it has assumed an obligation. This is what is behind the often-heard denunciation by one state of another's interference in its 'internal affairs' (more common in the Cold War, perhaps, than it is now). No state has a right as such to dictate to another how it should arrange things politically or economically, how it should promote the common good or protect its citizens.

The third principle is that the state must go to war with the right intention, namely the desire to obtain a good or prevent an evil. Even if the cause is just, motives of greed, cruelty or malice are not acceptable. There has to be a specific grievance that the state wants to remedy.

5.3.2 Just cause

Naturally, it is the 'just cause' provision around which there has been most debate. It is one thing to say that there must be just cause for going to war, and another to specify what is and is not just.

The central idea is that a just cause is provided by the fact that a nation has done or menaces an injury to another nation, where that injury cannot be repaired without military action and is so serious that the evils of war are less than those that would result from tolerating the injury.

To say that the injury cannot be repaired without war is to say that war must *always be a last resort*: all other means must have been exhausted, that is, tried but without satisfaction. Hence there must already have been serious (not superficial or for public relations only) attempts at negotiation, arbitration, diplomacy and mediation; and other non-military measures must have had no effect or be out of the question for one reason or another, such as economic sanctions, blockades, boycotts, protests, threats, non-cooperation in other areas, and the like. After the Falklands War in 1982, for instance, it was said by some, not least American, mediators that Britain could have tried more in the way of diplomacy and negotiation than she was prepared to. It may well be that domestic conditions (Margaret Thatcher's unpopularity at home due to economic recession, and her shrewd guess that a relatively painless but spectacular adventure would enhance her prestige at little cost) made the war against Argentina more likely than it should have been. The fact, however, that the latter country had already carried out aggression by invasion, rather than merely threatening to do so, made a forceful response by Britain more pressing, and mitigated to some extent the lack of British enthusiasm for negotiation.

PDE means that war is never justified for a small injury, given that the cost is always so great. No country should go to war over a small insult, a slight to her reputation, minor economic damage whether negligent or malicious (assuming this is not the precursor of something worse), a minor skirmish or provocation, or over something of relatively small importance, such as an insignificant amount of territory. For instance, it would have been quite wrong for the USA to have declared war on the Soviet Union for the shooting down of one of its U2 spy planes in 1962 (whether or not it had been in Soviet airspace). Also, every so often civilian aeroplanes are shot down for one reason or another, sometimes because they are mistaken for spy planes or are in forbidden airspace, and whilst the tragedy of such accidents is always great, it is not enough to justify a declaration of war, which would make the shooting-down of a plane look very small by comparison. There was a period in the 1960s and 1970s when there were regular skirmishes between Chinese and Soviet troops, but the thought of the destruction a war would bring between these two huge countries rightly made them shy away from the prospect.

The more devastating war is, as in the modern age with its atomic, chemical and biological weapons, the potential for laying waste whole cities and regions and for devastating the environment for decades to come, the more we can say that only the gravest reasons justify resort to full-scale conflict. Even if a state has justice on its side, it is prudent and charitable to the rest of humanity (and to the aggressor) to desist, as did America during the Cuban missile crisis of 1962 when the prospect of all-out nuclear war loomed large. Perhaps it is right for the just-war theorist to say that in the modern age – and here he will still differ from the true modern-age pacifist, while taking on much of what he says – nothing short of a nation's very survival will justify a war that is likely to bring mass destruction. Maybe nothing less than a threat to what might be called spiritual values will do, such as tyranny, a genocidal attack, enslavement or religious oppression. In the modern age, when a state considers whether to wage war, it must consider not just the effect on the enemy and itself, but on the world as a whole, including posterity: future generations might have to pay dearly for a war fought before they came into existence in a way that was unthinkable only a couple of centuries ago. We can see this in the effect of radiation on the Japanese in Hiroshima and Nagasaki, and in the damage to infrastructure that can take a nation decades to rebuild.

On the other hand, the modern-age pacifist is wrong to think that all modern war is 'total' war. In fact, when we look at many conflicts of the last half of the twentieth century, we see mainly 'limited' wars which stay confined to certain areas, do not involve every citizen in the nation, do not involve atomic, chemical or biological weapons, and do in the end cause a settlement of one kind or another, sometimes for the better. For instance, whatever the destruction and the hardship, the South Koreans had every right to resist the North Korean communist attack that would have turned the entire peninsula into a gulag. Whether the Americans were right to assist is another matter, though the post-Second World War climate, when communist Russia had taken over half of Europe and China had gone communist only a year before, suggests the Americans had every right to fear a potential world communist movement that could end up lapping at her own shores. Despite some fears over China, the war remained confined to the Korean peninsula and succeeded in keeping the North at bay.

The Falklands War and the Gulf War are other examples of limited conflicts. In the latter case one might debate the benefits that were secured by reducing Iraq to a state of poverty and seething vengeance for

years afterwards, but *if* it is true that the West's oil supplies were under
serious threat, and *if* it is true that all other means for resolving the conflict had been exhausted (both at least arguable assumptions), then the
fact that the war was a modern one did not preclude its justification: it
clearly was not a 'total' war. What the modern-age pacifist does not take
on board when looking at military conflict in our day is the *benefit* that
technology can bring, in the form of 'smart' weapons that, when used
properly, can destroy an intended target with very little collateral damage. The use of computers, satellites, remote sensing, precision bombing,
and state-of-the-art communications makes it much easier to control what
an army does and to pinpoint enemy targets. On the other hand, the pacifist is correct to point out the dehumanising effect 'remote' war can have
on those who fight it. It is very hard to forget the way in which the Gulf
War commanders in 1991 showed footage of 'smart' bombs destroying
Iraqi targets as though it was taken from a video game, joking about 'the
luckiest guy in Iraq' who missed being blown up by seconds. And it is
hard to forget the film of helicopter pilots picking off Iraqi soldiers and
civilians on the Basra Road, all of them *fleeing*, with the pilots acting as
though they were in a video arcade playing the latest hi-tech game. And
yet the technology *allowed* them to behave in this way, so efficient is it.
This is the double-edged sword that technology always is, capable in war
both of minimising damage and of dehumanising those who employ it.

What if there is fault on both sides in a conflict? After all, the more one
digs into the facts of a war, the harder it sometimes is to work out just
who was right. In the Mexican – American war over Texas, who had
justice on their side? The Texans voted for annexation by the USA more
than once, but the land belonged to Mexico. Both Mexicans and Anglo-
Americans had settled there. The more one delves, the more confused by
facts one can be. There is often no black-and-white situation, with one
side wholly in the right and the other wholly in the wrong. According to
just-war theory, when the injuries by each side to the other are about
equal, then neither is in a position to attack the other. If both sides break
treaties, renege on undertakings, refuse to co-operate, make grabs for each
other's land, and so on, then neither party has right on its side. If, on the
other hand, the injuries are unequal, or one side shows a willingness to
cease injuring the other, then the less guilty nation can have a just cause
for making war if the other persists in its injustices or has inflicted an evil
for which only war can make satisfaction.

If it is possible for a war to be fought in a limited fashion without threatening mass destruction, without spreading like wildfire, and without involving the entire citizenry, then any one of the following might constitute a sufficient cause: (1) a grave insult or humiliation to a government which threatens morale and promotes civil unrest; (2) an attack on property, territory or independence; (3) the recovery of stolen land; (4) the violation of a state's neutrality with respect to another war; (5) the protection of a state's citizens from physical danger in any part of the world (think of the Israeli raid on Entebbe Airport in 1976 – note that all military action, short of full-scale war, is governed by the same principles); (6) the protection of a state's commerce or free action in its own sphere; (7) the upholding of treaties and international laws and obligations; (8) the defence of a third party unjustly attacked, whether there is a treaty of protection or the countries are simply allies; (9) the defence of a weaker nation against a bully (Kuwait?); (10) the defence of a government attacked by its subjects (assistance to the White Russians following the Russian Revolution?).

What about one of the most common kinds of war, namely one fought to bring 'the benefits of modern civilisation' to another country, whether it be, say, nineteenth-century imperial wars or late twentieth-century wars aimed at bringing 'reform' and 'democracy'? Colonial war usually has both the motive of supplying benefits and the motives of greed and expansion. These latter reasons are not in themselves good ones, since greed is a vice whether of individuals or of states. On the other hand, it would be an exercise of the virtue of charity for one state to use force in assisting a people to set up a government where they did not already have one. Some political organisation is better than none, so if a state saw the possibility of bringing order where there was previously anarchy, it is hard to see why this would be in itself wrong. If, however, a nation already has a workable government providing law, order and basic services, military action would not be justified merely for the motive of bringing 'better' government.

The reason for disallowing action by one state to 'improve' conditions in another state derives from the idea that states ought to be allowed, wherever possible, to sort out their own affairs according to the Principle of Subsidiarity. This principle, which politicians in Europe are more fond of stating than implementing, is as follows: the family is prior to the state; the state exists for the good of its members; the state has the right and duty to direct, aid and supplement the activities of persons, families and other social groups in doing what promotes the common good; but the state is forbidden to take over the functions of private persons, families and other groups, and may not destroy or impair any natural rights of association or action by such persons and groups. To put all these elements into a nutshell, the Principle of Subsidiarity says that the state may not act contrary to the common good, beyond the common good, or contrary to private good in matters that are best taken care of by private initiative and free effort. For example, it is not for the state to tell parents how to bring up their children; to tell families how to manage their budgets; to interfere with the organisation of trade-union and workers' associations genuinely devoted to protecting the rights of workers; to centralise at a national level the day-to-day management of local communities and neighbourhoods. What is best left to the individual, the family or the community should be handled by them, not by the state. But then, it follows from the Principle of Subsidiarity that where the state *is* best placed to promote the common good – say, by regulating the system of government, elections and the like – it should maintain those functions in the absence of a higher authority *better* placed to perform them. And no state is higher than another state. So it is not for one state to take it upon itself to provide 'better' government for another by force. (A state might *request* help from another in this area, say in the supervision of a transition from dictatorship to democracy, but that is another matter.)

The job of a state, then, is to protect its legitimate interests and those of its citizens, not to dictate to other countries how they should organise their affairs. But the boundaries are easily blurred, as they were during the Cold War. To what extent is a state permitted to use force against the *evil* regime of another? It is one thing to help a government attacked by its subjects, but what if the subjects are attacked by their government? What actions were legitimate against Hitler's Germany before the Second World War, when the state unjustly persecuted whole racial and religious groups, or against Communist Russia with its repression, forced starvation through collectivisation, show trials and gulags? Does one state have the right to attack another to bring an end to, say, cannibalism, human sacrifice or the systematic murder of innocent human beings?

In general, we should say that no state can act as moral policeman for the world, much as some would like to. It is wrong for any person to force another to love virtue or detest vice, and the same goes for states. On the other hand, while it is not the duty of a person to make another do more works of charity, for instance, it may, as we have seen, be legitimate to stop one person attacking another, if not always a duty. Here, it appears, we do have a parallel between the individual and the state, but there are important qualifications. Just as the order of charity dictates that a person must love himself before others, and his family and those to whom he has special responsibilities before total strangers, so the state must consider the welfare of its own citizens first and foremost. A person with no strong emotional attachments or responsibilities might, in a society with a high level of violence, devote his life to protecting the elderly and the vulnerable against attack. (Suppose the police and other structures are ineffective.) In such a case he has only himself to think about and is in a position to take great risks. If a person has a family, however, he has to think very carefully before taking risks to life and limb in order to protect strangers – he has his own people to think about first. On the other hand, the state *always* has its citizens to think about first. It is never in a position to use force to protect third parties without having to consider carefully the impact on its own citizens. To commit them to the hardship of war in the protection of the rights of people who are not its subjects, therefore, is an extreme decision, and it is hard to see how anything less than the gravest violations of human rights, on a massive scale, would justify it.

I presented above a list of causes for war which can be considered just, all things being equal. Some causes that would be *insufficient* to justify military action are: (1) greed, envy, glory, the enlargement of territory, all of these exhibiting vicious motives; (2) commercial advantage; (3) distractions from domestic problems (the 'Wag the Dog' scenario, made famous by Hollywood and exemplified by Bill Clinton with his bombing of Sudan and Afghanistan at a politically opportune moment); (4) injuries resulting from provocation (qualification: a state can still exercise limited self-defence against an attack it provokes itself (as with individuals), but may not use it as a pretext for a declaration of war or for a response aimed at conquest. Germany was permitted to defend itself against Polish action that it had itself *provoked*, but this gave it no right to invade and conquer Poland); (5) unfriendliness by a state or commercial non-cooperation short of active injury (no state has the *right* to another's friendship or co-operation, any more than an individual does – in the absence of prior undertakings).

5.3.3 Questions about the justice of the cause

How certain must a state be of the justice of its cause before it goes to war? The answer is – as certain as it can be. Some say the state must be *morally* certain, that is, not absolutely certain, but so sure that if it turned out to be wrong it would not have been culpable for being so. (If Celia tells Dianne the test is on Friday, and Celia is otherwise trustworthy and Dianne has no other way of checking, Dianne can be *morally* certain the test is on Friday: even if the test is on Thursday and she fails to turn up, Dianne is not to blame for her error, having relied on an otherwise trustworthy source of information.) The point is that going to war is such an extreme decision to take that a state must have eliminated every reasonable doubt about the rightness of its cause before it resorts to the use of force. It is rather like a jury deciding whether to find someone guilty of murder, if the penalty is mandatory execution: war is a kind of death sentence for both sides, so the state should be as certain as a jury must be when deciding the life or death of an accused person.

The same goes for individual citizens deciding whether to volunteer for a war. They are obliged to convince themselves beyond reasonable doubt that what they are volunteering for is just. If they are not so convinced, they are bound to follow their consciences and refrain from volunteering. Many people, especially in the First World War when so few men knew what modern war was all about, volunteered for what they thought was a great adventure that would take them to Berlin, where they would 'teach Kaiser Bill a lesson'. They soon found out the reality. It is very difficult indeed to see how the First World War was anything but a bloody waste of life, serving no just cause on either side. If individuals had thought more about the facts and less about the promised adventure, millions of lives could have been saved (the assumption, perhaps rash, being that it would have been relatively easy to see through the government propaganda spewed out on both sides).

When it comes to conscription, however, the matter tilts in a slightly different direction. It is a reasonable assumption that a state will not force its citizens to go to war unless it believes there is a pressing need to do so, one that strikes at the state's vital interests. Where a citizen has a doubt, even reasonable, about the rightness of a cause for which he is being conscripted, he should generally obey the government because of the defeasible presumption that the government knows what it is doing. Note that this does *not* imply the attitude 'my country right or wrong', or that a citizen is obliged to fight in a manifestly unjust cause. Plenty of tyrannical governments throughout history have conscripted people to fight for nothing more than greed and glory, and it is right to resist such conscription. But where there is doubt, the presumption should lie with the government: the natural assumption is that governments are not evil and are not bent on harming their citizens, and would only bring great hardship on them for a good reason. But the assumption, and presumption that goes with it, are *defeasible*. If a conscript is morally certain that the cause is *unjust*, he should obey his conscience and refuse to fight. (Mere objection from religious or philosophical principle is not enough to justify conscientious objection if the conscript culpably believes false principles, such as the idea that all violence is wrong in itself.) To take an analogy, once a war has begun, a soldier is bound to obey his commanding officer even if he has reasonable doubts about the wisdom or morality of the order: the presumption must be that the commander is in a position to know what is best. (Example: is this installation military or civilian?) But if an order is flagrantly immoral – say, to execute a manifestly innocent civilian – the soldier must disobey. Hence the invalidity of the excuse former Nazis used at Nuremberg, 'I was only obeying orders.' But note that it is not enough for the commander to be *himself morally wrong* in issuing the order (say, to destroy a military installation for little benefit, or at great risk to his men); it has to be morally wrong *for the soldier to obey it* (as would be the case if it involved the killing of innocent civilians). The same goes for the state: the conscript cannot object simply because the war is, say, risky, costly or likely to bring mass destruction; it has to be the case that he would be fighting in a manifestly unjust cause, such as theft of territory or property, or a war of genocide or an attack on an innocent population.

We frequently read in the history books of states that go to war both chanting 'God is with us!' Every state thinks it has justice on its side. We saw that if both sides have equal fault, neither is in a position to attack the other, just as when two people provoke a quarrel with equal guilt. But can justice be on both sides? *Objectively* speaking, only one side can ever be right in a war, just as only one side of a moral debate can ultimately be correct. But there is a *subjective* aspect to justice, the aspect concerned with *decision-making*. Suppose Helen wants to take Joanna's copy of *War and Peace*, believing Joanna stole it from her. Joanna says Helen gave it to her as a present. Who is right? Objectively, only one of them can be, but there is a further question of the blameworthiness of actions. If Helen knows full well she gave the book to Joanna but insists on taking it back, she is not in good faith and acts wrongly. But if she is persuaded she is right, and is not acting from *culpable* ignorance (she should have known better), she is in good faith when she takes back the book and not to be

blamed on that account. Needless to say, Joanna might be equally persuaded that the book is hers, and would be right to resist. The same goes
for inter-state conflict. If a government sincerely and *reasonably* believes
in the justice of its cause, it is right to act on this belief, and its citizens are
also obliged to follow their state, subject to the principles set out above.

Can there be justice and injustice on the *same* side? Clearly there can, in
at least three situations: (1) a state has a just cause but uses unjust means,
such as massacring non-combatants or engaging in lies and deceit; (2) a
state has a just cause that mutates into an unjust cause (for example, a
war to regain territory might turn into a war of conquest after the achievement of the legitimate end; in this sense the USA was right not to forge
ahead to Baghdad in 1991 with the aim of deposing Saddam Hussein,
because the war was for the express purpose of liberating Kuwait); (3) a
state may have a just *immediate* cause, but not have right on its side if one
traces back through history (this might be said of the situation regarding
the Falklands). In the first case, the end never justifies the means. In the
second, the state must restrict its action to the legitimate end. In the third,
history is important in assessing interstate conflicts, but there is a point
when its relevance lapses. It is no exaggeration to say that just about
every modern state has a legitimate grievance against every other, if you
go back enough centuries. But to preserve order and peace wherever possible, lapse of time must extinguish some causes eventually, especially if
the aggrieved state acts in such a way as to show that it accepts the status
quo. For instance, the Palestinians have never renounced their claim to
the Holy Land, and so at this point lapse of time has not extinguished
whatever justice there is on their side. The same could be said of the Jews
with respect to the same territory, though they have had many more centuries during which lapse of time could have had an effect. A similar situation exists with regard to Northern Ireland. Naturally, we cannot possibly
evaluate the relative merits of each case without detailed examination of
the facts; but the principle is clear that at some point history 'cuts out',
and when this happens is determined largely by the way nations behave,
and what they say about themselves both to themselves and to others.

Before beginning a war, a nation must do the following things: (1) examine the facts with very great diligence indeed, seeking advice wherever
possible, both from friends and from impartial observers, and taking counsel from its own citizens; (2) weigh the merits of the cause *objectively*,
ignoring both vested interests (always the most potent, but covert, in such
situations) and foreign agitation. If it has a reasonable doubt it must re-

frain from military action; (3) judge whether it has a *well-grounded expectation of victory*. States that go on military adventures act like criminals, exposing their citizens to immense hardship without bothering to see whether they have a chance of achieving their end. The cost of war is so great that the government must have a solid belief in the chance of winning (part of the double-effect reasoning that must be gone through); (4) try all other means first, short of force, as suggested above. Once the decision at least to prepare for war is made, but before actual commencement, the state must: (1) issue an ultimatum to the other side; (2) allow all foreigners to leave, including, of course, citizens and representatives of the potential enemy.

In summary, can war in the modern age ever be justified? From what we have seen, the answer is yes: (1) if the supreme interests of the nation are at stake, such as independence, interests vital to the state's existence, and treaty obligations, then the state may be allowed to act, for it cannot surrender its right of self-defence any more than an individual can, nor its solemn undertaking to defend others; (2) if something less that supreme interests are at stake, war is much less hard to justify, given both the terrible potential cost of modern war and the range of available options for solving conflicts, short of violence. Using double-effect reasoning, the less important a state's interest the more limited a war must be, with the state using all available technology to minimise death and destruction.

5.4   Conduct During War

The theory of the just war does not apply only to the evaluation of *whether* to go to war, but also of how to act *in* a war. The just-war theorist rejects the notion that 'war is hell' in the sense that it is beyond all morality. As a matter of fact, there is hardly a war in history that has not involved atrocities, injustices and flagrant immoralities. All this shows, however, is that in extreme situations morality is as necessary as ever to restrain human evil and prevent soldiers from acting like barbarians.

The primary purpose of a war, once begun, is to fight to win. It is wrong to fight just for a stalemate (as happened in the First World War) or for the needless prolongation of a war (as arguably happened in the Second World War: the reader is encouraged to look at Major-General

Richard Rohmer's book *Patton's Gap*[10]). But 'fighting to win' does not equal 'fighting with all means necessary'. As was said earlier, some means are morally unlawful, every bit as wrong as they would be if implemented by an individual in peacetime. Some of them are the usual wrongful acts relating to the taking of life and destruction of property, but on the larger scale that war involves. As prime examples, we can note the following: (1) murder, that is, the direct killing of innocent and unarmed persons, which includes non-combatants such as old people, women and children (if they are in combat they are legitimate targets, of course, though mercy should be exercised where possible), soldiers who are surrendering, destruction of transport vehicles (ships, aeroplanes and cars) carrying non-combatants and not themselves on military errands (the passenger ship *Lusitania*, whose sinking in 1915 was the official cause of the American entry into the war in 1917, was carrying weapons, though whether this justified the immense loss of life is another matter), and massacres of civilian and defenceless populations; (2) rape or the establishment of brothels (for example, the 'comfort women' used by the Japanese in China and during the Second World War); (3) theft and pillage; (4) wanton destruction of places of worship; (5) attempts to lure enemy soldiers away from loyalty to their commanders (this is at least dishonourable); (6) lying, breach of treaties and solemn undertakings, forgery, false atrocity stories (spread by both sides in the two world wars, though we usually only hear of the lies from the other side); (7) the use of innocent people as 'human shields' (a common practice nowadays, as seen in the deliberate location of military installations in civilian areas); (8) extermination and depopulation, even of combatant areas, which is almost always a disproportionate means.

Does the prohibition on lying prevent any kind of deception? Clearly not, or else war could not be fought at all. There is nothing wrong with concealment of information from those (the enemy) who have no right to know. There is nothing wrong with ambushes, which take advantage of an enemy's ignorance or vulnerability. Deliberate and explicit misrepresentation of the facts is another matter, however. Modern war always uses disinformation and spurious intelligence, but this looks like outright lying. For instance, the Allies misrepresented to the Germans in 1944 that they were going to land at Calais rather than Normandy. It was perhaps not a straight lie to send ships and material to Calais in order to make it look like there would be a landing there, but to the extent that false intelligence was sent out *saying* so, this was arguably impermissible. 'How ridiculous,' you will reply, 'it is all right to misrepresent without being explicit – just don't *say* X, but make it *look* like X is the case! And anyway, how can you win a war without lying?' This is no place to enter into the complex issue of the morality of lying. Suffice it to say that many wars have been won without outright falsehoods being told. Truth is a good, and to lie is to attack it head on. You may conceal, you may equivocate, you may send out ambiguous signals, feinting and weaving so that the enemy is not sure what the truth is; but then you obviously have no obligation to *enhance* the enemy's knowledge, any more than I have an obligation to enhance your knowledge! Something less than explicit misrepresentation is not evidently an attack on truth, even if it does not promote truth, and even if it places truth as a good in a subordinate place to some other good, such as life.

Reprisals against innocent civilians may be prohibited, but what about reprisals in general? If the enemy chooses to use a particularly nasty kind of weapon, say gas or cluster bombs, it is not obviously wrong for the other side to respond in kind, with the aim of punishing and deterring such behaviour. In other words, if one side 'ups the ante', there is no reason as such why the other side cannot take up the challenge. But it is absolutely wrong to respond to one immoral action, say the murder of innocents, by committing another, as two wrongs do not make a right. (If traditional ethics does not teach this, it teaches nothing.) The only proper course is either to protest vigorously or to increase the pressure on legitimate targets.

It is the combatant/non-combatant distinction that has been the focus of so much attention by contemporary writers. It is one thing to speak blithely of those in uniform and those not, of civilians and soldiers, of legitimate and illegitimate targets. But can such distinctions really be made in modern warfare, in the era of 'total war' when all the resources of a nation are devoted to supplying and maintaining the military machine? The French soldier Marshal Pétain, reflecting on the First World War, said: 'Henceforth the object of war appears in all its amplitude and all its cruel simplicity: it has become the destruction not of an army but of a nation.'[11] One might take this as an endorsement of the idea that 'war is hell', or as a *reductio ad absurdum* of the very concept of a modern just war. Both these positions are, however, mistaken. To speak of 'the destruction of a nation' is itself misleading. Certainly there have been wars in which at least one side has aimed at this, and even achieved it; but that tragic fact does not make such an aim morally legitimate. No cause can ever justify the wiping out of a nation. But modern war can be fought, and has been fought, without such an objective. Furthermore, if the idea of 'total war' is supposed to imply that no meaningful distinction can be made between combatants and non-combatants, the implication is false. As Dr Johnson said, the existence of twilight does not mean that you cannot distinguish day from night. We no longer live in an age where armies are relatively self-contained and distinctive units fighting each other on battlefields far removed from civilian activity. (This was true, to a large extent, in the classical and medieval periods.) Modern armies require a continuous supply of matériel, and when a nation enters into full-scale war, as in both world wars, almost every citizen will participate in some way, however indirectly, even if it means sending food parcels or morale-boosting letters, or working in a factory producing material destined for some sort of military use, even if not the manufacture of armaments as such. But participating indirectly in a military enterprise does not make one a combatant *ipso facto*. And the general principle should be maintained that an army may not intentionally kill non-combatants, any more than if one person attacks another, the second is entitled to attack the aggressor's friends and supporters, even those who provide assistance that does not amount to fighting or activity essential to fighting (words of encouragement, for example).

Those who are direct combatants in a war are, of course, the soldiers (on land, sea and air) and those commanding them. Indirect combatants are the unarmed auxiliaries providing logistical support such as munitions manufacture, supply, transport, engineering, communications and computing. The question of who is wearing a uniform is not as helpful as it ought to be. All direct combatants will be in uniform, but some auxiliaries (such as weapons manufacturers) will not be. But some non-combatants will also be in uniform. Non-combatants include enemy subjects who are not direct or indirect combatants as well as those people and nations observing neutrality (whatever their sympathies). Among non-combatants there are persons in civil life and occupation, the old, the sick, women and children (though all of these might be and have been called up for action, especially when a nation is desperate). Two tricky categories are medical personnel and military chaplains. Both of these, at least when in a combat zone, are typically in uniform, and yet neither should be regarded as combatants, direct or indirect. Chaplains are obviously concerned with the soldiers' spiritual well-being, not their military activity as such (whatever tasks they may perform in an emergency), and so do not themselves fight or materially support combat, at least as their primary object. (They also help soldiers to control their fear and deal with other psychological problems that may impede their fighting activity; so they do assist in combat in a secondary sense.) The position of medics is a bit more difficult: after all, if it is permissible to attack people who repair tanks, why not people who repair soldiers? The traditional position is that medics and chaplains simply do not make a significant enough contribution to the prosecution of a war as their primary *raison d'être* for them to be considered combatants, and also that even if they do assist materially to some degree, the humanitarian purpose of their activity makes it an act of cruelty and inhumanity to treat them as legitimate targets.

Whatever the blurred edges and hard cases created by modern war, then, we can and should maintain a distinction between combatants and non-combatants. The question that needs to be asked is: Now that war is going on, what is the *primary* purpose or function of this individual's regular activity? Someone who goes on doing exactly what he was doing before the war, say working in the same supermarket, in the same clerical job, in the same school, retains his civilian status. If a person's kind of job stays the same but becomes devoted to helping the war effort, such as the manufacture of ball-bearings that were intended for cars but are now for tanks, he becomes an indirect combatant. The mere fact that someone helps combatants directly or indirectly, however, does not of itself make him a combatant if what he is doing is primarily humanitarian or charitable. If someone is helping the war effort but in a minor way (helping to boost morale, for instance), he does not become a combatant. And if he is not helping the war effort at all (whatever his sympathies), he will be as far from combatant status as is possible in a society at war.

The principle governing the combatant/non-combatant distinction is that combatants may legitimately and intentionally be killed, wounded, assaulted, attacked, harassed, blockaded, besieged, starved, intimidated and threatened. Cruel, malicious or vindictive action as such is wrong – the action must be a genuine element in a tactic or strategy for winning the war. So, for instance, one might question whether the Germans' long siege of Leningrad during the Second World War was a legitimate war aim. (One would have to examine the military facts, but it is at least arguable that the siege was governed more by malice than by a coherent strategy, and that the primary aim was the unacceptable one of demoralising non-combatants.) As far as non-combatants go, PDE must be applied:

does the legitimate military action against combatants justify the harm that is likely to be caused to non-combatants? It is permissible to attack a military target even if civilians will be killed, for example civilian ships and planes carrying arms. It is permissible to cut supplies to troops even if civilians will starve. The same goes for bombing a military target located in a civilian area. But the question must *always* be whether the good to be achieved, the positive contribution to overall strategy and tactics, justifies the scale of the damage civilians will suffer.

The problem with modern war is that it is so hard *physically* and *geographically* to keep military and civilian targets separate. In earlier times armies kept themselves quite distinct, indeed, they wore bright and colourful uniforms partly for this reason, and they fought in fields and open spaces. Commanders and strategists then began to think how 'ridiculous' this was from a purely military point of view: why advertise yourself? Why not fight in a 'dirtier' way, using what we now call 'guerrilla' tactics, camouflage, hit and run, mixing in with the local population and emerging only to carry out raids? This was especially successful in the American War of Independence and led to the British army's being outwitted and outmanoeuvred again and again.

The consequence is the same as it has always been in our 'enlightened' age when advances in technology and logistics are made: morality suffers a setback. It is now standard operational procedure for an army to camouflage itself as much as possible, to carry out 'black' or underground operations alongside the more obvious campaign, to make good use of the local population as 'human shields'. Needless to say, not every army employs every tactic in the book, but gone are the days when soldiers lined up in massed ranks against each other. As a result, distinguishing combatants from non-combatants is often very difficult, and attacking the former while preserving the latter is more often than not an impossibility. This is one of the unspoken reasons why the Gulf War in 1991 was psychologically fairly easy for Western societies to support: it was in the desert, far away from civilians, a sheer test of firepower between combatants. Of course the reality was more complicated, and when the Iraqis showed film of civilians killed by American or British bombing, the truth became more apparent and harder to swallow (not much harder, though, given the low level of casualties on the British/American side).

Modern-age pacifists, then, are quite right to point to the difficulties inherent in this aspect of contemporary warfare, but it remains the case that civilian casualties can be justified as a foreseen side effect of achieving a sufficiently important military objective. There is no mathematical calculation that can be performed, no equation to solve – we are, here, in a murky part of moral theory, forced to use terms such as 'significant', 'important', 'major', 'minor'. But without the principles just-war theory provides for dealing with hard cases, the whole idea of the ethical regulation of war vanishes. It becomes a free-for-all, as no doubt some people think it should be, or it is ruled out from the beginning – something I have argued cannot be supported. Moreover, there are plenty of cases where there is an obvious answer to the question: can this target be attacked? It would be wrong to bomb a civilian area containing thousands of non-combatants and only a few hundred infantry; to torch a village on the off-chance that it contains a spy; to attack a munitions factory surrounded by hospitals. 'But why should the other side be allowed to get away with it by exploiting our ethical standards, standards they do not even share?' This is a question that may be asked in many areas of life, including everyday personal relations. Principled people are regularly exploited by the unprincipled, and the former have a choice: to descend to the level of the rest, that is to *compromise* themselves; or to maintain their integrity.

What PDE tells us, though, is that the death of non-combatants can never be used as a *means* to the achievement of a legitimate military objective, no matter how important. Mass civilian bombing, a conspicuous feature of the Second World War, Korea and Vietnam (to name a few), is one of the actions pacifists readily – and rightly, I believe – point to as a totally unacceptable part of modern warfare. Mass bombing of *military* targets would only be justified if the damage done to the war effort was proportional to any damage to the civilian population. The German bombing of British centres of heavy industry during the Second World War, even though there were thousands of civilian deaths, was justifiable on the assumption that the aim was to disrupt the war effort. On the other hand, the Blitz on London, and the bombing of other overwhelmingly civilian targets (itself provoked by earlier British raids on Berlin), were aimed solely at demoralising the population by massacring civilians. Exactly the same can be said for the Allied destruction of Dresden in 1945, one of the great crimes of the Second World War. Even if the 135,000 civilian deaths had been only a foreseen effect of a legitimate objective, they were grossly disproportionate to whatever good was secured, as Dresden's military importance was next to zero. In fact, however, there was no military objective – the aim was precisely to demoralise the German population by wiping out non-combatants and flattening one of Europe's most beautiful cities. In the words of just-war theorist Paul Ramsey:

> fact that Dresden was of no military importance at all commensurate with the destruction let loose upon it, that it was an undefended city swollen with refugees, and that achieving the maximum destruction of human lives without discrimination through fire-storm and by concentrating on residential sectors and not on industries was 'an integral part of the strategy' – all this defines the wickedness done at Dresden.[12]

The same goes for the firebombing of Tokyo, and the atomic bombings of Hiroshima and Nagasaki, with the addition in the latter two cases that innocent people are continuing to feel the effects of these war crimes, via birth defects and deformities passed on through mutated genes. Only those who refuse to look at the facts would continue to agree with President Harry S. Truman that the bomb on Hiroshima was aimed at a 'purely military' target, as he wrote in his diary (about what the prospective target should be). The city did house the headquarters of the Second Army, responsible for the defence of southern Japan. It was also a communications centre and an assembly area for troops. In August 1945, however, there were 43,000 soldiers stationed there, with another 280,000 civilians, giving a civilian/military ratio of over six to one.[13] In his memoirs, Truman said: 'I wanted it dropped on a military target. I had told [Secretary of War] Stimson that the bomb should be dropped as nearly as possibly [sic] upon a war production center of prime military importance.'[14]

It is doubtful, from what Truman said both before and after the bombing of Hiroshima, that he believed it involved anything other than the intentional killing of large numbers of Japanese civilians as a *means* of ending the war. And Stimson himself clearly believed the bombings were straightforward civilian massacres justified by the quick ending of the war and the sparing of the lives of hundreds of thousands of American soldiers.[15] Whether a 'purely military target' or a 'war production center of prime military importance', it was clear that the purely *military* damage that could be done to Hiroshima would not end the war. Hence Truman's repeated references to the 'terror' the bomb would instil in the Japanese population at large, and to its demoralising effect. (One wonders also about the integrity of Truman's having refused to make Tokyo an atomic bomb target whilst ordering the firebombing of the city, which took as many lives and caused as much damage as the bomb over Hiroshima. Nor did he countenance making Kyoto an A-bomb target, since it was a sacred religious city for Japanese Buddhism; and yet he approved the atomic bombing of Nagasaki, which was Japan's most important Christian centre.) Here we can see the way in which, as I argued in chapter 3 of *Moral Theory*, the application of PDE requires the gathering and interpretation of evidence as to an agent's state of mind. Did Truman and Stimson actually intend to kill civilian non-combatants as a means to ending the war? They may not have said as much explicitly – that is the exception rather than the rule – but their other words and the circumstances of the case suggest that this was their intention.

Suppose, as Truman, Stimson, and the rest of the US command believed, that many more combatant lives were indeed spared than non-combatant lives taken by the use of atomic weapons and firebombing (around 300,000 were killed in Tokyo, Hiroshima and Nagasaki) – though even this is debatable. Did the end justify the means? If the theory I have been defending is correct, it did not. Size and numbers do not matter: whether it is one murder to save two lives, or the massacre of tens of thousands to save hundreds of thousands, the killing of the innocent is a crime against humanity. In all three cases it was used as a *means* to demoralise the population, in defiance of all norms of right conduct. The acts were every bit as bad as the killing of prisoners of war, the rape of women, and the collective punishment of the innocent for the acts of others – all of which were committed by both sides during the Second World War. In the words of the philosopher Elizabeth Anscombe, when she bravely opposed the granting of an honorary degree by the University of Oxford to Mr Truman in the 1950s:

[W]ith Hiroshima and Nagasaki we are not confronted with a borderline case. In the bombing of these cities it was certainly decided to kill the innocent as a means to an end. And a very large number of them, all at once, without warning, without the interstices of escape or the chance to take shelter, which existed even in the 'area bombings' of the German cities.

I have long been puzzled by the common cant about President Truman's courage in making this decision. Of course, I know that you can be cowardly without having reason to think you are in danger. But how can you be courageous? Light has come to me lately: the term is an acknowledgement of the truth. Mr. Truman was brave because, and only because, what he did was so bad. But I think the judgement unsound. Given the right circumstances (for example that no one whose opinion matters will disapprove), a quite mediocre person can do spectacularly wicked things without thereby becoming impressive.[16]

The objection, 'But there was no other alternative', is doubly wrong. First, there is nearly always an alternative: in this case, whatever the protestations by some historians, a demonstration atomic bombing could have been carried out that would have killed no one and ended the war just as quickly. (Still, one might question the morality of such an act, which would have amounted to a threat to commit evil, one the USA would not have been allowed to act on. There is no space here to debate the use of threats to employ evil means.) Second, the absence of an alternative does not turn an inherently bad act into a good one: there are no 'necessary evils'.

5.5 Globalism

There are many topics in the ethics of war we have not looked at, such as the treatment of prisoners, the conduct of diplomacy, the ethics of neutrality, and others. But the basic principles of just-war theory have been outlined and shown to be both plausible and workable, no more in fact than the extension of everyday traditional morality to an extreme situation. And yet one question still looms large, and can only be touched on here. *If* there were a higher, supranational authority regulating relations between states, would this not make the resort to war as unjustifiable as private vendettas and vigilante justice? Just as the state has the role of administering justice within a society, couldn't a world authority do the same for governments, relegating war to the history books?

In the age of 'globalisation', the 'world economy' and the 'interdependence of nations', this is the question ethical and political thinkers ask themselves more than ever. In the words of Tennyson's poem 'Locksley Hall', many long for a world where

the war-drum throbb'd no longer, and the battleflags were furl'd
In the Parliament of man, the Federation of the world.
There the common sense of most shall hold a fretful realm in awe,
And the kindly earth shall slumber, lapt in universal law.

There are two questions, however: could such a system work? and should there be such a system in the first place? As to the first, such a system *could* work, though what we have seen so far is not promising. Since the end of the Cold War, the UN has taken on more effectively its intended role as regulator of international conflict. Whatever its facilitation of diplomacy, however, it has not yet been able to prevent war, only to regulate when and where it takes place (and to some extent how). In fact, it is debatable whether the UN has actually prevented one single war from taking place. But this does not mean more powers and greater jurisdiction would not go some way to achieving the globalists' goal of world peace and disarmament. The problem is that even if states are prevented from making war themselves, this will only succeed if the UN itself is in the position of being able to use force to maintain the peace (recall the argument against absolute pacifism above). In other words, short of a complete change in the human condition, war will never disappear; if not practised *by* states, it will still have to be practised *on* states in order to secure compliance with the directives of the New World Order of peace and harmony. And one wonders whether such an arrangement would not be far more invidious than the one we now have: a World Government and a World Army, if truly supranational and not just the puppets of the states (which would mean the continuation of the present dispensation by other means), would be accountable to no one. At least, in the present system, states are accountable to other states for much of their geopolitical conduct.

'But a World Government would be accountable to morality itself, to the Moral Law you have been harping on about for so many pages. Isn't that good enough?' There is some weight to this objection, which leads to the second question. In *principle*, a supranational authority governing the geopolitical conduct of states is not objectionable. It is not intrinsically immoral. It could do good. It might even cause the beating of swords into ploughshares and spears into pruning hooks. But if the story of the Tower of Babel is anything to go by, the promise is likely to be greater than the reality. To engender true and lasting co-operation between states, given the radical diversities of culture, language and religion, would require nothing short of the extinction of these. Nationalism, already a dirty word in 'progressive' quarters, would have to be outlawed except at international football matches. Self-determination would have to become a by-word for selfishness.

Furthermore, a system of law and government is not worthy of admiration, or perhaps even allegiance, if it does not dispense justice impartially and with consistency. What would we say about a legal system that had one law for the rich and another for the poor? one law for blacks and another for whites? one law for presidents and another for postmen (as is now manifestly the case in the USA)? Similarly, a legal system of international scope must not be hypocritical or incapable of imparting justice blindly. So we should expect of a system of world government (what the globalists call 'global governance', as though 'government' sounds too dictatorial) that it punish not just alleged Balkan war criminals, or ageing Nazi camp commandants, but also the thousands of criminals of the former Soviet Union who murdered millions of their compatriots in crimes against humanity every bit as bad as any seen this century, and the thousands of communist Chinese who have massacred, and continue to oppress, millions of their fellow countrymen. Can any of us realistically envisage the UN even beginning to pursue these murderers, let alone pursuing them with the same vigour and commitment to justice and humanity that it displays in its pursuit of Serbian generals and Middle Eastern dictators? Of course the UN would not dare to challenge the Chinese or the Russians – but that is the whole point. If it cannot challenge them, or will not, then it does not impart justice without fear or favour. And if it cannot do that, it does not satisfy even the minimum requirement for political and juridical legitimacy.

The reality is that you cannot buy perpetual international peace without buying a World Government, a World Army, a World Culture, a World Language, and a World Economy. Perhaps we have the last three already. Globalists regularly talk about the first two. But the Orwellian nightmare such a prospect suggests might be too much for sturdy lovers of peace to bear. Peace and harmony between nations is a prize for which everyone must strive, not just pacifists. War is one of the most terrible activities in which human beings can engage. And yet it appears to be part of the human condition, just another aspect of the selfishness, violence, aggressiveness and arrogance that have bedevilled mankind since the beginning of time. To eliminate it would require nothing less than the mutation of human nature. To control it, on the other hand, is a real possibility requiring eternal vigilance.

The international banker James Warburg told a US Senate subcommittee on 17 February 1950: 'We shall have world government whether or not we like it. The only question is, whether world government will be achieved by conquest or consent.'[17] Whether or not Mr Warburg was correct (and the facts are beginning to bear him out), the truth may lie with the Roman military writer Vegetius (AD 379–95), who said: 'Si vis pacem, para bellum' – 'If you want peace, prepare for war.'[18] And with Aristotle, who said: 'We make war that we may live in peace.'[19]

Notes and Further Reading

Chapter 1

1 The abortion figures cited for the USA, Britain, Australia and Russia are readily available from pro- and anti-abortion groups and government sources.

2 For the views of Morowitz and Trefil, see their book *The Facts of Life: Science and the Abortion Controversy* (Oxford: Oxford University Press, 1992). On the question of foetal pain, see pp. 123–5, 157–9. On brain development, see chs 5 and 6. Note that at p. 86 they reproduce with approval the now discredited and almost certainly fraudulent embryological drawings of the German biologist Ernst Haeckel: see the work of Dr Michael Richardson, reported in *The Times* (London), 11 August 1997, and his 'There is no Highly Conserved Embryonic Stage in the Vertebrates: Implications for Current Theories of Evolution and Development', in *Anatomy and Embryology* 196 (1997), pp. 91–106.

3 P. McCullagh, *The Foetus as Transplant Donor* (Chichester: John Wiley, 1987), p. 129.

4 From the Movement for Christian Democracy, 'Foetal Pain Briefing' (n.d., mid-1990s; I have not been able to trace the original source). An excellent and seminal paper by Professor Liley on the nature of the foetus is his 'The Foetus as a Personality', *Australian and New Zealand Journal of Psychiatry* 6 (1972), pp. 99–105.

5 The abundant evidence (including citations) for foetal sentience can be found in McCullagh, *Foetus* and in the report by the Commission of Inquiry into Foetal Sentience established by the charity CARE, 'Human Sentience before Birth'. Whereas the standard view once was that babies were less sensitive to pain than adults, and foetuses less sensitive than babies, if not totally insensitive, recent research now seems to be showing that the very *opposite* is the case. See the report of recent experiments in the *Sunday Telegraph* (London), 2 August 1998, p. 9.

6 In X. Giannakoulopoulos et al., 'Fetal Plasma Cortisol and Beta-Endorphin

Response to Intrauterine Needling', *The Lancet* 344 (1994), pp. 77–81, at p. 77.

7 Peter Singer, *Practical Ethics* (Cambridge, Cambridge University Press, 1993; 2nd edn), p. 86. (All references to this book are to the second edition unless stated otherwise.)

8 Ibid., pp.142–3.

9 See Roger Lewin, 'Is Your Brain Really Necessary?', *Scientific American* 210 (December 1980), pp. 1232–4, reporting the research of Professor John Lorber, which no one seems to be following up; this shows an unfortunate lack of curiosity on the part of the scientific community, but also may have important implications for the treatment of anencephalic infants, who currently are treated 'selectively' or 'conservatively', that is, killed or allowed to die.

10 On the problems surrounding the concept of 'brain death' as a mark of human death, see Martyn Evans, 'Against Brainstem Death', in R. Gillon (ed.), *Principles of Health Care Ethics* (Chichester: John Wiley, 1994), pp. 1041–51, and 'Death in Denmark', *Journal of Medical Ethics* 16 (1990), pp. 191–4. For a comprehensive survey of the debate concerning 'brain death', and the rejection of it as a criterion of death by a neurophysiologist who once espoused it, see D. Alan Shewmon, MD, 'Recovery from "Brain Death": A Neurologist's Apologia', *Linacre Quarterly* 64 (1997), pp. 30–96.

11 Tooley, *Abortion and Infanticide* (Oxford: Clarendon Press, 1983), pp. 169–70.

12 Jarvis Thomson, 'A Defense of Abortion', reprinted in J. Feinberg (ed.), *The Problem of Abortion* (Belmont: Wadsworth, 1973), pp. 121–39, at p. 121, and originally published in *Philosophy and Public Affairs* 1 (1971), pp. 47–66.

13 Ibid., p. 122.

14 On fertilisation as a biological process, see Stephen Buckle, 'Biological Processes and Moral Events', *Journal of Medical Ethics* 14 (1988), pp. 144–7, and the response by D. S. Oderberg in *Journal of Medical Ethics* 15 (1989), p. 166 (where 'fifteen days' should read 'one full day').

15 For a detailed exploration and refutation of (1) the objection from fission and totipotency and (2) the objection from cloning and parthenogenesis, see D. S. Oderberg, 'Modal Properties, Moral Status and Identity', *Philosophy and Public Affairs* 26 (1997), pp. 259–98, responding to arguments by Peter Singer and others in P. Singer, H. Kuhse et al., *Embryo Experimentation* (Cambridge: Cambridge University Press, 1990). References to Warren Quinn in my article should also be consulted.

16 For a standard but brief account of cloning, see W. Becker, J. Reece and M. Poenie, *The World of the Cell* (Menlo Park, CA: The Benjamins/Cummings Publishing Company, 1996; 3rd edn), p. 614. On the famous case of Dolly the sheep, see I. Wilmut et al., 'Viable Offspring Derived from Fetal and

Adult Mammalian Cells', *Nature* 385 (1997), pp. 810–13.

17 Judith Jarvis Thomson's classic article, 'A Defense of Abortion', is cited above. For a contrary view see John Finnis, 'The Rights and Wrongs of Abortion: A Reply to Judith Jarvis Thomson', *Philosophy and Public Affairs* 2 (1972), pp. 117–45.

18 Tooley, *Abortion and Infanticide*, p. 170.

19 Ibid., p. 349.

20 Singer, *Practical Ethics*, pp. 98–9.

21 Peter Singer, 'On Being Silenced in Germany', which first appeared in the *New York Review of Books*, 15 August 1991, pp. 36–42, and is reprinted as an appendix to his *Practical Ethics*, pp. 337–59, at p. 345 (see further ch. 2, n. 20).

22 Singer, *Practical Ethics*, pp. 357–8.

23 Tooley's consideration of electronic and mechanical potential *persons* is in *Abortion and Infanticide*, pp. 178–83, from where the quotations are taken.

24 Readers who want to learn about the way the abortion debate went in the 1960s and 1970s in the USA should look at the fascinating behind-the-scenes account by Dr Bernard Nathanson, an abortionist who was at the very heart of the pro-abortion activist network (he helped to found NARAL, the National Association for Repeal of the Abortion Laws), and who later became convinced he was wrong, turning with equal passion to the defence of life. See *The Abortion Papers* (New York: Frederick Fell, 1983). On the truth about mortality from illegal abortions, and the shameless lies told by the pro-abortion movement, see pp. 41–2.

Chapter 2

1 Ronald Dworkin, submission to the House of Lords Select Committee on Medical Ethics, in their report on euthanasia, vol. 1, sec. 39 (London: HMSO, 1994).

2 The figures for euthanasia in the Netherlands make depressing reading. According to the government-commissioned Remmelink report, 130,000 people died there in 1990. Of these, 2,300 people (nearly 2 per cent) died as a result of physicians intentionally killing them at their request, by lethal injection. Another 400 people killed themselves with the assistance of their doctors. Another 1,000 were killed *without* being asked. Most of these people were allegedly incapable of giving their consent, but a significant number were fully competent. If this is not bad enough, it gets worse. The Remmelink report states that another 8,100 people were killed by the administration of pain-relieving drugs with the *intention* of hastening their deaths. Of these,

1,350 people were killed by physicians whose *primary* intention was to hasten death, whereas the remaining 6,750 were killed by physicians who primarily intended to relieve pain but *also* to end their patients' lives.

Although 27 per cent of the 8,100 who were intentionally killed by pain-relieving drugs were capable of giving their consent, most of them (60 per cent) were never asked. Why were these additional 8,100 deaths not classified in the report as euthanasia? The reason is that although the deaths were brought about intentionally, they were caused by drugs designed to relieve pain. So the deaths are misleadingly listed under the heading 'Alleviation of Pain Symptoms'.

The 1990 report also reveals that a *further* 7,875 people were killed in that year by withholding life support from them without their consent.

See P. van der Maas et al., 'Euthanasia and other Medical Decisions Concerning the End of Life', *The Lancet* 338 (1991), pp. 669–74; and letter by K. F. Gunning, Secretary, Dutch Physicians' League, *The Lancet* 338 (1991), p. 1010.

Since 1990 the situation in the Netherlands has deteriorated. See P. van der Maas et al., 'Euthanasia, Physician-assisted Suicide, and other Medical Practices Involving the End of Life in the Netherlands, 1990–1995', *New England Journal of Medicine* 335 (1996), pp. 1699–1705. And for a comparable story in Australia, see Helga Kuhse, Peter Singer et al., 'End-of-Life Decisions in Australian Medical Practice', *Medical Journal of Australia* 166 (1997), pp. 191–6. See also 'Involuntary Euthanasia is Out of Control in Holland', *The Times* (London), 16 February 1999.

3   The countenancing of involuntary euthanasia by Jonathan Glover can be found in his *Causing Death and Saving Lives* (London: Penguin, 1977), pp. 191–2.

4   Singer, *Practical Ethics*, p. 99; and see also p. 201.

5   The New Zealand case of the baby who was allowed to die even though her parents wanted her to live was reported in the British magazine *Southern Cross*, 30 September 1998, from where I took my information, but also in all the major daily newspapers in New Zealand, Australia, Britain and elsewhere.

6   The first two quotations at the beginning of the section on voluntary euthanasia are taken from *People's Weekly* magazine, 25 November 1991. The third is from Derek Humphry, *Let Me Die Before I Wake* (Eugene, OR: Hemlock Society, 1991), p. 25.

7   Humphry, *Let Me Die*, p. 61.

8   Singer, *Practical Ethics*, p. 195.

9   The following critique of voluntary euthanasia adapts material from D. S. Oderberg, 'Voluntary Euthanasia and Justice', in D. S. Oderberg and J. A. Laing (eds), *Human Lives: Critical Essays on Consequentialist Bioethics*

(London/New York: Macmillan/St. Martin's Press, 1997), pp. 225–40.

10 Ibid., p. 182.

11 Ibid., p. 90.

12 Ibid., p. 182.

13 Ibid., p. 183.

14 Singer's defence of the replaceability of babies is in ibid., pp. 185–8, and the phrase 'adverse effect[s] ...' is on p. 186. For a critique, see S. Uniacke, 'Replaceability and Infanticide', *The Journal of Value Inquiry* 31 (1997), pp. 153–66; S. Uniacke and H. J. McCloskey, 'Peter Singer and Non-Voluntary Euthanasia: Tripping Down the Slippery Slope', *Journal of Applied Philosophy* 9 (1992), pp. 203–19, at pp. 214–16. The general critique in the second article of Singer's arguments for non-voluntary euthanasia is well worth reading.

15 Jacqueline Laing, 'Innocence and Consequentialism: Inconsistency, Equivocation and Contradiction in the Philosophy of Peter Singer', in Oderberg and Laing (eds), *Human Lives*, pp. 196–224, at p. 209.

16 Singer, *Practical Ethics*, p. 183.

17 P. Singer and D. Wells, *The Reproduction Revolution* (Oxford: Oxford University Press, 1984), p. 149.

18 The analogy between the value of life and the value of art was suggested to me by Rick Momeyer, though I hasten to dissociate him from any of the conclusions reached in this chapter.

19 Singer, *Practical Ethics*, p. 189.

20 R. M. Hare, letter of support for Peter Singer to the German euthanasia advocate George Meggle, 1 July 1989. The letter was written during the controversy over the fifteenth International Wittgenstein Conference. It was cancelled owing to protests by disabled rights and other groups against the invitations to Singer *and* to Hare to speak at the conference.

On the issues surrounding the protests against Singer and the charge that his views on euthanasia are comparable to those of the Nazis, see P. Singer, 'On Being Silenced in Germany', which first appeared in the *New York Review of Books*, 15 August 1991, pp. 36–42, and is reprinted as an appendix to *Practical Ethics*, pp. 337–59, at p. 345; P. Singer, 'A German Attack on Applied Ethics', *Journal of Applied Philosophy* 9 (1992), pp. 85–91; J. Teichman, 'Humanism and Personism: The False Philosophy of Peter Singer', *Quadrant* (Australia), December 1992, pp. 26–9; J. Teichman, 'Freedom of Speech and the Public Platform', *Journal of Applied Philosophy* 11 (1994), pp. 99–105, reprinted in her *Polemical Papers* (Aldershot: Ashgate, 1997); D. S. Oderberg, 'The Singer Controversy', *Quadrant* (Australia), September 1993, pp. 74–6; D. S. Oderberg, 'Academia's "Doctor Death"?', *Human Life Review* (Fall 1998), pp. 31–40, and other contributions in that issue; H. Pauer-Studer, 'Peter Singer on Euthanasia', *The Monist* 76 (1993), pp. 135–

57; P. Singer and H. Kuhse, 'More on Euthanasia: A Response to Pauer-Studer', *The Monist* 76 (1993), pp. 158–74.

21 The claim that the 'family as a whole' can decide if it is in their own best interests to kill their child is in Singer, 'A German Attack on Applied Ethics', p. 86; similar claims are made in the pages from *Practical Ethics* cited above, and in Peter Singer and Helga Kuhse, *Should the Baby Live?* (Oxford, Oxford University Press, 1985); see also James Rachels, *The End of Life* (Oxford, Oxford University Press, 1986), p. 157; and various of the writings of R. M. Hare.

22 Glover, *Causing Death and Saving Lives*, p. 115.

23 Singer, *Practical Ethics*, p. 205.

24 Ibid., p. 206.

25 Ibid., p. 210.

26 The Tony Bland case was covered in British newspapers throughout 1993: see, for instance, *The Times* (London), 22 December 1993. The implications of the case are well covered in the submission to the House of Lords Select Committee on Medical Ethics by the Society for the Protection of Unborn Children, June 1993. The committee was convened as a result of controversy surrounding the Bland case, and reported in January 1994 (London, HMSO, HL Paper 21-I). It recommended no change in the law prohibiting euthanasia, but failed to recognise that the killing of Tony Bland was indeed euthanasia; its discussion of that case, while flawed, is worth reading.

27 Quoted in Peter Singer, *Rethinking Life and Death* (Oxford: Oxford University Press, 1994), p. 24. I have made use of Singer's revealing discussion of the definition of death in giving my own summary. The reader should consult chapters 2 and 3 of Singer's book.

28 Ibid., p. 25. See this page and following for the quotations from the Harvard committee report.

29 Ibid., p. 27.

30 Cited in Singer, *Rethinking Life and Death*, p. 58.

31 Lord Keith of Kinkel, cited in L. Gormally (ed.), *Euthanasia, Clinical Practice and the Law* (London: Linacre Centre for Health Care Ethics, 1994), p. 150.

32 On the important discoveries of the brain's hormonal operations, see Richard Bergland, *The Fabric of Mind* (London: Penguin, 1985).

33 Singer, *Rethinking Life and Death*, p. 32.

34 M. Evans, 'Against Brainstem Death', p. 1043. See further ch. 1, n. 10, on the question of 'brain death'.

35 *Daily Iowan*, 15 February 1996; *Seattle Times*, 16 February 1996; *The Australian*, 17 February 1996; *Detroit News*, 16 April 1997; *Chattanooga Times*, 16 and 17 April 1997. See also the case of Maria Lopez, who 'had been in a coma for a month. Doctors didn't expect her or the twins in her womb to

survive. Her family prepared to remove life support and called in a priest.'
Mrs Lopez, having 'coughed and moved' soon afterwards (the doctors told
her family this was merely due to reflexes), awoke and 'can ... communicate
by wiggling her fingers. She gave birth to two girls last month': Associated
Press, 8 July 1999.

36   On misdiagnosis of 'persistent vegetative state', see K. Andrews et al.,
     'Misdiagnosis of the Vegetative State: Retrospective Study in a Rehabilita-
     tion Unit', *British Medical Journal* 313 (1996), pp. 13–16.

37   On clinicians' views of management of patients in 'persistent vegetative state',
     see A. Grubb et al., 'Survey of British Clinicians' Views on Management of
     Patients in Persistent Vegetative State', *The Lancet* 348 (1996), pp. 35–40.

38   Dr Leo Alexander, 'Medical Science Under Dictatorship', *New England Jour-
     nal of Medicine* 241 (1949).

39   Hare, letter to Georg Meggle, cited in n. 20.

40   An excellent recent book on Nazi euthanasia policy is Michael Burleigh, *Death
     and Deliverance: 'Euthanasia' in Germany 1900–1945* (Cambridge: Cam-
     bridge University Press, 1994). It should be noted that a number of American
     doctors were keen advocates of early German and Nazi policies with respect
     to euthanasia and eugenics. One infamous example is the sterilisation of tens
     of thousands of 'defectives' in Virginia, notably Lynchburg. This was with
     judicial approval.

41   An important book surveying the reality of the slippery slope is Wesley J.
     Smith, *Forced Exit: The Slippery Slope from Assisted Suicide to Legalized
     Murder* (New York: Times Books, 1997).

42   For an excellent discussion of the proper role of the doctor with respect to
     euthanasia, see J. Cottingham, 'Medicine, Virtues and Consequences', in
     Oderberg and Laing (eds), *Human Lives*, pp. 128–43.

Chapter 3

1   See T. Regan, *The Case for Animal Rights* (London: Routledge, 1984). Even
    if you do not agree with his defence, the book is worth reading for its excel-
    lent critique of consequentialism.

2   Ibid., p. 243.

3   Ibid., p. 246.

4   Ibid., p. 417.

5   Ibid., p. 87.

6   Davidson on animal beliefs: see 'Thought and Talk', in his *Inquiries into
    Truth and Interpretation* (Oxford: Oxford University Press, 1984), and 'Ra-
    tional Animals', in E. LePore and B. McLaughlin (eds), *Actions and Events*

(Oxford: Blackwell, 1985). For a succinct summary and critique of Davidson's position, see P. Carruthers, *The Animals Issue* (Cambridge: Cambridge University Press, 1992), pp. 126–31.

For a Wittgenstenian critique of the idea of animal belief coming from the same direction as Davidson, see M. Leahy, *Against Liberation* (London: Routledge, 1994, first published 1991), *passim*, especially pp. 49–56, 121–2. Leahy also draws heavily on the work of R. G. Frey: see Frey's *Interests and Rights: The Case Against Animals* (Oxford: Clarendon Press, 1980).

7   For critical surveys of the possibility of chimpanzee language (which also contain citations of the more favourable literature), see S. Pinker, *The Language Instinct* (London: Penguin, 1994), pp. 335–49; J. M. Pearce, *An Introduction to Animal Cognition* (Hove: Lawrence Erlbaum, 1987), ch. 8 (where other species are considered as well); H. S. Terrace, L. A. Pettito et al., 'Can an Ape Create a Sentence?', *Science* 200 (1979), pp. 891–902; J. Wallman, *Aping Language* (Cambridge: Cambridge University Press, 1992). Jane Goodall presents her conviction that Washoe and other chimpanzees have genuinely learned language in her book *Through a Window* (London: Penguin, 1991), pp. 16–19.

8   Pinker, *Language Instinct*, pp. 337–8.

9   Ibid., p. 339.

10 Carruthers on contractualism, language and intelligent but uncommunicative Martians: *Animals Issue*, pp. 139–43.

11 On animal self-consciousness, see ibid., pp. 184–7.

12 On deception by apes, see R. Byrne and A. Whiten, 'The Thinking Primate's Guide to Deception', *New Scientist*, 3 December 1987, pp. 54–7. The story of the baboon Paul is on p. 54. (The tautology 'young juvenile' is in the text.)

13 A. Kenny, *Will, Freedom and Power* (Oxford: Blackwell, 1975), p. 20.

14 A. Fagothey, *Right and Reason* (St Louis, MO: C. V. Mosby Co., 1963; 3rd edn), p. 208.

15 Kenny, *Will*, p. 20.

16 Richard Feynman on the behaviour of the paramecium: see E. Hutchings (ed.), *'Surely You're Joking, Mr. Feynman!'* (New York: Norton, 1985), pp. 91–2.

17 William James, *The Principles of Psychology*, vol. 2 (London: Macmillan & Co., 1891), p. 383.

18 For Richard Feynman's amusing stories illustrating the programmed behaviour of ants, see Hutchings (ed.), *'Surely You're Joking'*, pp. 93–7. For more serious research, see the observations reported in H. Muckermann, SJ, *The Humanizing of the Brute* (St Louis, MO: Herder, 1906), pp. 77–99.

19 The report on the wasp *Cerceris ornata* is cited in Muckermann, *Humanizing*, pp. 41–2, the part in quotation marks taken from G. W. Peckham and E. G. Peckham, *On the Instincts and Habits of the Solitary Wasps* (Madison,

WI: State Publisher, 1898), pp. 219–20. See also the rigidly programmed behaviour of the wasp *Sphexichneumonea*, reported in ibid., p. 212, and by Carruthers, *Animals Issue*, pp. 123–4.

20　Tinbergen's classic work is *The Study of Instinct* (Oxford: Clarendon Press, 1951).

21　Carruthers, *Animals Issue*, p. 135.

22　Ibid.

23　D. DeGrazia, *Taking Animals Seriously* (Cambridge: Cambridge University Press, 1996), pp. 209–10.

24　Singer, *Practical Ethics*, p. 67.

25　Ibid., pp.78, 77, 78.

26　For but one example of the use of humans as guinea pigs in horrific experiments, see the revelations concerning the administration of radiation to prison inmates and babies (mostly black) in America in the 1950s, as part of 'military research'. The story was reported in the Australian newspaper *The Age*, 1 January 1994, and throughout the American and European press.

27　Singer, *Practical Ethics*, pp. 186, 133.

28　Ibid., p. 132.

29　On the pointlessness of much animal research, see for instance H. Ruesch, *Slaughter of the Innocent* (London: Futura, 1979).

30　In the Draize eye test, named after J. H. Draize, concentrated solutions are dropped into the eyes of animals, mainly rabbits, and the effects noted, such as swelling, redness, and damage to the eye. This has been, and continues to be, a standard method of testing the safety of shampoos, cosmetics and cleaning liquids.

Chapter 4

1　For general information about capital punishment, see R. Hood, *The Death Penalty: A World-Wide Perspective*, Report to the UN Committee on Crime Prevention and Control (Oxford: Clarendon Press, 1985). See also P. Hodgkinson and A. Rutherford (eds), *Capital Punishment: Global Issues and Prospects* (Winchester: Waterside Press, 1996). On capital punishment in the USA, see P. Hodgkinson, H. Bedau et al., *Capital Punishment in the United States of America* (London: Parliamentary Human Rights Group, 1996).

2　For an excellent survey and discussion of punishment and the theories concerning it, see J. Cottingham, 'The Philosophy of Punishment', in G. H. R. Parkinson (ed.), *An Encyclopedia of Philosophy* (London: Routledge, 1988), ch. 33. On retribution in particular, where a number of interpretations of the concept are distinguished and discussed, see Cottingham, 'Varieties of Retribution', *Philosophical Quarterly* 29 (1979), pp. 238–46.

3 For a useful (but difficult) discussion of forfeiture of rights, see J. J. Thomson, *The Realm of Rights* (Cambridge, MA: Harvard University Press, 1990), pp. 361–73.

4 Bentham, *An Introduction to the Principles of Morals and Legislation*, ed. J. H. Burns and H. L. A. Hart (London: Methuen, 1970), ch. XIII.i.2, p. 158.

5 Cottingham, 'Philosophy of Punishment', pp. 771–2.

6 Kant, *Rechtslehre* (1796), Part II, sec. 49E. See discussion in Cottingham, 'Varieties of Retribution', pp. 243–4.

7 Reproduced in P. Singer (ed.), *Applied Ethics* (Oxford: Oxford University Press, 1986), pp. 97–104.

8 Ibid., p. 102.

9 Ibid., pp. 98–9.

10 Ibid., p. 101. The original is spelt 'effeminancy'.

11 Ibid, p. 99.

12 For empirical information on the deterrent value of capital punishment, from which the figures in the text have been taken, see Hodgkinson and Rutherford (eds), *Capital Punishment*, pp. 162, 201–2; Hood, *Death Penalty*, pp. 126–7, 130–1.

13 J. G. Murphy, 'Cruel and Unusual Punishments', in M. A. Stewart (ed.), *Law, Morality and Rights* (Dordrecht: Reidel, 1979), pp. 373–404, at p. 401.

14 Ibid., p. 403.

15 Cottingham on Murphy: 'Punishment and Respect for Persons', in Stewart (ed.), *Law*, pp. 423–31.

16 Singer, *Applied Ethics*, p. 102.

17 Letter from Hare to the German bioethicist Professor Georg Meggle, cited in ch. 2, n. 20. I am not suggesting that Hare himself opposes capital punishment; as a utilitarian, he at least implicitly accepts it in cases where the net benefits are great enough. I am only using his words as an example of a common attitude among supporters of euthanasia.

18 For a useful series of articles on capital punishment, see A. Simmons, M. Cohen, J. Cohen and C. Beitz (eds), *Punishment: A Philosophy and Public Affairs Reader* (Princeton: Princeton University Press, 1995), Part III: articles by D. Conway, J. Reiman, S. Nathanson and E. van den Haag.

Chapter 5

1 The first couple of pages on the mysterious nature of war are taken almost verbatim from an unpublished typescript by N. M. Gwynne, entitled *War:*

Part 1, to whom gratitude is expressed for consent to reproduce this material.

2   Quoted in A. J. Coates, *The Ethics of War* (Manchester: Manchester University Press, 1997), p. 27, quoting from F. Veale, *Advance to Barbarism* (London: Mitre Press, 1968), p. 123.

3   For some useful surveys of pacifism, see: Coates, *Ethics*, ch. 3; J. Teichman, *Pacifism and the Just War* (Oxford: Blackwell, 1986, chs 1–3); P. Ramsey, *The Just War* (Lanham, MD: University Press of America, 1983, first published 1968), ch. 12. See also the critique by J. Narveson, 'Pacifism: A Philosophical Analysis', *Ethics* 75 (1965), pp. 259–71, reprinted in R. Wasserstrom (ed.), *War and Morality* (Belmont, CA: Wadsworth, 1970), pp. 63–77.

4   For a brief sketch of Gandhi's understanding of non-violence (from which my information is taken), see Coates, *Ethics*, p. 95, n. 14.

5   A typical example of disagreement among traditional ethicists over the parallels between self-defence and capital punishment (in particular whether state execution is wrong precisely because it is an intentional killing) can be seen in J. Finnis, J. Boyle and G. Grisez, *Nuclear Deterrence, Morality and Realism* (Oxford: Clarendon Press, 1987), pp. 312–17, especially p. 317, where one of the authors (presumably Finnis) overtly breaks ranks with the other two and supports the traditional position for which I argue, that state execution is a case of permissible intentional killing *despite* being in a different category from self-defence. The other two authors maintain, against the tradition, that capital punishment is by its very nature impermissible *because* it is in a different category from self-defence, that is, is a deliberately inflicted death. The authors are, then, united in denying that the death penalty is justified, like self-defence, as an *indirect* killing, contrary to the opinion of some traditional writers. I agree with them on this point. (As an example of a traditional writer who defends capital punishment as an exercise of self-defence by the state, see T. J. Higgins, SJ, *Man as Man: The Science and Art of Ethics* (Rockford, IL: Tan Books, 1992 [1958], pp. 512–13). The reasoning seems consequentialist, even though Higgins accepts the fundamentally retributive nature of punishment at p. 512.)

6   The classic defence of capital punishment on the ground of the Principle of Totality is in St Thomas Aquinas, *Summa Theologica* II–II, q. 64, art. 2.

7   The passage of Orwell's that I summarise and quote from is reproduced in Coates, *Ethics*, p. 83, and is taken from his essay 'England Your England', reprinted in his *Inside the Whale and Other Essays* (London: Penguin, 1962), at p. 63.

8   For some of the facts surrounding the Six Day War, see R. Ovendale, *The Origins of the Arab–Israeli Wars* (London: Longman, 1984), ch. 10.

9   For the use of US force against Caribbean nations to secure debt repayment, see R. J. Regan, *Just War: Principles and Cases* (Washington, DC: Catholic

University of America Press, 1996), p. 58.

10 R. Rohmer, *Patton's Gap* (London: Arms and Armour, 1981).

11 Quoted in Coates, *Ethics*, p. 236.

12 Ramsey, *Just War*, p. 353.

13 The information about the status of Hiroshima as a military target is taken from Richard Rhodes, *The Making of the Atomic Bomb* (New York: Touchstone, 1988), p. 713; for his citation of Truman's Potsdam diary regarding 'purely military' targeting of the atomic bomb, see pp. 690–1.

14 Harry S. Truman, *Memoirs*, vol. I (New York: Doubleday, 1955), p. 420.

15 Evidence that Stimson knew that large numbers of civilians would be killed, and moreover that this was a legitimate *means* of ending the war, can be found in R. J. Donovan, *Conflict and Crisis: The Presidency of Harry S. Truman 1945-8* (New York: Norton, 1977), pp. 67–8.

16 G. E. M. Anscombe, 'Mr. Truman's Degree', originally published in 1957, reprinted in her *Ethics, Religion and Politics: Philosophical Papers*, vol. III (Oxford: Blackwell, 1981), ch. 7, p. 64. See also her important articles, 'War and Murder', ch. 6, and 'The Justice of the Present War Examined', ch. 8 (written in 1939).

17 Quoted in different versions in various places, this one coming from D. Griffin, *Descent into Slavery?* (Clackamas, OR: Emissary, 1988), p. 214. I have not verified the accuracy of the quotation.

18 The quotation from Vegetius is precisely: 'Qui desiderat pacem, praeparet bellum', from *Epitoma Rei Militaris*, book 3, prologue. I have used the more common form.

19 Aristotle, *Nicomachean Ethics*, book 10: 1177b 5–6.

Index